Books in the series 'The Colonial Economy of NSW 1788-1835'

A Brief Economic History of NSW

The Colonial Economy of NSW 1788-1835–
A retrospective

The Government Store is Open for business–
the commissariat operations in NSW 1788-1835

The Enterprising Colonial Economy of NSW 1800-1830–
Government Business Enterprises in operation

Guiding the Colonial Economy–Public Funding in NSW 1800-1835

Financing the Colonial Economy of NSW 1800-1835

Essays on the colonial Economy of NSW 1788-1835

Industries that Formed a Colonial Economy

INDUSTRIES that FORMED A COLONY

(The growth of industrial development in the new colony of NSW from 1788, including a study of the formation and operations of the VDL company)

GORDON BECKETT

For book orders, email orders@traffordpublishing.com.sg

Most Trafford Singapore titles are also available at major online book retailers.

Printed in Singapore.

ISBN: 978-1-4669-2774-2 (sc)
ISBN: 978-1-4669-2775-9 (hc)
ISBN: 978-1-4669-2776-6 (e)

Trafford rev. 08/06/2012

 www.traffordpublishing.com.sg

Singapore
toll-free: 800 101 2656 (Singapore)
Fax: 800 101 2656 (Singapore)

CONTENTS

Industries

The VDL Company

INDUSTRIES

CHAPTER 1

INTRODUCTION

In 1882 Charles Lyne wrote a book about Colonial industry of the time– *The industries of NSW*. He reviewed a total of 35 articles about Colonial Industry in the last quarter of the 19th century, for industries such as Hunter Valley Farming, Lithgow Coal, and Pottery & Brick-making. This was a landmark analysis and the first and last of such studies. Subsequent studies have been more of an overview of industrialists and their activities rather than detailed studies of specific industries.

This present study is that of tracking early manufactures and their growth over time. Innovation and growth involved entrepreneurs, privatisation and a great deal of foreign investment.

For many years, Australia was essentially a primary-producing country. Manufacturing was geared largely to supplying local domestic requirements. The discovery of minerals, a growing population and military equipping created a profitable home market and led to an expansion of this sector.

Manning Clark writes (Vol 1, *A History of Australia*–P.249) 'Up to 1810 and the time of Macquarie, neither the convict stain nor clothing, lodging, or way of life distinguished the bonded (convicts) from the free workers. Nor within the free group was it possible to distinguish the ex-bond from the native-born and the free immigrant. Tradesmen were much in demand in the building trade; others (*ex land grant owners who had failed or been turned off their land*) found employment in the small industries of the colony, in the pottery, the hat-manufactory, the tannery, the brewery, or

1

with the shoe-maker, the tailors or the tin-smiths; others took to the sea, on coastal vessels, or a ship trading with the Islands'

The last significant study of colonial manufacturing was completed by G. J. R. Linge in *Industrial* Awakening published in 1979. In 2000 it is timely that a further review be made of the earliest industry not of 1900 but of 1800.

The reasons that early governors sponsored developing industries in the early colony are various and commence with basic survival

Of course Governor King faced his own series of challenges. He began his term of office under strained relations with Hunter and, naturally, Macarthur. Macarthur wanted to boycott this new governor and his new policies of controlling the public herds and their grazing whereabouts. However, under King, the colony made great strides in new business activities. After Macarthur was transported to England for trial, King saw that whaling was the only 'staple' and envisaged great secondary industries and huge colonial profits. An export trade in coal began from Coal Harbour (Newcastle), which received government support through a large allocation of convict labour. Coal was sent to both India and the Cape . . . Some timber was exported, but did not receive a good reception at its destination. A source of cheap salt pork was found in Tahiti. Then in August 1800, King announced 'the manufacture of linen and woollen goods has begun with some success. Tuppence a pound was paid for local wool, which was woven into blankets. The raw wool was paid for by exchange of blanket material. This could well have been the start of the flourishing future wool industry.

The Naval Officer, (Harbour master) shared his revenues between the Orphan Fund and the Police Fund. This was the start of taxation in the colony and to an extent gave the colony an imprimatur of a successful colonial trading post.

Of all the early industries, it was the timber industry that was most important. After food provision, the governor's chief role was to create housing and barracks for free immigrants, convicts, and military personnel. Not until Macquarie's arrival did any significant planning for public buildings and infrastructure begin. The timber gathering and processing by its very nature was left to convict workers, and Ralph Hawkins (The timber-getters of Pennant Hills) provides a scenario of timber–gathering in the Hornsby Shire.

Governor Phillip encouraged sealing as an entrepreneurial activity and as an alternative and supplement to his policy of independent farming and Agri-production through 30 acre land grants.

1. Sealing also supported a fledgling boat-building and provedore industry and became the first export industry. Up to 1841 whaling and sealing exports were greater than wool, coal or timber.
2. New industries such as tallow, soap, tannery, linen, hats, slops, blankets were encouraged to serve a local market (some of these were government-sponsored eg linen, clothing, distillery), but Macquarie saw the limitations of the size of the local market to manufacturing industries; he also saw the convict labour as a means of creating output with minimal if not competitive costs, especially where local raw materials were involved. He then built a public works program around his output until the output itself created a catalyst for new manufactures.
3. The Lumber Yard and its associated operations, in employing over 3,000 convicts had the opportunity for using any skilled labour arriving in the colony, and for making a wide-range of items in local demand, and which were encouraged as being import replacers.
4. His decision to privatise many established L/Y operations created a grass roots manufacturing industry, which although it may have been assumed by private entrepreneurs, would have been a lot longer in arriving. Entrepreneurial encouragement by Macquarie also over-rode any endeavours by Macquarie to have monopoly operations in the L.Y.
5. Thus the L.Y. was the real catalyst for growth of a manufacturing sector, mostly because of the positive policies of Macquarie and the heads of the commissariat

Thus the direct link between the commissariat L/Y and the rise of manufacturing!!

Upon his arrival, Bligh was appalled by the conditions of the colony and told Windham back in London (HRA 1:6:26) that much needed to be improved in the colony. He also wrote that of his being convinced that the immediate economic future lay in the encouragement of agriculture rather than in the development of commerce (for example the development of the wool trade) or the Bass Strait and overseas trade, for they were extremely trifling (HRA 1:6:121).

Clarke records (A History of Australia, Vol 1, P.331)

> *'by 1820 Simeon Lord had turned the profits of marriage, fishing in the south seas and trade in the Pacific Islands into a manufactory at Botany Bay where he employed convicts and from 15 to 20 colonial boys making blankets, stockings, wool hats, kangaroo hats, seal Hats, possum skin hats, all shoddy but cheaper than the imported English hats, boot leather, trousers, shirts, thread, kettles and glass tumblers. The bulk of the wool grown in NSW was shipped direct by the growers to England, and Lord was the exception to the principle that the settlers should use their great natural advantages of grass and climate to grow food and wool and import the other goods they needed'.*

Bigge reported glowingly about the future prospects for grazing and agriculture but also recorded a downside to the growth in the agricultural economy; 'between 1810 and 1820, the numbers of sheep trebled, and some settlers were finding it more profitable to sell the fleeces rather than the carcasses (J.T. Bigge: Agriculture & Trade Report–p16-18)

The Macquarie legacy was described by the retiring governor during the handing-over ceremony with Governor Brisbane. 'I found the colony in a state of rapid deterioration: threatened with famine, discord and party spirit prevailing, and the public buildings in a state of decay. I left it a very different place: the face of the country was greatly improved; agriculture flourishing, manufactories had been established and commerce revived; roads and bridges built and inhabitants opulent and happy'. (HRA 1:12:331)

This same principle of comparative advantage was considered carefully by the Commissariat and the Macquarie Administration before the decision to expand the numerous government business enterprises which were responsible for employing convict labour was implemented and became fully operational. The colony, it was decided, needed a manufacturing and industrial base to work in conjunction with the agricultural enterprises, and to supply the government with its public works materials from local sources, rather than rely on imports from Britain.

It was a source of great delight to Macquarie that he had brought about such change, and what a difference in approach and attitude between the two governors. In fact, although Phillip, Hunter and King could have contributed little more than they did towards trade, commerce and industrial development, it was the Macquarie pro-entrepreneurial policies that brought about such great progress in both industrial and economic development

Ralph Hawkins in '*The Convict Timber-getters of Pennant Hills*' writes

> "*The Chief Engineer's department enquired after the trades of convicts after arrival and kept the most useful of them in Government employ. The Engineer's department systematised the labour of the convicts, classifying men according to their trades and instructed those unskilled and young enough or willing enough in a suitable trade. The Lumber Yard in Sydney was the centre of industrial operations in the colony. Here men practiced both timber and metal trades, preparing useful products for the government. A number of outlying gangs prepared raw materials for the public works programme. The brickmaker's gang worked At Brickfield Hill, the Shell gang gathered oyster shells for lime from the Aboriginal middens along the foreshore of the harbour and the Lane Cove River. The quarry gang prepared the stone, while further afield in the woods to the north-west of Sydney at Pennant Hills was the Timber-getting gang. This latter gang was a gang of men chosen for their skills and not a gang of men under secondary punishment. These men were mostly drawn straight from the arriving ships and worked shorter hours than most other*

5

convicts. They were of sufficient confidence to go on strike in 1819. Macquarie needed their services and they returned to work after only 3 weeks."

In the listing of key events, certain sectors of the secondary industry economy have been selected for a time-line of progress. There are reasons for specific industries being selected.

A brief outline of events before 1810 draws attention to a number of circumstances that are of fundamental importance to an understanding of early industrial development:

i.   There was a general shortage of labour
ii. Circumstances combined to prevent real income and output from small settlers from rising
iii. monopoly position of military officers buying incoming provisions from visiting ships and retailing at exorbitant prices and profits
iv. most small farmers had neither the knowledge nor the capital to improve their farming techniques or to buy stock and equipment
v.   the need to take people off the store
vi. the arrival of only a few free migrants
vii. large increase in arriving convicts

References Used and Literary Review

Of particular note is that the following literature is made up of economic history writings and general history. No other economic historian has made anything of the link between the operations of the commissariat and the rise of a manufacturing sector in the colony.

This link assumes that the commissariat business enterprises under the Macquarie Administration commenced the initial manufactory before transferring operations from the public to the private sector where practical, and then allowing competition to develop, in further satisfaction of the mechanism of a market economy. This process was under the overall encouragement of free enterprise by Macquarie, and was designed to create a support sector for the already strong agri-business sector, to attract free skilled labour to the colony and to attract investment to the colonial economy as well as being an import replacement facility. Manufacturing in the Lumber Yard was intended to satisfy an artificial government market whilst transference to the private sector

1. HRA
2. HRNSW
3. Coghlan (x 3)
4. Butlin (x 2)
5. Steven
6. Blayney
7. Linge
8. Lyne
9. Hainsworth
10. Abbott & Nairn
11. Maloney: History of Australia
12. Clark: History of Australia
13. Barnard: History of Australia
14. Hawkins: The Timber-getters of Pennant Hills
15. Hainsworth: 'In search of a staple–the Sydney Sandalwood trade 1804-09'
16. Abbott, G.C. 'Staple theory and Australian economic growth 1788-1820'

These <u>Key Events</u> are set down by industry group as a means of demonstrating the surprising amount of originality within the economy and the potential for men of education with a flair for innovation and access to capital. They are later sorted onto a time-scale.

A. Fishing & Whaling

1. **Sealing in Bass Strait** (1797) **commenced**
2. **Boat building** for hunting seals (1798)
3. By 1804 11 privately owned sloops were engaged in Bass Strait sealing
4. Between 1800 and 1806, over 100,000 seal skins landed in Sydney

7

5. **Whaling began** (1802)
6. **Boat building** for hunting whales
7. By 1830, 17 ships operated from Sydney, and by 1835, 76
8. Whaling stations established in NSW (1830), Victoria (1831) and S.A.(1837)
9. In 1830, NSW exported £60,000 worth of whaling & sealing products with wool at £35,000. By 1835, wool had overtaken fishery products. By 1841 whale oil exports peaked at £150,000 p.a.; by 1850, this had declined to £28,000. The decline was accelerated by the gold rushes which caused a shortage of labour for the whaling ships. In 1851, the whaling stations in Mosman's Cove closed. By 1853, exports from NSW had fallen to £16,000
10. By 1841 there were 41 bay-whaling stations in Tasmania. In the 1840s, over 400 vessels were built in VDL boat-yards

B. Timber

1. 1788 First Fleet cuts Sydney Cove timbers as clearing of land for initial settlement.
2. Earliest tree trunks not dried and when used *in situ* warped, twisted and bowsed.
3. Phillip sent out scouts to seek better quality timber and came across the Pennant Hills Timber-getting area.
4. Government Farms

   i. Within the commissariat, responsibility was allocated for the supervision of convicts undertaking government work. Even after London had directed cost cutting for convict maintenance a certain number of convicts were kept for government service, and during the King, Bligh and Macquarie Administrations government farms were established in 5 rural locations, not only to provide fresh fruit vegetables and meat for use within the colony but to manage the labour and output of over 500 convicts.

C. Manufacturing

1. 1788 First bricks used for building (Darling Harbour, Brickfield Hill, St. Peters, Granville, Gore Hill, Rosehill
2. Pottery works produced plates, jars, clay pipes (1788). By 1804 several other pottery works were operating
3. 1789–first vessel built for ferrying passengers between Parramatta and Sydney
4. 1795–Sydney's first windmill had been imported and erected on Observatory Hill
5. 1795–First ale brewed at Parramatta
6. 1796–Naval Dockyard established in Sydney Cove
7. 1799–Government broom factory opened with 1 man making 6 dozen brooms each week
8. 1800 Linen manufacturing on the Hawkesbury from locally grown flax
9. 1800 House of Industry, the women's section of Parramatta Gaol and later, the Female Factory made linen and other clothing items (hats, slops, blankets)
10. 1815 Steam powered flour mill
11. 1820 Local paper mill supplying all material for publishing *Sydney Gazette*
12. 1820 carriage and harness making in Sydney
13. 1824 Sugar made from local cane for first time
14. By 1838, NSW had 2 distilleries, 7 breweries, 12 tanneries, 5 brass and iron foundries, 77 flour mills and single factories producing salt, hats, tobacco and other goods
15. In 1839, Australian Sugar Company formed in NSW

C. Mining

1. 1797 Coal found on banks of Hunter River
2. 1801 All coal and timber declared by Governor King to be property of the Crown
3. 1801 Robert Campbell shipped coal to Calcutta and Cape of Good Hope

4. 1823 Commissioner Bigge recommended Newcastle coalfields be privatised
5. 1824 AAC company opens up 1 million acres
6. 1839 Gold discovered but kept quiet
7. 1841 Silver-lead ore discovered in Adelaide and 10 ton exported to Britain
8. 1846 Tin discovered in S.A.

D. Agri-Business

1. 1788 First Fleet arrived with livestock, seeds and young plants. However, the small cattle herd and sheep mostly died; only 2 horses survived more than 2 years
2. Phillip established a 3.6 ha farm where the Botanical Gardens now stand.
3. 1789 First Government farm commenced at Rose Hill. James Ruse received one acre at Rose Hill for wheat /grain experimenting.
4. 1791 The Ruse grant was increased shortly to 30 acres.
5. 1791 First tobacco grown
6. 1792 Planting of citrus trees along Parramatta River
7. 1795 Horses imported and by 1810 there were 1134 horses in NSW
8. 1797 NSW held about 2500 sheep
9. 1797 Governor Hunter reported the first planting of grape vines; by 1802 12,000 vines had been planted around Parramatta. Original cuttings had arrived with First Fleet
10. 1807 Samuel Marsden took first cask of cross-bred wool to England for testing.
11. 1813 First crossing of Blue Mountains
12. 1816 Botanic Gardens in Sydney developed
13. 1816 First wheat grown near Bathurst
14. 1820 First dairy industry established in Illawarra district

E. Exports & Trade (202,152,177,186,221)

1. 1790 The *Sirius* under John Hunter (Phillips' intended successor), returned with a cargo of flour, seed wheat and barley, and a year's provisions. Phillip had despatched the ship to acquire rations for the colony as the second fleet had been delayed and the colony was starving. The brig *Supply* was also despatched to Batavia for a supply of rice and other provisions

2. 1792 Army officers traded in goods from visiting vessels–a pattern which was to last for many years. Dutch and Indian vessels brought further supplies for trading and officers realised huge profits. Further plans were made for ships from Cape Town, Batavia and India to bring other tradable items. Strong trading links developed between Sydney and Batavia.

3. 1798–The Commissariat's first commercial purchase of grain from local farmers–1500 bushels of wheat were purchased from Hawkesbury farms.

4. 1798 The first boiling works was opened on Cape Barren Island, where they collected over 12500 seal skins and 3000 litres of seal oil for export to China

5. 1801 Robert Campbell exported 100 tons of Hunter Coal to Calcutta and 100 tons to Cape of Good Hope.

6. Although colonial trade in sealing, whaling, sandalwood and trepang (sea slug) was well underway by 1806, export was still hindered by the British Navigation *Acts* and the East India Company monopoly.

7. In 1810, Wentworth, Riley and Blaxall signed a contract to build a new main hospital in the settlement in exchange for a monopoly on import of spirits

8. 1812, first wheat purchased by NSW from VDL

9. 1813, Scarcity forced corn prices up from 5/–a bushel to 15/–per bushel. And wheat from 6/3 to £1/8/-

10. 1814, nearly 15,000 kg of wool was exported

F. Newspapers

1. 1795 A wooden-screw press, brought with the first fleet, was used to print the first official directive by Gov. Hunter
2. 1803. First newspaper (*Sydney Gazette*) founded by Gov. King mainly for government orders and proclamations. The weekly was edited by ex-convict, George Howe.
3. 1824 The weekly *Australian* first appeared owned by W. C. Wentworth and Robert Wardell. It was published without a licence. It was printed until 1848
4. 1826. The *Monitor* was first published by E. S. Hall, who became an antagonist of Governor Darling and spent numerous times in gaol.

G.   Banking

1. 1811 Macquarie considers the need for banking upon his arrival, but is directed by the Secretary of State not to proceed
2. 1817 Macquarie issues banking licence for a private investment group to start the *Bank of NSW*.
3. Bigge determines the licence is illegal but recommends the continuation of the enterprise provided directors and stockholders assume all liability for deposits. No responsibility is to fall to the Government. The licence is ratified. and
4. The Bank of Australia commences in 1826

H.   Roads and Bridges

1. 1788 Governor Phillip prepared the first town plan
2. 1788 First wooden log bridge built over the tank stream
3. 1794 Timber bridge built over the Parramatta River at Parramatta
4. 1810 Macquarie introduced a toll and turnpike system for major arterial roads from Sydney
5. 1811 Engineer John O'Hearne built a stone bridge over the tank stream

6. 1813 A large span bridge built over Hawkesbury at Windsor–65 metres long
7. 1814 Old South Head Road built and Sydney–Liverpool road built
8. 1815 Road down Bulli pass built to Wollongong
9. 1818 Oxley charted what is now the Oxley Highway to Port Macquarie
10. 1826 Great North Road commenced
11. 1830 Sydney–Goulburn Road surveyed
12. 1835 Track linking Sydney–Melbourne completed

Timescale of Manufactures

1788   1. 1788 First Fleet cuts Sydney Cove timbers as clearing of land for initial settlement.

1788   2. Earliest tree trunks not dried and when used *in situ* warped, twisted and bowsed.

1788   3. Phillip sent out scouts to seek better quality timber and came across the Pennant Hills Timber-getting area.

1788   1. 1788 First bricks used for building (Darling Harbour, Brickfield Hill, St. Peters, Granville, Gore Hill, Rosehill)

1788   2. Pottery works produced plates, jars, clay pipes (1788). By 1804 several other pottery works were operating

1788   1. 1788 First Fleet arrived with livestock, seeds and young plants. However, the small cattle herd and sheep mostly died; only 2 horses survived more than 2 years

1788   2. Phillip established a 3.6 ha farm where the Botanical Gardens now stand.

1789   3. 1789–first vessel built for ferrying passengers between Parramatta and Sydney

1789   3. 1789 First Government farm commenced at Rose Hill. James Ruse received one acre at Rose Hill for wheat /grain experimenting.

1790	1. 1790 The *Sirius* under John Hunter (Phillips' intended successor), returned with a cargo of flour, seed wheat and barley, and a year's provisions. Phillip had despatched the ship to acquire rations for the colony as the second fleet had been delayed and the colony was starving. The brig *Supply* was also despatched to Batavia for a supply of rice and other provisions
1791	4. 1791 The Ruse grant was increased shortly to 30 acres.
1791	5. 1791 First tobacco grown
1792	6. 1792 Planting of citrus trees along Parramatta River
1792	2. 1792 Army officers traded in goods from visiting vessels–a pattern which was to last for many years. Dutch and Indian vessels brought further supplies for trading and officers realised huge profits. Further plans were made for ships from Cape Town, Batavia and India to bring other tradable items. Strong trading links developed between Sydney and Batavia.
1795	4. 1795–Sydney's first windmill had been imported and erected on Observatory Hill
1795	5. 1795–First ale brewed at Parramatta
1795	7. 1795 Horses imported and by 1810 there were 1134 horses in NSW
1795	1. 1795 A wooden-screw press, brought with the first fleet, was used to print the first official directive by Gov. Hunter
1796	6. 1796–Naval Dockyard established in Sydney Cove
1797	**1. Sealing in Bass Strait** (1797)
1797	1. 1797 Coal found on banks of Hunter River
1797	8. 1797 NSW held about 2500 sheep
1797	9. 1797 Governor Hunter reported the first planting of grape vines; by 1802 12,000 vines had been planted around Parramatta. Original cuttings had arrived with First Fleet
1798	**2. Boat building** for hunting seals
1798	3. 1798–The Commissariat's first commercial purchase of grain from local farmers–1500 bushels of wheat were purchased from Hawkesbury farms.
1798	4. 1798 The first boiling works was opened on Cape Barren Island, where they collected over 12500 seal skins and 3000 litres of seal oil for export to China

1799	7. 1799–Government broom factory opened with 1 man making 6 dozen brooms each week
1800	8. 1800 Linen manufacturing on the Hawkesbury from locally grown flax
1800	9. 1800 House of Industry, the women's section of Parramatta Gaol and later, the Female Factory made linen and other clothing items (hats, slops, blankets)
1801	2. 1801 All coal and timber declared by Governor King to be property of the Crown
1801	3. 1801 Robert Campbell shipped coal to Calcutta and Cape of Good Hope
1801	5. 1801 Robert Campbell exported 100 tons of Hunter Coal to Calcutta and 100 tons to Cape of Good Hope.
1801	6. Although colonial trade in sealing, whaling, sandalwood and trepang (sea slug) was well underway by 1806, export was still hindered by the British Navigation *Acts* and the East India Company monopoly.
1802	**5. Whaling** (1802)
1803	**6. Boat building** for hunting whales
1803	2. 1803. First newspaper (*Sydney Gazette)* founded by Gov. King mainly for government orders and proclamations. The weekly was edited by ex-convict, George Howe.
1804	. By 1804 11 privately owned sloops were engaged in Bass Strait sealing
1806	4. Between 1800 and 1806, over 100,000 seal skins landed in Sydney
1807	10. 1807 Samuel Marsden took first cask of cross-bred wool to England for testing.
1810	7. In 1810, Wentworth, Riley and Blaxall signed a contract to build a new main hospital in the settlement in exchange for a monopoly on import of spirits
1812	8. 1812, first wheat purchased by NSW from VDL
1813	11. 1813 First crossing of Blue Mountains
1813	9. 1813, Scarcity forced corn prices up from 5/–a bushel to 15/–per bushel. And wheat from 6/3 to £1/8/-
1814	10. 1814, nearly 15,000 kg of wool was exported
1815	10. 1815 Steam powered flour mill
1816	12. 1816 Botanic Gardens in Sydney developed

1816	13. 1816 First wheat grown near Bathurst
1820	11. 1820 Local paper mill supplying all material for publishing *Sydney Gazette*
1820	12. 1820 carriage and harness making in Sydney
1820	14. 1820 First dairy industry established in Illawarra district
1823	14. 1823 Commissioner Bigge recommended Newcastle coalfields be privatised
1824	13. 1824 Sugar made from local cane for first time
1824	5. 1824 AAC company opens up 1 million acres
1824	3. 1824 The weekly *Australian* first appeared owned by W. C. Wentworth and Robert Wardell. It was published without a licence. It was printed until 1848
1826	4. 1826. The *Monitor* was first published by E. S. Hall, who became an antagonist of Governor Darling and spent numerous times in gaol.
1830	7. By 1830, 17 ships operated from Sydney, and by 1835, 76
1830	. In 1830, NSW exported £60,000 worth of whaling & sealing products with wool at £35,000. By 1835, wool had overtaken fishery products. By 1841 whale oil exports peaked at £150,000 p.a.; by 1850, this had declined to £28,000. The decline was accelerated by the gold rushes which caused a shortage of labour for the whaling ships. In 1851, the whaling stations in Mosman's Cove closed. By 1853, exports from NSW had fallen to £16,000
1831	Whaling stations established in NSW (1830), Victoria (1831) and S.A.(1837)
1838	14. By 1838, NSW had 2 distilleries, 7 breweries, 12 tanneries, 5 brass and iron foundries, 77 flour mills and single factories producing salt, hats, tobacco and other goods
1839	15. In 1839, Australian Sugar Company formed in NSW
1839	6. 1839 Gold discovered but kept quiet
1841	10. By 1841 there were 41 bay-whaling stations in Tasmania. In the 1840s, over 400 vessels were built in VDL boat-yards
1841	7. 1841 Silver-lead ore discovered in Adelaide and 10 ton exported to Britain
1846	8. 1846 Tin discovered in S.A.

CHAPTER 2

THE GROWTH AND STRUCTURE
OF THE COLONIAL ECONOMY

The main characteristics of the colonial economy in transition [1](before 1832) are

- The Colonial Government adopted the policy of free enterprise and free trade, during and following the administration of Lachlan Macquarie.
- Out of necessity there was a dominance of agriculture in the economy—this was a social phenomenon because of the needs and availability of convict labour.
- Social problems with bad treatment of aborigines and convicts curbed the otherwise 'clean' image of a successful economy.
- Lack of catalysts for British private investment prevailed until Macquarie converted the colonial image in the 1810-1820 period with new buildings, cleaning up the slums of the 'Rocks' area, and encouraging new enterprise.
- Wealth creation was taking place through capital investment and speculation.
- The growing need for financial institutions came with the commencement of borrowing and capital migration.

---

[1] Beckett, G 'The economics of Colonial NSW' (colonial press 2003)

- The need for private borrowing overseas occurred because of the lack of savings, wealth and financial institutions in the economy before 1830.

On the other hand the key factors of the (gradually) maturing colonial economy changed slightly (after 1832)

- Transportation and the convict labour program was the catalyst for growth until growth plateaued and transportation became more of an economic burden that could not continue to be tolerated
- The importance of the on-going British treasury support payments was that there was a steady flow of funds arriving in the colony, not only as support payments for the convicts, but they also had a flow-on effect through the commissary into the pockets of small farmers, pastoralists and vegetable growers as well as to the numerous cottage industries springing up throughout the settled areas of Sydney, Parramatta, Liverpool, Newcastle and the Hawkesbury.
- The role of free immigration and the accompanying capital contributions was essential to the constant demand for labour, enterprising operators and the capital formation within the colony. They brought capital goods, capital ideas and just plain capital to the colony.
- The role of land sales[2] was that it provided the colony with the funding boost it required to diversify the colony. Land revenues provided the direct funding for immigrants, aboriginal support, and a small amount of supplemental discretionary funding for the governor.
- The rise of the pastoral industry was crucial for trade, attracting immigrants, British investment and then to the attracting of manufacturers associated with the agricultural industries, including the extraction industries.
- The growth of manufactures[3] closely followed the growth of the agricultural sector and attracted another source and variety of capital and direct investment
- British capital investment and speculation was encouraged by the creditworthiness of the colonies, by direct investment of

---

2   Butlin 'Forming the colonial economy'
3   Hainsworth 'The Sydney Traders'

landowners from Britain and by migrant flow. British newspapers gave many column inches to events in the colony and there was a constant stream of books being written about life and exploits and successes in the colony.

- Population growth[4] was constant and fast and was supported by emancipated convicts, and convicts whose sentences had expired, by free immigrants and even by British ex-Military personnel attracted to the colony from India and post-Napoleonic Europe.

- The importance of education cannot be overstated. The illiteracy rate between 1788 and 1802 was high, but Marsden led the movement for schooling young people as well as creating literacy programs for the mature aged worker[5].

- Statistics collected for the period come from a variety of sources such as 'The blue books' original records held by the (NSW) State Records Office, from the HRNSW and the HRA. Some of the pre-1822 statistics are questionable but with nothing better, they offer a limited picture of life in the colony. Coghlan was the official collector of statistics for over 30 years and his 'Wealth & Progress' provides a vital contribution to our understanding of fiscal events, trends and achievements within the colony as well as a graphic comparison of the six colonies.

Each of these elements contributes to the growth of the colonial economy.

Thus, this is 'how' the economy grew[6], the 'why' is another matter. The why was, in reality, to further the goals of British colonial policy–to create a strategic base for defence and foreign policy rationales, as an investment outlet, as a source of trade, both with raw materials being exported to Britain and British goods being imported–a Navigation Act scenario, and mostly, in practice as a transference of some of the worst social ills in Britain to a colony' out of sight'. Wrapping all these aspects together was the goal of self-sufficiency and self-support.

---

4   Hartwell 'Economic Development of VDL'
5   Abbott–Chapter 3 in Economic Development of Australia
6   Beckett 'The Economics of Colonial NSW' Chapter 3–Policies & Planning

As in any modern economy, the colonial economy had practical and physical limitations[7].

- The trade and economic cycles in the colony were influenced by events overseas, as well as local.
- Droughts and floods, insect plagues and livestock disease.
- Grazing land had limited availability until explorers found a way across the Blue Mountains in 1816.
- The Depressions of 1827 and 1841-1843 were man made and largely the result of British speculators, but the negative effects were largely offset by the boom times which attracted the investors and speculators, improved the trading between the two countries and improved the overall standard of living at a rate far greater than if there had been no cycles.

To offset these limitations[8], there were a number of positive aspects within the economy

- There was a continuous and growing flow of convicts between 1820 and 1842. In all over 160,000 convicted souls found their way to the colonies in Australia.
- Ever increasing physical and fiscal resources were provided by Britain to the colonial economy.
- There followed the creation of basic capital accumulation by individuals.
- Sustained higher living standards were underpinned by British fiscal support.
- The growing population was underpinned by the progressive freeing of prisoners, as well as by sponsored immigration, which in turn brought a constant social change.

---

[7]   Based on Beckett, G 'The Public Finance of Colonial NSW' (colonial press 2002)

[8]   Based on Butlin, S.J. 'Foundations of the Australian Monetary System 1788-1851'

Other commentators and writers comment on the source of growth in the colonial economy. Abbott and Nairn[9] introduce a number of specialist economic historians in their edited version of 'The economic Growth of Australia 1788-1820' Hartwell[10] writes of the Economic Development of VDL 1820-1859, and Fitzpatrick[11] offers another opinion in 'The British Empire in Australia'.

Butlin, N.G[12] suggests his own formula of economic growth factors in 'Forming the Colonial Economy'.

However, Abbott in his Introduction[13] points out the dearth of any written treatment of the early phases of Australian economic development in publication between 1939(Fitzpatrick) and Shaw's Convicts and Colonies[14] in 1966. Abbott & Nairn try to fill that gap through a collection of short papers, usually an abbreviated version of the author's full account elsewhere in print. They believe (as stated in their Introduction) that the 'economic advantages to the colony included the resources made available by Britain, although the convicts provided merely the means, not the end of settlement'[15]. They also insist that the economic and strategic motives ascribed to Britain in the settlement of the colony must include the 'examination of the decision to transport convicts to Botany Bay in terms of British colonial policy before 1786, and of the prevailing social and economic conditions in Britain and their possible relation to crime[16].

Having considered the how of the equation seeking to determine the contribution to growth of the colonial economy, now we need to consider the reasons why.

---

9   Abbott & Nairn (eds) Economic Development of Australia
10   Hartwell 'Economic Development of VDL'
11   Fitzpatrick 'The British Empire in Australia'
12   Butlin, N.G. 'Forming the Colonial Economy'
13   Abbott & Nairn 'The Economic Growth of Australia'
14   Shaw, A.G.L. 'Convicts & Colonies'
15   Introduction to Economic Development of Australia 1788-1821
16   Abbott & Nairn (eds) 'The economic Growth of Australia 1788-1821'

The economic growth of the colony was but one of the considerations necessary to meet the defence, foreign policy, economic and social goals of the British settlement plan. An undeveloped colony did not gain the British any credibility in meeting their goals, and it was the transfer of the convicts to this alternative penal settlement that provided the workhorses of development to meet their full objectives. In addition, at least in Governor Phillip's settlement implementation plan, the convicts would be used to develop the infrastructure whilst at the same time encouraging the extraction and utilisation of available raw materials ready for shipping back to Britain.

We will now consider the key factors set down above, within the space constraints of this exercise. Each one would be the subject of a broad study in chapter length[17], under a number of category headings viz. Colonial Economic Statistics; Capital Formation in the Colonial Economy; Sequencing the Growth (an Abbott concept); The Patterns of Growth and The Cottage Industries.

A. Statistics

The statistical[18] summaries[19] show numerous highlights of the colonial economy and can be listed as follows:

o   The population growth[20] was regular and challenging, although the surplus of males over females was disparate and potentially detrimental. We should be mindful of the number of children and their specific needs. The nexus between total population and those 'on the store' was broken and reduced year by year. This progress affected the role, influence and operation of the commissary. Two other observations on the population growth can be made. Firstly,

---

[17]   Refer Beckett who includes chapter length discussions in 'The Economics of Colonial NSW'

[18]   Sourced from Beckett, G 'Handbook of Colonial Statistics' (colonial press–2003)

[19]   Reproduced in the appendix to this study

[20]   Source HRA, *passim*

the growth rates in the Town of Sydney followed similar trends to those later found in Parramatta, Liverpool and Windsor. This means that selected decentralisation locations were attractive to new settlers and met the needs of these settlers. Secondly, as the earliest settlement outgrew its natural boundaries (of the Blue Mountains, the Hawkesbury to the north and the Nepean to the south), the new expansion settlements of Bathurst (ten (10) small land grants were initially made 1815-1818) and Newcastle (twenty-three (23) small agricultural grants were made in 1821) supported Lord Bathurst's policy of large-scale land grants to be a catalyst to growth.

o   The number of convicts[21] arriving in New South Wales made a big difference to the colony in transition

o   The volume of treasury bills[22] drawn by the colony, especially in those first important 30 years, reflected two facts–the amazingly low cost to the British Treasury of operating the colony (that Treasury goal was being achieved) and of just where the 'capital formation' in those early years was coming from.

o   The return of livestock[23] shows the successful pasturing of sheep and cattle and the quality of management, climate and husbandry proffered this burgeoning industry.

o   Trade statistics[24] (imports) shows the source of such imports and the need for securing the Asian trade routes, for the majority of imports arrived from India and China and only in 1821 were the majority of imports from Britain.

o   From as early as 1810, private farming[25], based on evidence to the Bigge enquiry as contained in his subsequent report, was dominant, successful and essential to the needs of the colony. The accuracy of some of the statistics is questionable but they are the only statistics available. The total acres appear to be well balanced between grazing (sheep, cattle and hogs all grew rapidly with little

---

[21] Shaw, A.G.L. *Convicts & the Colonies* pp363-8

[22] Bigge, J.T.–Appendix to Report III (1823)

[23] Source: Select Committee of the House of Commons on Transportation 1838

[24] Wentworth, W. C. 'History of NSW '

[25] Bigge evidence

sign of breeding loss or slaughter for food) and grain, with wheat and maize sharing the farming land.

o   By reviewing the prices obtained at the London auctions of NSW Wool between 1818 and 1821[26], we can understand Bathurst's goal of growing 'fine' wool, which he thought would have averaged 12s per pound rather than the 2s 10p it actually achieved.

o   Wool shipments[27] soared between 1807 and 1821 and grew from 13,616 lb to 175,433 lb annually during that time.

o   An early 1821 map of Sydney[28] shows the location of the emerging manufactures of the colony. The second slaughterhouse had opened, a sixth mill was opened and we find the locations of boat-building, tanneries, salt works, furniture, candles, earthenware, tea and tobacco and a brewery, all serving the colony. Manufacturing was not the largest employer but in terms of import replacement goods, was the most important employer. Agriculture won the export stakes and supported the colonial local revenue base by allowing imports to match exports, and supporting a duty and tariff on all imports. This local discretionary revenue started off small and convenient, but grew rapidly into a major government source of revenues to cover every expenditure apart from the direct costs of the convict system.

o   A listing of major Public Works[29] helps us understand the benefits to the colony of the free settlers, the convicts, the contractors and the entrepreneurs. In summary, the period between 1817 and 1821 witnessed the development of 6 main roads, of major government buildings, of churches, of military barracks and growing infrastructure. Mostly the period witnessed the success of the Macquarie administration and his major contribution to the colonial economic growth.

o   This writer's assembling of raw colonial economic statistics[30] (refer appendix) suggests a positive balance of payments growth during the 1826-1834 period with growth, but sometimes negative

---

26   Macarthur Papers Vol 69

27   ibid

28   NLA Map Collection–Sydney Map published 1822

29   Cathcart, L–Public Works of NSW

30   Beckett 'Handbook of Colonial Statistics (colonial press 2003)

balance of payments at other times. Imports took a dip in the depression years of 1827 and 1828 but grew dramatically until the next depression of 1842-1844. Local revenues, which the British treasury relied upon to replace contributions from Britain, also grew as a reflection of the burgeoning colonial economy. If we use 1826 as a base year then growth to 1834 became a cumulative factor of 280% over those 8 years or a remarkable 4% per annum.

All in all, the statistics acquaint the reader with a fairly comprehensive picture of 'how' (much) the colony was growing, especially during those important formative years. The colonial establishment had laid the basis for a successful colony and for supporting the future rounds of convict transfers.

CHAPTER 3

THE COLONIAL ECONOMY
GROWING TOWARDS
SELF-SUFFICIENCY

Early Intentions, Policies & Plans

It was British policy to retain the concept of a prison settlement but only if the colony could pay its own way. Such dual desires were in conflict. Autocracy (as in being necessary to operate a prison) would destroy any freedom of enterprise, which in any other circumstances was essential to the growth of colonial income. Would social and political progress come with economic advances?

Wealth would increase continuously between 1802 and 1850, not due to any industrialisation, but due to an entry into a cycle of investment in pastures and sheep–'the golden age'. Wealth was measured in purely tangible forms–Coghlan in '*The Wealth & Progress of NSW*–1886', computed the wealth of the colony at that time, in terms of the value of rural holdings, the value of residential town developments, the value of government buildings, of roads and other infrastructure, plus the value of all usable plant and equipment. Needless to say, this measurement got unwieldy and did not last as a statistical guide to the success of the colony. Probably Coghlan was being forced to compare the colony of NSW with other colonies in Australia as well as with similar countries overseas, for political purposes. Coghlan produces a table comparing the NSW wealth per head with that of numerous overseas countries, with little point except to comment that measuring standards were different elsewhere.

The cycle rolled forward–opening up new land, adding the grazing of sheep, adding to 'national income' followed by more investment–and the cycle rolls around again. Diversification of the economy soon followed and led to an ever-increasing standard of living, which, in itself sustained further growth.

Capital formation followed, mostly in agriculture but increasingly in manufactures[31]. Such steps usually relied on borrowing externally, but such borrowing must have been accompanied by development of financial institutions.

A society, which cannot by its own savings finance the progress it desires must strive, in the alternative, to make itself credit worthy and will only succeed if it follows market opportunities and adopts comparative advantage.

Because future prospects depend so much on present imports, the colony must look for profitable export industries[32]. It must also offer prospects of gain to people of enterprise.

Let me restate the salient points of the above synopsis.

The main characteristics of the colonial economy in transition[33](before 1832) are

- The Colonial Government adopted the policy of free enterprise and free trade, during and following the administration of Lachlan Macquarie.
- Out of necessity there was a dominance of agriculture in the economy–this was a social phenomenon because of the needs and availability of convict labour.

---

[31] Butlin–Forming the Colonial economy
[32] Based on Hainsworth–The Sydney Traders
[33] Beckett, G 'The economics of Colonial NSW' (colonial press 2003)

- Social problems with bad treatment of aborigines and convicts curbed the otherwise 'clean' image of a successful economy.
- Lack of catalysts for British private investment prevailed until Macquarie converted the colonial image in the 1810-1820 period with new buildings, cleaning up the slums of the 'Rocks' area, and encouraging new enterprise.
- Wealth creation was taking place through capital investment and speculation.
- The growing need for financial institutions came with the commencement of borrowing and capital migration.
- The need for private borrowing overseas occurred because of the lack of savings, wealth and financial institutions in the economy before 1830.

On the other hand the key factors of the (gradually) maturing colonial economy changed slightly (after 1832)

- Transportation and the convict labour program was the catalyst for growth until growth plateaued and transportation became more of an economic burden that could not continue to be tolerated
- The importance of the on-going British treasury support payments was that there was a steady flow of funds arriving in the colony, not only as support payments for the convicts, but they also had a flow-on effect through the commissary into the pockets of small farmers, pastoralists and vegetable growers as well as to the numerous cottage industries springing up throughout the settled areas of Sydney, Parramatta, Liverpool, Newcastle and the Hawkesbury.
- The role of free immigration and the accompanying capital contributions was essential to the constant demand for labour, enterprising operators and the capital formation within the colony. They brought capital goods, capital ideas and just plain capital to the colony.
- The role of land sales[34] was that it provided the colony with the funding boost it required to diversify the colony. Land revenues provided the direct funding for immigrants, aboriginal support,

---

[34] Butlin 'Forming the colonial economy'

and a small amount of supplemental discretionary funding for the governor.

- The rise of the pastoral industry was crucial for trade, attracting immigrants, British investment and then to the attracting of manufacturers associated with the agricultural industries, including the extraction industries.
- The growth of manufactures[35] closely followed the growth of the agricultural sector and attracted another source and variety of capital and direct investment
- British capital investment and speculation was encouraged by the creditworthiness of the colonies, by direct investment of landowners from Britain and by migrant flow. British newspapers gave many column inches to events in the colony and there was a constant stream of books being written about life and exploits and successes in the colony.
- Population growth[36] was constant and fast and was supported by emancipated convicts, and convicts whose sentences had expired, by free immigrants and even by British ex-Military personnel attracted to the colony from India and post-Napoleonic Europe.
- The importance of education cannot be overstated. The illiteracy rate between 1788 and 1802 was high, but Marsden led the movement for schooling young people as well as creating literacy programs for the mature aged worker[37].
- Statistics collected for the period come from a variety of sources such as 'The blue books' original records held by the (NSW) State Records Office, from the HRNSW and the HRA. Some of the pre-1822 statistics are questionable but with nothing better, they offer a limited picture of life in the colony. Coghlan was the official collector of statistics for over 30 years and his 'Wealth & Progress' provides a vital contribution to our understanding of fiscal events, trends and achievements within the colony as well as a graphic comparison of the six colonies.

---

35 Hainsworth 'The Sydney Traders'

36 Hartwell 'Economic Development of VDL'

37 Abbott–Chapter 3 in Economic Development of Australia

Each of these elements contributes to the growth of the colonial economy.

Thus, this is 'how' the economy grew[38], the 'why' is another matter. The why was, in reality, to further the goals of British colonial policy–to create a strategic base for defence and foreign policy rationales, as an investment outlet, as a source of trade, both with raw materials being exported to Britain and British goods being imported–a Navigation Act scenario, and mostly, in practice as a transference of some of the worst social ills in Britain to a colony' out of sight'. Wrapping all these aspects together was the goal of self-sufficiency and self-support.

As in any modern economy, the colonial economy had practical and physical limitations[39].

- The trade and economic cycles in the colony were influenced by events overseas, as well as local.
- Droughts and floods, insect plagues and livestock disease.
- Grazing land had limited availability until explorers found a way across the Blue Mountains in 1816.
- The Depressions of 1827 and 1841-1843 were man made and largely the result of British speculators, but the negative effects were largely offset by the boom times which attracted the investors and speculators, improved the trading between the two countries and improved the overall standard of living at a rate far greater than if there had been no cycles.

To offset these limitations[40], there were a number of positive aspects within the economy

---

[38] Beckett 'The Economics of Colonial NSW' Chapter 3–Policies & Planning

[39] Based on Beckett, G 'The Public Finance of Colonial NSW' (colonial press 2002)

[40] Based on Butlin, S.J. 'Foundations of the Australian Monetary System 1788-1851'

- There was a continuous and growing flow of convicts between 1820 and 1842. In all over 160,000 convicted souls found their way to the colonies in Australia.
- Ever increasing physical and fiscal resources were provided by Britain to the colonial economy.
- There followed the creation of basic capital accumulation by individuals.
- Sustained higher living standards were underpinned by British fiscal support.
- The growing population was underpinned by the progressive freeing of prisoners, as well as by sponsored immigration, which in turn brought a constant social change.

Other commentators and writers comment on the source of growth in the colonial economy. Abbott and Nairn[41] introduce a number of specialist economic historians in their edited version of 'The economic Growth of Australia 1788-1820' Hartwell[42] writes of the Economic Development of VDL 1820-1859, and Fitzpatrick[43] offers another opinion in 'The British Empire in Australia'.

Butlin, N.G[44] suggests his own formula of economic growth factors in 'Forming the Colonial Economy'.

However, Abbott in his Introduction[45] points out the dearth of any written treatment of the early phases of Australian economic development in publication between 1939(Fitzpatrick) and Shaw's Convicts and Colonies[46] in 1966. Abbott & Nairn try to fill that gap through a collection of short papers, usually an abbreviated version of the author's full account elsewhere in print. They believe (as stated in their Introduction) that the 'economic advantages to the colony included the resources made available by Britain, although the convicts provided merely the means, not the end

---

[41] Abbott & Nairn (eds) Economic Development of Australia
[42] Hartwell 'Economic Development of VDL'
[43] Fitzpatrick 'The British Empire in Australia'
[44] Butlin, N.G. 'Forming the Colonial Economy'
[45] Abbott & Nairn 'The Economic Growth of Australia'
[46] Shaw, A.G.L. 'Convicts & Colonies'

of settlement'[47]. They also insist that the economic and strategic motives ascribed to Britain in the settlement of the colony must include the 'examination of the decision to transport convicts to Botany Bay in terms of British colonial policy before 1786, and of the prevailing social and economic conditions in Britain and their possible relation to crime[48].

Having considered the how of the equation seeking to determine the contribution to growth of the colonial economy, now we need to consider the reasons why.

The economic growth of the colony was but one of the considerations necessary to meet the defence, foreign policy, economic and social goals of the British settlement plan. An undeveloped colony did not gain the British any credibility in meeting their goals, and it was the transfer of the convicts to this alternative penal settlement that provided the workhorses of development to meet their full objectives. In addition, at least in Governor Phillip's settlement implementation plan, the convicts would be used to develop the infrastructure whilst at the same time encouraging the extraction and utilisation of available raw materials ready for shipping back to Britain.

We will now consider the key factors set down above, within the space constraints of this exercise. Each one would be the subject of a broad study in chapter length[49], under a number of category headings viz. Colonial Economic Statistics; Capital Formation in the Colonial Economy; Sequencing the Growth (an Abbott concept); The Patterns of Growth and The Cottage Industries.

---

[47] Introduction to Economic Development of Australia 1788-1821

[48] Abbott & Nairn (eds) 'The economic Growth of Australia 1788-1821'

[49] Refer Beckett who includes chapter length discussions in 'The Economics of Colonial NSW'

A. Statistics

The statistical[50] summaries[51] show numerous highlights of the colonial economy and can be listed as follows:

o   The population growth[52] was regular and challenging, although the surplus of males over females was disparate and potentially detrimental. We should be mindful of the number of children and their specific needs. The nexus between total population and those 'on the store' was broken and reduced year by year. This progress affected the role, influence and operation of the commissary. Two other observations on the population growth can be made. Firstly, the growth rates in the Town of Sydney followed similar trends to those later found in Parramatta, Liverpool and Windsor. This means that selected decentralisation locations were attractive to new settlers and met the needs of these settlers. Secondly, as the earliest settlement outgrew its natural boundaries (of the Blue Mountains, the Hawkesbury to the north and the Nepean to the south), the new expansion settlements of Bathurst (ten (10) small land grants were initially made 1815-1818) and Newcastle (twenty-three (23) small agricultural grants were made in 1821) supported Lord Bathurst's policy of large-scale land grants to be a catalyst to growth.

o   The number of convicts[53] arriving in New South Wales made a big difference to the colony in transition

o   The volume of treasury bills[54] drawn by the colony, especially in those first important 30 years, reflected two facts—the amazingly low cost to the British Treasury of operating the colony (that Treasury goal was being achieved) and of just where the 'capital formation' in those early years was coming from.

---

[50]   Sourced from Beckett, G 'Handbook of Colonial Statistics' (colonial press–2003)

[51]   Reproduced in the appendix to this study

[52]   Source HRA, *passim*

[53]   Shaw, A.G.L. *Convicts & the Colonies* pp363-8

[54]   Bigge, J.T.–Appendix to Report III (1823)

o The return of livestock[55] shows the successful pasturing of sheep and cattle and the quality of management, climate and husbandry proffered this burgeoning industry.

o Trade statistics[56] (imports) shows the source of such imports and the need for securing the Asian trade routes, for the majority of imports arrived from India and China and only in 1821 were the majority of imports from Britain.

o From as early as 1810, private farming[57], based on evidence to the Bigge enquiry as contained in his subsequent report, was dominant, successful and essential to the needs of the colony. The accuracy of some of the statistics is questionable but they are the only statistics available. The total acres appear to be well balanced between grazing (sheep, cattle and hogs all grew rapidly with little sign of breeding loss or slaughter for food) and grain, with wheat and maize sharing the farming land.

o By reviewing the prices obtained at the London auctions of NSW Wool between 1818 and 1821[58], we can understand Bathurst's goal of growing 'fine' wool, which he thought would have averaged 12s per pound rather than the 2s 10p it actually achieved.

o Wool shipments[59] soared between 1807 and 1821 and grew from 13,616 lb to 175,433 lb annually during that time.

o An early 1821 map of Sydney[60] shows the location of the emerging manufactures of the colony. The second slaughterhouse had opened, a sixth mill was opened and we find the locations of boat-building, tanneries, salt works, furniture, candles, earthenware, tea and tobacco and a brewery, all serving the colony. Manufacturing was not the largest employer but in terms of import replacement goods, was the most important employer. Agriculture won the export stakes and supported the colonial local revenue base by allowing imports to match exports, and supporting a duty and tariff on all imports. This local discretionary revenue

---

[55] Source: Select Committee of the House of Commons on Transportation 1838
[56] Wentworth, W. C. 'History of NSW'
[57] Bigge evidence
[58] Macarthur Papers Vol 69
[59] ibid
[60] NLA Map Collection—Sydney Map published 1822

started off small and convenient, but grew rapidly into a major government source of revenues to cover every expenditure apart from the direct costs of the convict system.

o   A listing of major Public Works[61] helps us understand the benefits to the colony of the free settlers, the convicts, the contractors and the entrepreneurs. In summary, the period between 1817 and 1821 witnessed the development of 6 main roads, of major government buildings, of churches, of military barracks and growing infrastructure. Mostly the period witnessed the success of the Macquarie administration and his major contribution to the colonial economic growth.

o   This writer's assembling of raw colonial economic statistics[62] (refer appendix) suggests a positive balance of payments growth during the 1826-1834 period with growth, but sometimes negative balance of payments at other times. Imports took a dip in the depression years of 1827 and 1828 but grew dramatically until the next depression of 1842-1844. Local revenues, which the British treasury relied upon to replace contributions from Britain, also grew as a reflection of the burgeoning colonial economy. If we use 1826 as a base year then growth to 1834 became a cumulative factor of 280% over those 8 years or a remarkable 4% per annum.

All in all, the statistics acquaint the reader with a fairly comprehensive picture of 'how' (much) the colony was growing, especially during those important formative years. The colonial establishment had laid the basis for a successful colony and for supporting the future rounds of convict transfers.

• Public Expenditure in the Colony

If the statistical summary shows how progress was made in the colonial economy then a brief study of the mechanics of 'capital formation' will evidence the fiscal factors underpinning that progress.

---

[61]   Cathcart, L–Public Works of NSW
[62]   Beckett 'Handbook of Colonial Statistics (colonial press 2003)

Capital formation in the colony during these early years can be focused on the massive building and construction program. In the new colony, there was a demand for convict and military barracks, housing and government buildings, storehouses for the commissary, docks, wharfs, draining programs, fresh water, and so on. The support services required a supply of bricks, tiles, timber, furniture, roads, boats, agriculture and farming for food production. *The core of government practical economic management between 1788 and 1830 was The Lumber Yard*[63]*, which included The Dockyard, the Stone Quarries, the Female Factory, and various timber harvesting, land clearing and road making enterprises.*

The capital for these government enterprises had been provided by the British Treasury, and certainly in greater quantities than originally estimated. Matra, in his 1776 submission to the British Government estimated an outlay of £3,500 for the first year and from then on self-sufficiency and no further cost to the British Treasury.[64] This estimate was not only optimistic but did not allow for adequate infrastructure once the colony was settled. Matra's plan was for a small convict contingent by the shore of the deep water mooring, with a fresh water stream close by, level ground for building log barracks and store buildings. No weather disturbances, no wild animals, no deleterious convicts, and a plentiful supply of wild animals and fruit and vegetables, good soils, and no interference from any natives. Matra's dream world was far from realistic and practical but his projections suited the senior government and parliamentary officials who approved a small impractical budget for the expedition.

The basic economic problem within the growing economy, and thus one of the early limitations to solid or speedy growth, was the provision of savings to sustain the army of unskilled and semi-skilled workers engaged in this construction and development work–this in turn, hindered private construction for other than settlers who had ready money to invest in such work, and thus most early residences were supplied and furnished

---

[63]   Refer Beckett' The Public Finance of NSW' where a full discussion is made of the Commissary and convict management including the various enterprises of the commissary operations.

[64]   HRNSW–Copy of Matra's letter to the British Colonial Secretary detailing the costs of establishing the new colony

by the government. However, in the absence of an adequate local supply, the greatest part of these 'investment' funds was to be drawn from outside Australia, in the form of imported British capital. This flow of British capital helps our understanding of the aggregate capital formation in the colony. British capital was important in inducing the smooth expansion during the first four decades of the colony, and it was a key factor in the subsequent economic declines in 1827 and in 1842-1844. For most of this period, prices and wages rose slowly if not persistently and inflation was imported on the back of speculative activities.

Obviously public authorities played an important role in capital formation[65] and the public sector seems to have contributed a declining portion of the aggregate from 100% to approx 50% during these first four decades. Four components dominated overall aggregate capital formation. These are ranked in terms of volume: Infrastructure such as roads, buildings, barracks etc; agriculture such as government farms, grain growing and livestock grazing; residential construction, and finally manufacturing. In broad terms, we can see that manufacturing investment in workshops and offices matched each other, and it is interesting to note that manufacturing investment did contribute to what was perceived as a dominant agricultural, pastoral and farming economy. It is also noteworthy that the British Government continued to pay for and thus contribute the convict and transportation system, the colonial defence and the 'civil list' for the colonial use.

C. The Role of the State[66]

If capital formation reflected the engine of growth and the statistics reflected the multifarious facets of growth, then the State became the conduit for growth[67]. Competent government policies, capable administration and sound conditions for enterprise were the essential ingredients for colonial economic growth, and even the dichotomy within the colony of 'free

---

[65] Based on Hartwell 'Economic Growth of VDL'
[66] Based on Fitzpatrick 'The British Empire in Australia
[67] Based on Beckett–Chapter 5–'William Lithgow' where capital formation and the role of government is discussed

enterprise' or 'government enterprise' could not slow the clamour for better living conditions, jobs and a controlled haven for entrepreneurs.

Fitzpatrick in *The British Empire in Australia* reminds us of the transition in 1834 from the point 'where the earliest community was primarily a state-supported establishment to the next point (after 1834) when imported capital applied to wool growing and associated or derivative industries rapidly endowed the community with the character of British private enterprise instead of public enterprise, and appointed the pastoral sector as a field for investment into a profitable colonial territory'[68]. The Forbes Act (by the Legislative Council) in 1834 offered inducements to British capitalists to invest in New South Wales, and as a result the colony of NSW, with three million people, had received twice as much British capital as the Dominion of Canada, with a population of nearly 4.5 million. There are obviously two distinct stages of state intervention in reaching out to overseas investors. Before 1834 the role of the state was to provide British capitalists with free land and labour in the colony, then came the development of sheep-raising of fine wool, and the sequel was, having facilitated the importation of capital for investment, its role was to provide services which would facilitate the earning of dividends on the capital invested. However, even though initial dividends were sent 'home' in ever-increasing quantities, the time came when local people and institutions were the recipients of these dividends and great enterprises were part owned within the colony.

The state had, according to Fitzpatrick[69], four main functions:

o Firstly, to take the responsibility for adjusting claims when the economic system reached crisis, as in 1827 and 1842, although Governor Gibbs acted reluctantly and belatedly in the latter crisis.
o Secondly, the state is to administer essential services, in the operation of which private investors could not derive normal profits.

[68] Fitzpatrick 'The British Empire in Australia
[69] ibid Page 347

o   Thirdly, the state must nurture enterprise, including well-capitalised undertakings, by means of tariffs, bounties and other concessions.

o   Fourthly the State is to take responsibility for restoring to private capital, power, which has been taken away from it.

Fitzpatrick can be challenged on, at least, this last point. It surely cannot be the role of the state to supplant, supplement or fiscally support private capital lost within the colonial economy. If private investment criteria is invalid or faulty, then within a free enterprise economy, even one adopting an extended use of government enterprise, private capital must be supported by or subjected to market forces and not 'restored' by the state.

The introduction of the railways, just outside our time-line is such an example. The British were strongly urging private operators to install and operate in-town rail services. The *Sydney Railway Company* was empowered by the Legislative Council to build a private line with the support of 'government guarantees', with the right of the government to resume operations with minimal compensation to shareholders if the enterprise collapsed. The enterprise did collapse, was taken over by government planners, financially restored to health and the railway system moved on to be become a successful government enterprise[70]. The role of the State, in this typical case, was not to guarantee speculators, but to protect the suppliers and contractors who placed their trust and faith in the free enterprise system. Fitzpatrick is confusing a touch of Marxist policy with a shackled government enterprise.

We can deduce that the state had an important role in the development[71] of the colonial economy and filled this role with supportive mechanisms and policies–especially guidance for financial institutions following overseas borrowing, overseas investment and land speculation.

---

[70]   Beckett 'The Public Finance of the Colony of NSW' (colonial press 2002)

[71]   See also Butlin, N.G. 'Forming the Colonial Economy' for a discussion of these factors leading to changes in financial institutions

D. Sequencing Economic Growth[72]

I come now to a brief study of 'in what sequence' did the economy grow, and as N.G. Butlin, in the Preface to *Investment in Australian Economic Development* writes "I have found no guidance on this question from the few essays which examine the early economy in identifying the sequence of economic growth in terms of both aggregate behaviour and the performance of major investment components".

One must fear to tread where Butlin finds weakness or gaps. This essay may still not fully satisfy the larger Butlin type questions but the immediate concern is about the 'hows' and the 'whys' of the colonial economic growth between 1788 and 1850 and as such there is an obligation, albeit ritualistic, to outline the main sectors of investment contributing to that growth. Since this study may cover many areas, methodology and circumstances of sequential development may not matter as much as first thought.

Some facts should perhaps be stated first as the basis for future conclusions:

- o Government enterprise towered above private enterprise[73] at least between 1788 and 1821 because the government had the sole access to capital, land and labour, and government enterprise met the needs of the colony and its community of free settlers.
- o Government enterprise was based on two facts–survival and self-sufficiency of the colony. From Phillip's livestock and building materials imported with the first fleet (including his 'portable' government house), government had undertaken to be the planner, the contractor, the financier and the provider of all labour and material resources in this new penal colony. That essentially was the nature of a penal settlement[74]. Then King decided he wanted a little 'spending money' outside the purview of the British Treasury, and this was a development unknown in normal prison or penal colonies but became the first step in the transition

---

[72] Based on Butlin, N.G. 'Investment in Australian Economic Development

[73] A concept of Marjorie Barnard in 'Macquarie's World'

[74] Based on Ellis Chapter 11 'Lachlan Macquarie'

to a semi-autocratic free settlement. If this is an anachronism, then substitute 'planned economy' into any government encouragement of free enterprise. Then add Governor Macquarie, who as a free spirit, developer extraordinaire and ego driven creator of entrepreneurship[75]. Macquarie's contribution is in itself extraordinary. He applied, wisely, firm private enterprise principals to planning and development and set his sights on bettering the colonists' standard of living, changing the reliance on government hand-outs (the colony had to stand on its own feet, which is subtly different to being entirely self-sufficient, but is a good first step to self-sufficiency) and encouraging entrepreneurship in the colony. In Macquarie's mind, the role of his administration was to reduce British Treasury support payments, increase discretionary local revenues, build desirable government buildings and infrastructure, and create the atmosphere for manufacturing in the colony.

o Obviously agriculture was the main objective of economic planning. It could use most of the convicts arriving in the colony[76]; it was minimalist in skills requirements, and relied more on natural events than most other colonial activities, but was mainly the most important of labour intensive undertakings. Agricultural operations would be extended to government farming, land clearing, timber harvesting and much of the work of the Lumber Yard. Its success was essential to maintaining the colony and making it self-sufficient As was pointed out above, agriculture contributed to more capital formation in the colony than did manufacturing but the rise of manufacturing mostly during and following the Macquarie administration created balance within the economy and created a support structure internally and an import replacement opportunity

o The growth of government enterprises such as the government farms, the Lumber Yard,[77] which in turn included the stone quarries, and the timber forests, the Female Factory and the Dockyard, encouraged rather than damaged any move to free enterprise operations. The earliest private enterprises, other than

---

[75] Concept from Barnard 'Macquarie's World'

[76] Refer Shaw 'Convicts & Colonies'

[77] Refer Beckett 'The Economics of Colonial NSW'

pastoral establishments, were government contractors. Little capital was required, only limited skills (other than a nose for making money) were necessary, and there was plenty of work available and not a lot of competition.

o   British private capital was uncertain and untried in the colonial context; investment within Britain or in the tropical colonies was considered more profitable and safer; of the hundreds of companies floated in the United Kingdom between 1820 and 1850, only five important companies were formed for investment in Australia. The Land Grant Companies–these were the three (3), plus two banks, within the Australian context–The Australian Agricultural Company (AA Coy), The Van Diemen's Land Company[78] (VDL Coy), The South Australia Coy (SA Coy), Bank of Australasia and The Union Bank of Australia–filled a role as catalyst for attracting new investment and even offered some official sanctioning and support parameters for colonial investing[79].

o   A question should be posed, at this point, as assistance for understanding the sequence of development. Was the colonial NSW economy in 1830 a capitalist economy[80]? It was, as we learnt earlier, an economy in transition before and after that date. In so far as capitalism implies a rational, and acquisitive society, then NSW had been capitalist (urged along by Macquarie) ever since it had broken the bonds of being the self-contained prison promulgated in 1788. Capitalist techniques, as opposed to traditional techniques of economic planning, assisted with the transition from a penal to a free economic society. The transition included the organisation of production by the capitalistic entrepreneur for profit, by the combining of labour and materials into a marketable product. The capitalist enterprise portrayed itself in the banks, the insurance companies, merchant houses and the large-scale pastoral farms–all institutions, which were rationally

---

[78]   Refer Beckett, G. 'The economic circumstances of the Van Diemen's Land Company (colonial press 2003)

[79]   Hartwell refers to similar factors in 'The VDL Government 'Historical Studies ANZ, Nov 1950

[80]   Butlin, N.G. in 'Forming the Colonial Economy states that the colonial economy was 'capitalistic' This portion of the essay is examining this claim

organised for the pursuit of profits. The most important means of production–land–had fallen by the 1830s into relatively few hands–trade and finance were highly concentrated, most of the population were without ownership of property, and worked for a wage determined by the market. West, in *A History of Tasmania*[81], offers us a quotable insight into the settlement progression "The dignity and independence of landed wealth is ever the chief allurement of the emigrant. Whatever his rank, he dreams of the day when he shall dwell in a mansion planned by himself, survey a wide and verdant landscape called after his name and sit beneath the vineyard planted by his own hands"

o   Another brief quote may also be in order. Hartwell, writing in *The Economic Development of VDL 1820-1850* thinks "it is impossible to study the trade cycles without reference to general economic development, and the existing economic histories of Australia did not answer the kind of questions I was asking"[82]. His point is that he offered, in his work, a specialist account of economic development, as will this account try to be in relation to the growth of the colonial economy in New South Wales.

E. Patterns of Economic Growth[83]

Although Butlin raised an interesting question on sequences of growth, any reference to sequences can also be raised in terms of 'patterns'.

The highlights of any 'pattern' can be traced to the foundation of the colony. This will also serve to identify some of the 'whys' in the essay topic.

The colony was founded for the multiple purposes of creating an intermediate stopping point for British ships travelling to India and China, of provisioning them, offering some form of back loading for the return trip to Britain, after unloading goods at this Port of Botany Bay. It

---

81   West,' History of Tasmania–edited by Shaw in one volume
82   Hartwell 'Economic History of VDL' P.251
83   A Beckett concept developed in The Economics of Colonial NSW

was also considered to be of strategic value in limiting the expansion of Portuguese and Dutch interests in the sub-Asian region. Bonus reasons were considered to be that the East Coast region could be a source of raw materials for British industry[84], which was at that time coming to the implementation stage of the industrial revolution, and that any future colony would utilise British shipping and be an outlet for future investment and finally but almost as an after-thought any colony in so isolated a region could be a suitable location for a penal settlement.

Thus the growth in the colony followed first the formation of capital, then the importation preferences of capital, then the needs of the colony and finally the desires and preferences of the entrepreneurs and traders. This cycle continued right up to the discovery of gold, but it was not the traditional boom and bust cycle. It was a trade and investment cycle of designating an investment opportunity, bringing together the capital required, filling the opportunity and recommencing the cycle by starting all over.

The pattern changed somewhat in the mid-1830s (the colony was by now almost a mature 50 years of age) when the pattern of growth suddenly had a new spoke–local wealth, local ownership, locally retained dividends and the need for reinvestment. This change in pattern broke into the overseas raising of capital, and the overseas distribution of dividends and the overseas domination of manufacturing in the colony.

Local traders were gaining prominence in sealing, whaling, exporting and importing, merchant financing and the commencement of local auctioneering. Traditionally the Sydney markets had favoured enterprising practitioners who had surplus livestock or cottage industry manufactures, and these pursuits often led to more than the public markets as their distribution point. Simeon Lord, the master trader, bought a hat manufacturer in Botany whose rise had been exactly along those lines, cottage industry production, public markets distribution, rented premises, paid labourers, advertising, then buy-out and take-over.

---

[84] Proposed by Sir Joseph Banks (HRNSW–Vol 1)

Government policy fitted largely into this pattern and we have covered already the encouragement of business enterprise, however, the main role of government was to create the climate and the environment for entrepreneurs, borrowers, lenders and a satisfactory circumstance for making a profit and the return of capital. This came by way of successful business ventures, in both the agricultural and industrial enterprises. Because the skill levels within the colony were only gradually expanding and refining, there was official encouragement of British industry expanding with branch operations. Agricultural enterprise was encouraged by offers of land grants and then the cheap sale of land, and later the provision of either cleared land or convict labour.

Abbott[85] discusses the 'constituents' of the New South Wales colonial economy, and lists six. Agriculture; The Pastoral industry; Manufacturing; Trade within the colony; Exports other than wool; Government Works and Services.

Let me turn to some 'constraints' on the growth of the colonial economy; these include[86] Government policy; land, labour and capital.

There was an implied constraint to local colonial growth imposed by the Westminster parliament. The last of the series of Navigation Acts was in 1696 but stood unchanged until after the recognition of American Independence in 1783[87]. In general, until the legislation was passed,

British colonists had been free to trade with any country and to use ships of any nationality, and accept the cheapest freights. Following the passage of the legislation and the numerous amendments, they were obliged to use only British (including colonial) ships, to send all their exports direct to Britain and to import all their overseas goods direct from Britain. In this way, writes Abbott in *Economic Growth of Australia 1788-1821*, the colonists were virtually insulated from direct contact with the world economy.

---

85   Abbott & Nairn 'The Economic Growth of Australia
86   Abbott & Nairn 'The Economic Growth of Australia
87   Discussed in Hainsworth 'The Sydney Traders'

CHAPTER 4

THE GROWTH OF MANUFACTURING IN THE COLONY AS A RESULT OF COMMISSARIAT OPERATIONS

Hainsworth in the prologue to *The Sydney Traders* writes 'To study the 'entrepreneur' is to study the central figure in modern economic history–the central figure in economics'. The years 1788 to 1821 are the seed-time of Australian government'.[88]

Although it is difficult to connect the growth of economic development for any one sector in terms of percentage of contribution, we know that the more important sectors must be;

1. Growth of population
2. Government immigration policy
3. Foreign capital
4. The need for import replacement
5. The need for foreign exchange through exports.

In each of these sectors, the commissariat had a role and there was an important government need. The government had to grow the economy at the lowest practical cost, while also offering official services which would

---

[88] Hainsworth *Sydney Traders* prologue page 14

attract growth, trade and population. It achieved this, at least through 1821, by using the commissariat as the quasi-treasury, the manager of government business enterprises, and the employer of government-sponsored convict labour. The point here is that the economic model had to incorporate and reflect each of these 'input' factors. Here in brief is the methodology used.

The influence of the commissariat over foreign exchange, imports and exports, government-sponsored manufacturing and even attracting foreign investment capital is without comparison, but it is measurable. The economic model for the period does not nor cannot parallel Butlin's measurement of post-1861 GDP, but it does use basic ingredients like:

1. Computing the free working population
2. Computing the working convict population
3. Assuming a productivity adjustment for lower than expected convict output
4. Valuing productive labour at Coghlan suggested rates
5. Interpolating labour product to total output.
6. Comparing annual total production per head of population and per head of 'worker'
7. Estimating total output by industry and comparing this to underlying assumptions about labour output.
8. Extending the estimated GDP from 1800 to 1860 to ensure the recessions of 1810-1816, 1828-29 and 1842-45 as shown in the GDP figures were responsive to these downturns.
9. Comparing the growth of local revenues from 1801 and of trade, for the same period reflected changes to estimated GDP.
10. Announcing the adopted GDP figures for the period 1800-1860 and seeing how they blended in with the Butlin figures.

The results are assembled on a spreadsheet for each year, but a summary has been produced as an extract in order to evidence gains for each ten-year interval, and to show that the Beckett compilations and the Butlin compilations fit in with each other.

TABLE 7.1: ESTIMATES OF GDP BETWEEN 1800 AND 1900

Year	GDP per head of population	GDP per head of workforce
1801	13.61	35.10
1811	28.06	49.95
1821	33.54	59.70
1831	35.68	63.51
1841	39.66	70.60
1851	40.13	76.43
1861	46.00	85.00
1871	47.00	118.00
1877	57.00	139.00
1881	63.00	151.00
1889	67.00	158.00
1891	66.00	155.00
1900	57.00	132.00

Source: Beckett *Handbook of Colonial Statistics for period 1800-1860*
Butlin, N.G. *Investment in Australian Economic Development 1861-1900*

Certain conclusions can be reached about this table. GDP in the colony grew in each ten year period because the components of that GDP grew eg population, manufacturing enterprises, convict numbers, exports and immigration. As the colony went through its transition from penal to free, especially a free market-based economy, so government investment in services and infrastructure grew. Personal investment in housing increased and the wealth of individuals grew, as well as the collective wealth of the colony. The downturn in 1900 was due to the recession in the mid-1890s when many banks failed, unemployment increased and the previous land boom of the 1870-80s crashed, leaving many families and businesses in financial difficulty.

However certain questions remain: This model relates to restricted sectors of the colonial economy, but it only touches indirectly on important sectors such as the pastoral, whaling and seal industries. These sectors were indirectly reflective of a growing export market and a more detailed model with declared sub-elements would express the importance of the natural resource and primary production industries including timber, shipping, coal, minerals, wool and wool by-products.

There were some distractions from within the colony to Macquarie's aggressive enterprise policies. In a wave of perversion, William Charles Wentworth led an anti-Macquarie movement against local manufacturing in favour of importations. In January 1819, Macquarie gave permission for a group of clergy, merchants, settlers, and other gentlemen to convene a meeting in the court-room of the new General Hospital, to prepare a petition. The petition was for a redress of grievances and essentially sought expand rather than restrict imports into the colony. Macquarie, by trying to match exports with imports in value terms, was restricting the type of imports authorised. In a despatch to Bathurst of 22 March 1819, Macquarie notates[89] the resolution:

'1. *That a regular demand exists in the colony for British manufactures of nearly all descriptions, greater than the established mercantile houses here have supplied or are likely to supply regularly.*
2. *Restrictions prevent merchants from employing ships of less three hundred and fifty tons burthen (under the Navigation Acts)*
3. *That this meeting requests Gov Macquarie to try and expand shipping between Britain and Australia for transporting Manufactures and colonial produce.'*

The sentiments were laudable but the request baseless. The commissariat, with its huge buying opportunities, could have achieved the desired result as could merchants collaborating into a buying group. The obvious solution was to encourage the local production of all imported items at a lower cost. Macquarie made no recommendations to Bathurst, which meant that he had strictly fulfilled his role to the petitioners and left Bathurst with the opinion that the colonial manufacturers and merchants were ill-prepared to fight British exports.

In over 300 pages of text, John Ritchie[90] reviews the submissions made in the colony to Commissioner Bigge, but does not recite any submission

---

89 HRA 1:10:52 Macquarie to Bathurst 22nd March, 1819
90 Ritchie, John *Punishment and Profit–The Bigge Commission into NSW'*

made by merchants or manufacturers. However in the Bigge reports, we find details of evidence submitted by Simeon Lord about his manufacturing activities. At his factory at Botany Bay, he employed between 15 and 20 convicts in the making of:

Blankets	Possum skin hats	Glass tumblers
Wool hats	Boot leather	Kettles
Kangaroo hats	Stockings	Thread
Seal hats	Trousers	Shirts

Between 1810 and 1820 the number of sheep trebled, and many producers were finding it more profitable to sell carcasses rather than fleeces.

Local manufactured items did not entirely replace imports and items were still imported from India and China.

Local exports from India and China included:

Sugar Candy
Sandalwood
Spirits
Silks
Pearl Shells
Soap
Wearing Apparel
Bêche-de-Mer
Cotton goods
Whale Oil and Meat
Seal Oil

Trade exchange was made on a barter basis, of 'coarse cotton' and ironware for coconut and salt pork was carried on with a number of the Pacific Islands

Among other evidence to the Bigge Enquiry, there were numerous complaints by manufacturers about the limited supply of materials and the high cost of buying from government business enterprises—for instance the cloth produced by workers at the government female factory was 2/9d per yard, whereas at Mr Kenyon's private establishment it was only 11d. The manager of the Robert Campbell merchant business complained to Commissioner Bigge about the duties levied in England on whale and seal oil from the colony. He also criticised the port regulations which required captains to give 10 day's notice of intention to sail–he claimed this resulted in high wharfage charges. Ritchie '*Punishment & Profit*' concludes that, although Bigge wanted to encourage trade and certain manufacturing, he was reconciled to the fact that their promotion would not provide an adequate or proper solution to the question of convict employment, punishment and reform.[91]

Observations on Industry and Commerce in NSW

By 1820, Simeon Lord had turned the profits of fishing in the south seas and trade in the Pacific Islands into a manufactory at Botany Bay where he employed convicts and 15 to 20 colonial youths making blankets, stockings and hats of wool, kangaroo, seal and possum skin. All were shoddy but cheaper than similar items imported from England. [92]

The heavy influx of immigrants during the Darling Administration brought its own difficulties, especially when drought and depression descended on the colony at the end of the 1830s. This period led on to the severe economic depression of 1842 which had been fuelled by a reduction of foreign investment, a cessation of British speculation and a further withdrawal of absentee landlords. There were also numerous local factors, partly encouraged by Sir George Gipps, Governor Darling's successor. Between 1831 and 1841, imports had increased by 1257 percent to a total of over £2.5 million.[93] The severe drought of 1825-8 was unfairly blamed on Darling, as were the epidemics of 'hooping cough' and smallpox which afflicted the colony. Darling's own son died in the whooping cough epidemic.

---

[91] Evidence by sundry manufacturers to Commissioner Bigge Enquiry

[92] An quote extracted from Clark, A History of Australia sourced by Clark from 'An account of Mr Lord's manufactures, submitted to Commissioner Bigge, 1st February 1821

[93] Barnard, Marjorie *Story of a City* p.18

Between December 1831 and December 1832, 325,549 gallons of spirits and 109,406 gallons of wine were imported and at least another 11,000 gallons of gin were distilled locally–all for a population of only 15,000. As for the prices of consumer items, milk was 8 pence per quart, potatoes 15/–a hundredweight, beef had declined to 1 ½ pence[94], mutton 2 ½ pence, veal 5 pence, pork 4 ½ pence. Fowls cost from 1/9d to 2/3d per pair, whilst butter varied from season to season between 1/–and 3/–per pound and cheese sold at 4 pence per pound. Cape wine was 8d to 8½ per pint and port was 1/5 to 2/–per quart. Respectable lodgings were a £1 per week and a horse could be hired for 10/–a day and a gig for 15/–per day. Housing costs had risen to £530 for a six-roomed cottage.

The depression had lasted from the late 1830s to 1842 but it created a slow down in the colony which lasted until gold was discovered in 1852, causing an estimated 1638 bankruptcies. There was a glut of livestock and sheep were selling for 6 pence per head. Land sales ceased and there was an oversupply of labour for the first time in 50 years. Another blow to the struggling economy came with the discovery of gold in California, with estimates of 5757 houses being empty out of the 7100 houses in Sydney town.[95]

In the period up to 1800, the economy was based upon the limited trade monopolised by military men like John Macarthur, as well as a steady expansion of government-financed agriculture to feed the growing number of convicts. This expansion could only continue until the colony became self-sufficient in food; then an alternative product of sufficient value to be exported, would be required to generate the hard currency to pay for the increasing number of imports demanded by the growing economy. Only by developing such a staple export could the colony become economically viable and thereby partially relieve the Treasury of the burden of supporting it. With such a staple export attracting additional population, the colonists would also have some hope of eventually claiming the continent's wide interior.

---

[94] Beef during the Macquarie Administration was bought by the Commissariat at 5 pence per pound

[95] Barnard Marjorie *ibid*

By 1802, Governor King could report to London that seal skins were the way ahead in terms of exports. More than 100,000 skins were landed in and shipped from Sydney between 1800 and 1806. In 1804, 11 Sydney-based ships were engaged in the Bass Strait sealing trade, in addition to the large number of ships engaged in whaling.

By the early 1800s there were four main types of economic activity in the colony. Agriculture and grazing were making the colony almost self-sufficient in these products, and large landowners were undermining the governor's attempts to encourage yeomen farmers. Many of these large landowners also engaged in mercantile activities but a growing number of emancipated convicts became traders on their own account, with speculation in trade marked by gluts and scarcities. Many merchants also operated their own vessels, engaging in sealing and whaling. The number of whalers operating out of Sydney rose from 5 in 1827 to 76 in 1835. Between 1826 and 1835 the value of fishery products passing through Sydney reached £950,000 and in 1849, there were 37 boats based in Hobart employing 1000 seamen.[96]

Sealing and whaling exports were followed by wool. Although only 29 sheep had arrived with the First Fleet, successive convict fleets added to the flocks and numbers quickly expanded by natural increase. By 1805, there were 20,000 sheep in the colony, in addition to the 4,000 cattle, 5,000 goats, 23,000 pigs and 500 horses. The efforts of these large landowners, including John Macarthur, resulted in a dramatic change in the export statistics with the weight of wool exports rising from just 167 pounds in 1811 to 175,433 pounds in 1821.[97]

By 1835, the supremacy of pastoralism was beyond dispute, with exports of fine wool dominating the trade figures. The success of the pastoral industry defeated the British government's efforts to slow the invasion of the interior. The success was the result of a combination of factors—cheap land taken from the Aborigines, cheap labour in the form of convict

---

[96] Day, David *Claiming a Continent—A new History of Australia.* Pages 49,50,51

[97] Day, David *Ibid pages 52,53*

workers and even Aboriginal labour from those able to supervise large flocks over extensive unfenced grasslands in the interior.[98]

Not surprisingly the Europeans found the places they wished to settle were those the aborigines had found most desirable–land with water sources and native grasslands. By 1850 over 4,000 pastoralists with their 20 million sheep occupied 400 million hectares (1,000 million acres) of inland Australia.

Population growth contributed greatly to the rise of manufacturing and the general economic growth in the economy. NSW grew from 76,845 Europeans in 1836 to 187,243 in 1851, and growth in Port Phillip and South Australia was even more dramatic. By 1841, more than half the male population of NSW had been born in the colony or was an immigrant rather than convict, while convicts and emancipists comprised just over one-third of the total population. However males still outnumbered females by roughly two to one.

When it comes to identifying special and important exports, one aspect of trade is generally overlooked. Wool exports began to drop in the early 1820s, but most historians claim wool dominated agricultural exports and that opinion clouds the real truth. In fact in the 49 years from 1788 to 1828, if a reliable set of export statistics were compiled, it would be surprising if Australian-owned whaling and sealing vessels were found to be less productive than sheep. Figures do exist for the next six years from 1828 and for Australia as a whole. Whaling narrowly exceeded wool for that period whilst, as late as 1833, it was the main export industry of NSW. However, after that time, 'wool races away, yielding in the last three years of the 1830s almost double the export value of Australia's whale products' [99]

A secondary importance of the whaling industry is that each vessel is estimated to have spent an average of £300 whilst in port. This did not include the sovereigns spent by the crews in the inns and elsewhere.[100]

---

[98] Day, David *ibid* page 74
[99] Blainey, Geoffrey *The tyranny of Distance* Page 115
[100] Coughlin, T.A. *Labour & Industry in Australia* Volume 1, Page 367

There was also the work for the dockyards and shipbuilding was probably the largest and most dynamic colonial manufacture before 1850. Tasmania alone built 400 vessels, from small cutters to ships of 500 tons, which joined the England-Australia run. Blainey also observes that reluctance to put whaling into an accurate perspective in importance to the colonial economy stems from apathy towards maritime history. He claims that 'except for ship-lovers, the sea and ships are still virtually banished from written history'.[101]

In his third report in 1823[102,] Commissioner Bigge referred to the high level of efficiency amongst the convicts assigned to 'task work' for the government manufactures. He discovered that, at the close of the Macquarie period, the significance of the Government Store as a market for colonial produce and a source of foreign exchange were greater than ever. A heavy increase in the number of convicts transported after the end of the Napoleonic wars had correspondingly increased the government's demand for foodstuffs. Bigge reported that the concentration on producing foodstuffs had retarded the growth of export industries while encouraging the growth of agriculture–farming as opposed to grazing. He added: 'it is possible, given other circumstances the settlers might have turned their attention to the production of other objects than those that solely depended upon the demands of the Government'.[103]

Bigge also referred to the high level of skills used in the Government Business Centre–the Lumber Yard–and to the benefit derived by the colony from the local public sector manufacturing.

Commissioner Bigge reported on the extent of the trades utilised in the Lumber Yard and it was an impressive list[104]. The trades carried on in this

[101] Blainey *ibid* Page 116-7

[102] Commissioner Bigge's Estimate of the value of convict labour in Sydney for 1822

[103] Bigge, J.T. *Report on the Agriculture and Trade of NSW* 1823 Page 22

[104] Bigge, J.T. *Report on the Agriculture and Trade of NSW* 1823 Page 22

government business enterprise [in this case, the Lumber Yard] were also reported on by Major Ovens, the former Superintendent of Convicts[105]:

> *'In the Lumber Yard are assembled all the indoor tradesmen who work in the shops such as blacksmiths, carpenters, sawyers, shoemakers, tailors etc. The workmen, carrying on their occupations under the immediate eye of the Chief Engineer are probably kept in a better state of discipline than those, who working more remote, are dependent on the good behaviour of an overseer for any work they may perform. Whatever is produced from the labour of these persons[106], which is not applied to any public work or for any supply of authorised requisitions, is placed in a large store and kept to furnish the exigencies of future occasions.'*

In the colonial economy, growth came in numerous guises including as technological progress in industry and agriculture, transport and communication, population growth, the accumulation of capital; the discovery of raw materials and the spread of economic freedom.

The rise of a manufacturing sector relied on most of these areas, especially technological gains, supply of capital, immigration of skilled trades and Macquarie's sympathetic encouragement of entrepreneurs. Although not as vital as the agricultural sector, the manufacturing sector provided substantial employment, innovation, skills training, and a basis for potential decentralisation. Most importantly, during the Macquarie Administration, the manufacturing sector supported the colony's transition from a penal to free market economy. As it stabilised, it became attractive for a large number of British-based industries wishing to open branch offices in the colonies and invest in small-scale activities, often transferring skilled labour from Britain to underpin their colonial operations.

---

[105] Report by Major Ovens to Governor Brisbane on reorganisation for the Lumber Yard HRA 1:11:655-7

[106] Sawn timber for framing, roof battens, flooring, window frames, doors, nails, bolts, bellows, barrels, furniture–from Beckett *The Operations of the Commissariat of NSW 1788-1856*

Local industry also helped to develop local resources, both human and capital. Both coal and timber became important exports for the colony, whilst the list of other natural resources being developed for both local use and export continued to expand. New industry required new talents and skills, so a number of adjunct industries came into being–engineering design, equipment manufacturing and equipment maintenance. Not all new equipment was imported and, particularly for agricultural equipment suitable for local conditions, local manufacture and assembly was the norm rather than the exception.

Employment in the sector grew to an important level, with the number of factories in NSW increasing from 37 in 1829 to 174 in 1850[107]. Exports increased during the same period from £79,000 p.a. to over £8,000,000[108]. Boatbuilding peaked in 1843 at 46 vessels for the year, although the average size halved between 1841 and 1843. There were 102 vessels registered in the colony in 1841 displacing 12,153 tons; by 1843 this number had declined to 77 and it continued to decline until the 1900s.[109]

Even as late as 1827, the Colonial Office was still very suspicious about the expenses of the convict establishment. Lord Bathurst wrote of '. . . the difficulty I feel in reconciling the scarcity of assignable convicts . . . with the enormous and increasing expense with which this country is still charged'.[110]

Every effort to trim convict maintenance expenses or expand the assignment system impacted on commissariat business operations. The Superintendent of Convicts would agree to the training of apprentices only to find them sent off 'on assignment', whilst the best workers in the Lumber Yard were always in demand by private manufacturers and government building workers were constantly in demand by the private contractors.

---

[107] Butlin, Ginswick & Statham *The Economy before 1850* (Australians: Historical statistics–p.108)

[108] Butlin et al *ibid*–P. 109

[109] Sourced by Beckett from original data in *Australians: Historical Statistics*, Coghlan and Butlin

[110] HRA 1:8:221

There are few signs that the colonial governors attached great importance to colonial manufacturing. Bligh dismissed it as trifling and, while Lord's textile and hat ventures were launched whilst he was Governor and there is no evidence Macquarie appreciated the long-term significance of such enterprise; he only saw that Lord employed an average of about 20 convicts. However, the rise of manufacturing did not depend entirely on private enterprise, for there was plenty of government enterprise for instance the Female Factory at Parramatta, which enjoyed the dual role of maintaining about 300 single 'at risk' women and providing the spun yarn for slops. There was also the contribution made by privately-owned industries which became so important to the colony's development. The search for staple basic industries began early; shipping, sealing and whaling were the first industries followed by wool.

Since European settlement, there had always been two frontiers–the interior and the ocean. As noted by Hainsworth, 'between 1800 and 1821, the more enterprising settlers, found the oceanic frontier a more hopeful source of gain than the harsh and alien terrain at their backs'.[111]

Therefore, it was not illogical that the first activity undertaken by convicts and free settlers with the necessary skills was the building of boats. Boat building led on to the second phase of staple activity, the use of those boats for exploiting the ocean's possibilities. Not only was construction a challenge but the task of keeping them seaworthy year after year was even more formidable. As Hainsworth points out[112], to harvest export staples from the Pacific and Australian coastal waters, and to establish a colonial carrying trade with outlying settlements, the traders needed a large number of smaller craft. This rationale even sat comfortably with instructions to successive governors from Phillip to Macquarie, viz 'It is our royal will and pleasure that you do not on any account allow craft to be built for the use of private individuals.'[113] Activity was brisk and during the first 25 years of the colony's development, hundreds of vessels of up to 200 tons were built.

---

[111] Hainsworth, D.R *The Sydney Traders* page 115
[112] Hainsworth, D.R *The Sydney Traders* page 117
[113] From HRNSW I (part 2)–Phillip's instructions which became a model for Hunter, King, Bligh and Macquarie)

Sealing, the first staple export industry, followed because ' . . . the agriculturalists, knowing that exports in grain were altogether impracticable, resorted to the external, though near resources of the colony, viz: in procuring seal-skins about Bass's Straits'[114]. The story of sealing is that of a cruel industry set in a harsh environment. Total numbers were not recorded, but from Macquarie Island alone over 101,000 skins were taken[115] each season. In addition to the skins, which usually brought about 5/–each in the English market, hundreds of tons of oil were exported to Britain. It usually took about 3,000 seals to produce 100 tons of oil; and from the gross earnings the British Treasury extracted a duty of £24 a ton for oil. Many sealers working for small firms would be paid, not on a piece rate, but as a percentage of the gross value of the catch at Sydney prices.

The Need for Manufacturing

G.P. Walsh, a historian, has already made two significant contributions to the literature on the 'Dawn of Industry'. This writer's purpose is not to retrace the same ground but to examine closely how the traders supplemented or replaced government activity, and how they launched types of manufacturing which had no government involvement. At first, it was only natural that the government should play a dominant role, for it had the responsibility of clothing, housing, feeding and finding employment for its convict charges, both male and female. Thus it became the chief employer of labour, provider of capital and the chief consumer. The local government was also prepared to foster industrial enterprise, though their support was haphazard and random. In fact after they had

---

114 Collins, David; *An Account of the English Colony in NSW '–1806. Collin's reference notes also records (page 581) a report from Grose to Dundas of September 1793 (also found HRA 1:1:447) that 'Dusky Bay possessed all the advantages of Norfolk Island, but had a safe harbour and could become the centre of a sealing industry.*

115 The *Sydney Gazette* in 1815 made this comment, but also noted that the numbers declined rapidly as the trade became more competitive. The muster of July 1804 showed 123 'free men' (emancipists) 'off the store' and in the southern ocean 'sealing'. By 1805, one private firm (Lord, Kable and Underwood) alone reported 206 men sealing–HRA 1:5:371

launched brewing, salt-making, milling and crude textiles, and operated a number of crude industrial processes, needed for their convict charges, the government allowed some of these ventures to pass into private hands.

In Chapter 12 'Dawn of Industry' of '*The Sydney Traders*'[116,] Hainsworth guides us in a review of the growth of manufactures before 1825. He pointed out that 'Thanks to the initiative of Sydney traders, manufacturing and processing industries emerged very early and helped to transform NSW from penal settlement to colony'.

By 1800, sealing[117] was dominating the trading calendar. The official return for that year showed over 118,000 skins had passed through Sydney with Simeon Lord and his fellow ex-convicts, Kable and Underwood, handling over 72,000 from just one source–Antipodes Island. By 1815, the *Sydney Gazette* was reporting the sealing industry was in decline as this intense harvesting had lowered their natural numbers. However, the British Government was influenced by the 'whale lobby' to raise discriminatory duties against colonial oil, seal and whale. Spermaceti oil was to bear a duty of 15s 9d per ton for British ships but £24 18s 9d if obtained by colonial ships and £8 8s a ton were imposed on Black Whale oil from the Derwent estuary. Thus, through these discriminatory tariffs, colonial oil was virtually barred from London.

Cottage industries were not only the preserve of the small home-based manufacturers. Coghlan[118] points out 'those who had the enterprise and industry to devote land to gardening were amply repaid'. The broad acre crops raised were chiefly wheat and maize, with a little oats and barley, and some potatoes and other vegetables. Excellent opportunities for growing fresh fruit and vegetables were provided by the weather, the climate and the generally good soil around Sydney, but gardening was not generally undertaken except by the few who were conscious of home grown vegetables. They were able, says Coghlan:

---

116 Hainsworth, D.R. The Sydney Traders
117 Based on Hainsworth 'The Sydney Traders Ch12 'The Dawn of Industry'
118 Coghlan, T.A. 'Labour & Industry in Australia' (Page 117–Vol I)

'to grow almost all ordinary English vegetables, all the English fruits and some fruits, such as grapes, grew in abundance. Macquarie described his garden at Parramatta as 'full of vines and fruit trees and abounding in the most excellent vegetables.'

In 1805, stock-raising was given impetus when the two Blaxland brothers arrived in the colony, bringing a considerable amount of capital and more than a little acquaintance with cattle husbandry. In 1810, horned cattle numbers stood at 12,442. When Macquarie left 10 years later the herds numbered 102,939, an annual increase of 20.5%. Herd numbers were carefully guarded with no undue slaughtering and in 1814 salt beef was still being imported. Even so, the records show that beef was cheap with a herd selling at £8 per head. Horses, says Coghlan, 'throve[119] in the settlement from the beginning although their numbers increased very slowly'. In 1800 there were only 203 horses, but by 1810 numbers had grown to 1134 and they totalled 4564 by 1821.

Coghlan recognises the importance of the timber industry and writes

'. . . the export of timber became fairly considerable and in 1803, Governor King spoke of it as 'the only staple of the colony'–the inland forests could not be exploited because of the lack of any means of transport, and as a result 'numerous saw-pits were established on the inlets of Port Jackson, along the banks of the Hawkesbury, and later at Newcastle on the Hunter, where convicts were engaged cutting timber as well as in mining coal.'

Occasionally cargoes were shipped to India; in 1809 timber to the value of £1500 was sent there in part payment for a return shipment of rice.

'The presence of so much valuable timber would in ordinary circumstances have led to the establishment of shipbuilding yards. Vessels were built for sealing purposes as early as 1791, but the presence of craft capable of going to sea was considered

---

[119]   This is an editor's change–the Coghlan text states 'shrove'

> *a menace to the safe-keeping of the convicts and the governor*
> *directed no boats were to be built of greater length than 14*
> *feet.'*

In 1798, Hunter removed this restriction, and encouraged the shipbuilding industry by permitting a vessel of 'thirty tons to be built to procure seal skins and oil in Bass Straits'[120.] Campbell then built a vessel of 130 tons which was launched in 1805[121]. There was considerable activity mostly through the Dockyard, attached to the commissariat, in boat-repairs, refurbishing and provisioning, but the stoppage of the fishery in 1810 was a serious blow to the industry.

Between 1821 and 1826, immigration to the colony was mostly by way of assigned servants, but it was difficult to collect the payments due, and this made the whole notion impractical. Coghlan writes:

> *'in the matter of indentured service many employers,*
> *principally those in the country districts were willing to*
> *advance £8-10 towards the cost of each immigrant labourer*
> *obtained by them and in February 1832 Governor Bourke*
> *despatched a list of 803 labourers who might be sent out on*
> *these terms. It was on immigration at the cost of land revenue*
> *that the colonial authorities placed their confidence. They*
> *offered to set aside £10,000 from the land fund for emigration*
> *purposes; of this sum they desired that about two-thirds be*
> *devoted to promoting the emigration of unmarried women,*
> *as the proportion of men in the colony was excessive and*
> *that one-third should be used in loans for the emigration of*
> *mechanics.'*

After 1836, it was decided that the rapidly increasing land revenue of NSW should be entirely devoted to immigration[122] and in 1837 over 3090 immigrants were brought to the colony of whom 2688 were sponsored

---

[120] Coghlan, Labour & Industry Vol 1 Page 121-2
[121] Steven, Margaret 'Merchant Campbell 1769-1846'
[122] Coghlan 'Labour & Industry in Australia–Vol I Page 178

through the Emigration Commissioners in London and 405 were under the bounty scheme by colonial employers.

The need for manufacturing in the colony was created by local demand for tools, materials and supplies, largely for meeting general construction and housing needs. Manufacturing in the colony was carried out by both the private and government sectors. The private sector was sponsored by a handful of entrepreneurs or skilled settlers who sought to create a 'cottage industry' to satisfy local demand for their products, sales of which were affected by limited demand and a constantly changing market.

Through the commissariat, the public/government sector became involved. The aims were to put convicts to productive work, reverse the long lead time for purchasing urgent materials from Britain and more fully utilise the 'free' local resources such as timber and convict labour. Barnard observes[123]:

> *'The colony was never wholly penal, nor was it intended to be. It was, in due course, to be balanced by freed men, their children, and such other settlers, soldiers, seamen and the like who cared to take the reward for their services in land, of which the Crown had a superfluity. Actually, NSW suffered very little from being a penal settlement and was fortunate in that her first unpromising colonizing material was early swamped by infusions of new blood, that wool, land grants and then gold attracted free colonists. There were no foreign elements to arouse Imperial suspicion, no subject race to put what might have been considered a necessary brake on progress.'*

This statement by Barnard is a rewriting of history but it would be an ideal policy, if it were true. It was designed to be a penal settlement and every move made centred on the convicts–their work, protecting them from themselves, feeding, clothing and maintaining them and providing them with tools, equipment and supplies. Laissez-faire might have been the vogue in London but during the Phillip Administration the settlement

---

[123] Barnard, Marjorie *A History of Australia* 1962 (Page 304)

struggled whilst awaiting food and other supplies, and convicts were held tightly accountable for all their activities. Until 1823, the entire responsibility for the settlement rested on the Governor; upon him was bestowed a power to control lawlessness, and he effectively exercised it.

By 1821 at the end of the Macquarie Administration, the diversity of manufacturing in the colony was far more impressive than could reasonably be expected from a former penal colony transforming itself into a free market economy. Macquarie's enthusiasm for free enterprise and 'cost saving' led to a great deal of production sponsored by the commissariat. Convict labour was considered to be without 'cost' and therefore without 'value' as were local raw materials, so much of the output of the commissariat business enterprises left without recognition of their value, which well-suited Macquarie's purposes. As early as 1812, he had been sternly warned by Colonial Secretary Liverpool [124] that:

> '. . . the burden of the colony of NSW upon the Mother Country has been so much increased since the period of your assumption of the government of it, that it becomes necessary that you should transmit a more satisfactory explanation of the grounds upon which the unusual expenditure has been sanctioned by you.'

Liverpool admitted he had misgivings about this attack when he continued his letter to Macquarie in terms of: 'I can't point out what expenses have been unnecessarily incurred, and the only ground I have for forming a judgement is by comparison of the total amount of bills by your predecessors and yourself'.'

Naturally enough, the absolute totals became progressively higher but, in terms of bills drawn on the store per convict head on the store, the comparisons declined. Macquarie was actively creating an investment for the future so that at some point the colony could be self-supporting and outside the need for Treasury appropriations. However, in philosophical terms, why should local revenues be used to support any form of penal colony for Britain? Surely the population of free settlers could grow in

---

[124] HRA 1:7:476 Liverpool to Macquarie 4th May, 1812

conjunction with the transfer of convicts to the colony; whilst Britain supported the convicts and the colony supported its own operations. One of Macquarie's goals in encouraging active government business enterprises was the early achievement of self-sufficiency so that the colony would be out of the clutches of Whitehall. His thinking was only half right. He was so preoccupied with the colony's economic and fiscal arrangements that he lost sight of the overall plan. Local revenues were first raised in 1802, designed for 'discretionary' expenditure by the governor of the day. The reason for this loose arrangement was that the Treasury appropriated funds for specific purposes such as convict maintenance and civil establishment salaries, but did not see the need for maintenance works, repairs, infrastructure development and the like. Thus the money for these essentials had to be sourced locally and reserved for deployment by the government. Whitehall soon discovered this stream of revenue and, although the Treasury officials knew it was illegally-raised, they restricted its use by withholding British funds to the amount of revenue raised within the colony. Thus in Macquarie's administration, private enterprise figured as a means of both import replacement and cost saving and manufacturing filled the joint roles of availability of key/essential merchandise and of putting convicts to productive work.

Barnard records[125] that even:

> '. . . boys–some as young as eleven–were kept in Sydney at Carter's Barracks near Brickfield Hill and were working as a carpenter, shoemaker, stone-cutter, blacksmith, and other trades to which the boys were apprenticed. The product of their labour went into the public store, and a pool of much needed mechanics was created.'

This observation is rather unique; it is unsourced but it does not have the ring of accuracy about it. Barnard is implying that these trades were carried out at the Barracks, which means that materials and tools were brought there daily. With carts and manpower for hauling purposes being in very short supply, it seems unlikely that large lumps of stone or tree trunks would be hauled from Upper George Street (the Lumber Yard was

---

[125] Barnard, M *A History of Australia* Page 237

at the corner of George and Bridge Streets) all the way to Brickfield Hill for young boys to play with. Carter's Barracks were used for confinement and punishment, and there was little space for practicing woodcraft or stone masonry. It is much more likely that the boys were released under supervision on a weekly basis and taken to the source of the raw materials, for instance the stone-yard and the Timber Yard, which were both on George Street North. This is a rare unsourced and apparent contradiction by Barnard. She is probably incorrect when she states the output of the apprentices went to the public store–it is likely that it went to the Lumber Yard store,–where all building materials, supplies and tools were inventoried. The public store kept only for dry goods, fresh foods or grain.

The extent of private sector manufacturing ranged from clothing, castings and carts to soap, silver-smithing, tanneries and tin-smithing. Government manufacturing covered an equally broad range–from nails to timber framing, bricks, tiles and stone blocks, forged items and boot making. Because the small local population would not have supported such a sector by itself, the broad intent was two-fold–to replace imports and negate the timeframe of at least a year between the ordering and receipt of goods, and to create an export market of sorts.

According to Jackson[126], the population in the colony during 1820 was only 34,000, too small to create sufficient demand for private sector output and encourage economic development. The early entrepreneurs and their activities raise numerous questions which have not been studied in the literature to date. Hainsworth records[127]

> 'Simeon Lord cannot be described as a typical emancipist trader for his operations were too large and diverse, but he was a member of numerous local groups. Another was Henry Kable, whose commercial beginnings are still more shadowy–an illiterate man transported in the first fleet, Kable was for several years a constable of Sydney and probably profitably plied with liquor by the drunks he locked up.'

---

[126] R.V. Jackson *Australian Economic Development in the 19th Century*
[127] H.R. Hainsworth *Sydney Traders* P.41

By implication, Hainsworth is questioning how these two (of many) eventually became such successful traders? What was their source of start up monies? How did these emancipist traders get started? Hainsworth concludes 'the capital they mobilised for shipbuilding and sealing in 1800 must have come from trading'.[128] Other examples of early unexplained success include John Palmer and his close colleagues. Palmer was the third Commissary who began on 5/–per day and became the wealthiest man in the colony during the King Administration. Later his sister Sophia married the largest merchant in the colony, Robert Campbell. Palmer and his trading colleagues prospered in a colony where the commercial life was supposedly monopolised by an officer clique.[129]

Historians usually describe the officer class as having cast a large shadow in the early 1790s under Hunter but the officers could not stop an undertow of small dealers and emerging traders growing up around them. Rather the officers themselves brought this about by allowing the retail trade to fall into the hands of 'ambitious and able (if uneducated) men with no gentility to lose'[130] In many cases, because the wholesale market was officer-controlled and these emancipist retailers wanted to continue to expand and grow, they moved into 'cottage' manufacturing–often working with the commissariat to supply finished goods or raw materials for further processing by the Lumber Yard or Female Factory (such as tanned leather, scoured wool, and crushed grain). For many emerging entrepreneurs, this was the way they commenced their manufacturing activities–trader, marketer and then manufacturer.

According to Hainsworth[131], Simeon Lord was typical of the early merchant traders. When a shortage of circulating notes occurred, Lord (amongst others) requested his creditor customers to liquidate their debts to him by any means possible. The result was that Lord accepted grain, most of which he had bartered from his retail customers and then sold into the store on his own account. He also accepted payroll bills from military officers with

---

[128] Hainsworth refers his readers, on this point, to his inserts in the ADB for Lord, Kable and Underwood Volumes 1 & 2

[129] ADB Volume 2–John Palmer (Hainsworth)

[130] Hainsworth *The Sydney Traders* Page 42

[131] Hainsworth *Sydney Traders* Page 83

whom he was dealing on a wholesale basis and individual 'notes or bills' payable which were freely circulating and classed as petty banking. Lord would consolidate these bills and exchange them for one large bill drawn by the commissariat on the Treasury in London. He would then release this bill to his suppliers, usually visiting ships' captains, or transfer them to his Indian or Macao (Hong Kong) suppliers. Obviously the greatest limitation to entrepreneurial activity in the colony was 'the medium of exchange': the lack of a mint, a Treasury or even a private bank of issue. However with all its faults the system worked; it was the only system they had and the traders made the best use of it'[132] Thus private sector output was limited by government demand for food and materials.

The Jackson theory is that the sale of goods to the government store (commissariat) provided a major source of foreign exchange to the private sector because sale proceeds were made available in the form of Treasury Bills drawn on London.

Summary of Chapter 4

Of the nine economic drivers within the colonial economy, manufacturing had the most far-reaching and desirable results.

The Macquarie Administration decided to centralise and highly regulate the labour and output of the more than 50% of the convicts who were assigned to private or government work after their arrival in the colony. For those assigned to government labour, the broad range of activities required a smarter government store than had hitherto been the case. The store had to have on hand sufficient tools and materials to keep these people fully utilised. Those convicts assigned to land and road clearing needed grubbing tools and axes as well as hauling equipment and food supplies. Those allocated to public building and infrastructure projects required tools, bricks, blocks, tiles and a large array of sawn timbers.

The Governor ordered the commissariat to create a central facility for assembling and distributing these materials. Most items could have been

---

[132] Abbott & Nairn (*Growth)* Chapters 8 & 9

ordered in from Britain or elsewhere in Europe but the lengthy purchasing and requisition procedures required a lead-time of between 15 months and 2 years. Thus Macquarie's charge to the commissariat, to employ convict labour to manufacture locally as many imported items as possible created an import replacement program which resulted in employment and the rise of private sector entrepreneurs as well as generating the transition of local manufacturing from the public to the private sector.

The story of the rise of manufacturing in the colony of NSW is that of the business enterprises promoted and operated by the commissariat. The 900-page volume of the story of manufacturing in Australia, 'Industrial Awakening' by G.J.R. Linge, does not officially recognise the link between the growth of manufacturing and the commissariat business enterprises. After a few definitions of business enterprise, manufacturing and secondary industry, Linge claims on page 24 claims:

> ' . . . the importance of government activities during the whole of this first period can hardly be overstressed. To a considerable extent the administration controlled the factors of production: it regulated, restricted, and occasionally encouraged the private sector: it ran its own farms, herds and workshops and above all it was the main consumer of goods produced'.

In fact, there was no manufacturing prior to the introduction of the Lumber Yard. Although Linge and others refer to this merely as a workshop to keep convicts busy, the Lumber Yard was strategically located, well supervised and enjoyed a sophisticated production-planning regime that would still be admired in industry today. Just to place the Lumber Yard in perspective, it was not only as a means of 'working' convicts but a source of making locally many items needed within the settlement. You cannot have 2,000 convicts in a facility without producing some items of value and necessity. So the Lumber Yard commenced with the goal of using local resources and local labour to produce a wide range of products for local consumption and use.

Linge makes the comment on page 30-1 that 'at first most of the convicts worked for the government, but from late 1792 some were assigned to officers as agricultural labourers'. He refers extensively to the shortage of skilled labour as well as a general shortage of labour. What he does not recognise is that the forced labour of the Lumber Yard and its associated enterprises enabled this important, if not essential, business enterprise to get off the ground and created an opportunity for 'cluster' industries to be established, the starting point of the real secondary industries.

As was stated in the introduction to this chapter, 'out of necessity the demand for timber products, bricks, tiles, stones, rude furnishings and hand carts needed to be and could be supplied locally'. Wheelwrights forged simple iron rims, while coopers steamed woods for barrel making. Local timbers were cleared from suitable timbered hills on the north shore, clay was extracted from location at Brickfield Hill and on the south side of the Parramatta River, government buildings were being erected in Sydney and the new outlying towns, land was being cleared to the north, south, east and west of the settlement roads were under construction, and the commissariat was responsible for its coordination and planning. It was a massive planning exercise as well as a major exercise in saving government funds. Although no-one in the Colonial Office thought in terms of opportunity cost, there is sufficient evidence to suggest that import replacements were saving hundreds of thousands of pounds each year, and underpinning the desire for the colony to be self-sufficient.

The commissariat business enterprises drove the growth of the colony for over 30 years but most importantly, they created a manufacturing base for the colony and that, in turn, provided some balance to and support of the agricultural industry that was producing much needed foreign exchange and exports.

CHAPTER 5

INDUSTRIES ON THE RISE

Coghlan (in Vol 1 Labour & Industry in Australia) writes P.128 'a variety of the flax (*phormium tenax*) plant grew abundantly on Norfolk Island and extravagant hopes were developed on that point. Phillip and his N.I. settlement leader P.G. King expected to supply sufficient flax to make all the rope and canvas required in the settlement.

The results were not satisfactory as the flax proved difficult to work, mainly because the proper method for treating the material was not understood. Two New Zealand natives who were familiar with the right process were taken to the Island but were not able to assist. After many trials the best that was produced by 1796 was a 'course canvas'. Seeds were sent from England and grew successfully on the banks of the Hawkesbury River, sufficient to warrant in 1800 the manufacture of linen. At the end of 1800 new looms and appliances arrived in the colony. Two Irish convicts understood the new process and during the next twelve months 279 yards of fine linen and 367 yards of course linen were produced. A cottage industry grew with convict wives receiving incentives of cattle and livestock to hand spin and weave more linen. Production was centred around the 'House of Industry' at the Parramatta Gaol where nine looms were at work–two for fine line, two for duck, one for sacking and four for making hemp, sailcloth and woollens. About 100 yards of cloth was produced each week at 2/6d per yard.

Hemp seed was brought from India in 1803 where again it flourished along the banks of the Hawkesbury River. Its importance was in making rope and sail-cloth, materials likely to be in great demand as the Port of Sydney became a whaling ship centre. The industry succeeded for a few years and diminished as the whaling industry subsided.

By 1802 two woollen looms were at work but the output was of unsatisfactory coarseness. Unfortunately, according to Coghlan (P.131) 'the product of the looms was poor in quality and the output insignificant'.

'In 1806, a private entrepreneur set up looms and made cloth and blankets in small quantities; about the same time several tanneries were established and hides and kangaroo skins were tanned and a boot factory set up. The boots found a ready sale but were of poor quality, being too porous for use in wet weather' (Coghlan Vol 1, Page 131).

The manufacture of salt was first attempted by the commissariat, but then passed into private hands, and by 1811 sufficient local manufacture existed to replace all imports.

Hat-making was not as successful—hats were made from seal-skins, were cheap but not of the same quality as imported products.

Manufacturing grew increasingly as the domestic population grew. Manufacturing for export was essentially zero because of the distance from the 'centres of civilisation' and the industries that existed before 1856 were chiefly of a domestic character. Coghlan records that by 1838, in NSW, there were 77 grain-mills, 2 distilleries, 7 breweries, 5 soap works, 12 tanneries, 5 brass and iron foundries, 7 woollen factories, one salt, one hat and one tobacco works, as well as a few other manufactories. The number of persons employed was very small and in general, the output quality was inferior in quality to similar imported goods. The foundries were unable to turn out quality agricultural implements, and even basic tools were not well made. Growth took place in quality, quantity and diversity. In 1848, there were 272 industrial establishments in New South Wales. Distilleries, breweries, sugar refineries, soap and candle works, tobacco and snuff factories, woollen mills, hat manufactories, rope works, tanneries, salt works, starch manufactories, blacking manufactories, meat preserving and salting, potteries, glass works, copper-smelting works, iron and brass foundries, gas works, ship and boat building, flour mills, oatmeal and groat mills.

'During the 1830s and 1840s, sheep-farming was the most important industry in the whole country, with the quantity of wool exported showing a continuous increase in each year and advancing from 7,213,584 lbs valued at £442,504 in 1839 to 41,426,655 lbs, valued at £1,992,369 in 1850. Practically the whole of the wool shipped from Australia was carried to England. Australian exports represented only a little over 50% of the wool processed in England during this period. Of the exporting states, Victoria was in first position, marginally above the production of NSW, although the NSW fleeces brought a marginally higher payment per pound. Overall, during the period, 1836-1851 prices per pound varied between 10.5 pence to 2/-. The financial depression of 1843-1845 saw the price of wool drop to its lowest level but then pick up in 1846, although in 1849 prices were still slumped at 10.5 pence per pound. Even so wool still represented two-thirds of the value of all exports of the colonies, followed by tallow. Cattle breeding and production grew and numbers in 1850 had reached 1,900,000. Because local consumption was so small compared to available supply, the export trade of meat products, hides, tallow, bones became of great importance. The dairy industry gained rapid importance as the demand for butter and cheese grew. The colony became independent of imported supplies by 1845.

Economic cycles before self-government in 1856 had an impact on manufacturing in the colony. Farming ranked second in importance to grazing in the colony. In NSW, the area under cultivation increased from 95,000 acres in 1839 to 153,000 by 1850, half of which acreage was planted to wheat. Corn production did not reach market demand and so imports came from other colonies. Farming was still the occupation of small settlers, who made it a family affair to cultivate grain production–wheat being preferred because of the yield and the lower costs of landing the grain in Sydney

'The cultivation of grapes for wine and brandy received increased attention in the 1830s due to immigration of German families, who found both the soil and the climate well suited to growing vines. By 1850 over 1100 acres were under cultivation and producing 111,000 gallons of wine and 1958 gallons of brandy.' (Coghlan Vol 1, P.507)

Tobacco was growing in the Port Macquarie area as well as around Sydney. Over 500 acres were under crop.

In addition to wool, the principal exports in 1840 were tallow, oil, skins, bark, salt beef, and copper. Tallow to the value of £167,858 represented the production from nearly One million sheep boiled down for their fat.

By 1840 the whaling industry had declined very greatly with only 1854 tons of sperm oil and 4297 tons of black oil, along with a considerable quantity of whale bone and seal skins valued at over £150,000

The events of 1841 and the two following years effectively put stop to the investment of British Capital in the colony of NSW, and it was several years before the colony came back into favour as a recipient of foreign capital. Coghlan opines (P.512) 'in spite of the lack of British interest in Colonial affairs or perhaps because of it, local trade was placed on a sound basis free from liability to sudden and violent fluctuations. For the first time there arose a real disposition on the part of the settlers to cultivate the local market. *The original settlers had looked upon Australia as a place to be exploited'.*

Consequently after the financial crisis was over, there was much talk about the colonists supplying themselves with as many articles as possible instead of relying upon exports. Brewing and tanning increased production. Sugar-refining became a well established industry between 1841 and 1850 and achieved self-sufficiency by the end of that period. Soap-making now fully satisfied the local market, although the coarseness of local woollen cloth manufacture could not compete against the quality of imported goods. The salting and preserving of colonial meat began in 1841 and although of excellent quality the industry was not a financial success, even though in 1850 there were nine preserving plants in Sydney alone. Coal was easily extracted but created little interest in seeking other minerals. Coal extracted amounted to 84,000 tons of which 31,600 tons was exported. Copper discovered at Molong was being tested in 1850.

Coghlan reports (Page 513) that deep-sea ships entering Australian ports numbered 251 in 1841 but fell off to 80 in 1841 and did not rise again until gold discoveries of 1851.

Sydney was the centre of a very active coastal shipping trade, with small ships trading from this centre into Wollongong, Port Macquarie, the Hawkesbury and many other NSW ports. By this means were carried grain, meat, tallow, hides, butter and cheese, timber, coal, lime and all sorts of colonial produce. The cedar-producing districts shipped their product from Port Macquarie and more northern ports while lime came from Pittwater and Shoalhaven.

Then came the discovery of gold, the immediate effect of which was upon the small manufacturing industries of NSW–some were to be stimulated and others were to be extinguished. There was an increased demand for all classes of manufactured goods, but as a rule the most enterprising and resourceful men were the first to leave for the goldfields, and this desertion proved fatal to most of the minor industries.

Of the three industries that appeared strongest prior to gold discoveries, only one survived successfully. Woollen cloth manufacture, soap and candles and refined sugar went into the gold rush period, but only refined sugar came out as strong! For woollen cloth the market grew at the start of the gold discoveries but then tailed off and became almost extinct. Much the same trend took place in the making of soap and candles. Sugar refining just grew and grew, with raw material coming from the East Indies to the new mills in Victoria. NSW mills were supplied locally.

The desertion of labour from small business directed more attention to the use of machinery. In 1855 a steam engine was used in only one brickyard; in 1859 the number was thirty. In 1855 only 12 sawmills used steam-power; in 1859 the number was 38.

The Newcastle district of NSW held 17 coalfields, with Newcastle itself being the shipping port. Output slipped as workers tested the goldfields but most returned the following year and production boomed. In 1850 output was 71,216 tons; in 1852, output fell slightly to 67,404 ton but by 1860, output grew to 368,862 ton (valued at £226,493).

Wages and working hours

Governor Phillip was not an economist, but did have generous feelings towards his subjects; he was also a moralist, and these factors converged to help him determine which hours his men should labour. His laws were all conceived in the spirit of the underlying philosophy—one that designated work to be a punishment, the life of man a warfare and his time here below probation, to be spent in weariness and sorrow. The root idea of those who pressed for colonisation of the Australia was that the transfer of the bond population of England to a new land would be in itself a cleansing process and the habit of regular work,'especially in the open air', would bring health to soul and body. Phillip was of this mind and apparently thought there could not be too much of a good thing, so he fixed the working hours from sun-up to sunset. In summer this meant 5 AM to 7 PM, with intervals of 2 ½ hours for rest. The working day in summer was therefore 11 ½ hours long. These hours were to be adhered to 'until a fair and proper task had been established.

Task work soon reduced these working hours to a more comfortable 6-7 per day, or until the task was completed. At this point, the working day often finished at 2 or 3 PM.

In the wages regulations of 1800 the week's task work for various forms of agricultural labour was fixed 'for servants of the Crown employed by government and individuals', and in the same regulations, day work was fixed at 9 hours for 5 days of the week and 5 on Saturday. The majority of the men in government employ were on task work and there is abundant evidence that men on task work worked only about half the time their fellows on day work laboured.

In 1804 Bligh issued a regulation fixing the hours of agricultural labour from 5 AM to 7 PM but only for November and December, otherwise hours remained the same between 1803 to 1811 i.e. 9 hours for 5 days and 5 on Saturday.

When the governor granted to convicts in government employ the right to work 'on their own hands' his expressed wish was to encourage industry and his anticipation was that their labour would be principally employed in the small garden allotments which were granted to the industrious and secondarily in the service of private persons. The proclamation of the governor fixed the daily wage of a bond labourer working 'on his own hands' at 10 d., but did not specify the rates for fixed labourers. The cost of feeding and clothing a convict in the early years of settlement was usually reckoned as equal to 10 s. per week., and 'working on his own hands', a man could earn 5 s. more according to the regulation rate of pay, so that the weekly cost of to a master of his assigned servant's labour was about 15 s. with the hours of work being 5 AM to 7 PM.

In January 1797 the settlers complained that the wage demanded by the free labourers was 'so excessively exorbitant that it runs away with the greatest part of the profit of their farms'. At this time rates for certain kinds of agricultural labour were specified. Many were piece work rates, but the daily rates were also determined, viz 2 s 6 d without rations, and 1 s with rations provided. The regulation rations were to be 4 lbs of salt pork, or 6 lbs of fresh pork and 21 lbs of wheat with vegetables per week. Where a man was hired by the year, he was to be paid £10 with board and lodging. In the same general order, the rate for a 'government man' working in his own time was again fixed at 10 d per day. In December 1807, Bligh issued a proclamation fixing the scale of wages to be paid for reaping at 10 s per acre or a bushel of wheat, at the option of the labourer. If the master provided food, a deduction of 2s 6d per day was to be made The rate of 5 s per day for stacking and carrying was a noteworthy concession to the demands of the labourers and all the other rates were 10 to 20 percent in advance of those previously issued.

When Macquarie became governor in December 1809, he continued the rates existing when he assumed office. But there was no doubt that many rates were exceeded by certain classes of employers, especially when the exigencies of business demanded it. These higher rates were usually paid by the small settlers who had no assigned servants and who lacked the social or political connections which would make it dangerous for workers to press for wages in excess of regulation. According to testimony to an 1812 select Committee of the House of Commons, the commonest labourer earned from 5 to 7 s per day. Commissary Palmer gave evidence that the lowest weekly wage for which a labourer could be obtained was 24 s, whilst labour in the outlying districts was much dearer than in Sydney. Specialist craftsmen such as smiths, carpenters, tailors and shoemakers could earn an extra £4-5 per week. The new regulation forbid an assigned servant to work in his own time for anyone other than his 'master', but it established the custom of paying wages to all assigned servants, which policy was never contemplated when the system of assignment was introduced. Macquarie was a great builder. His roads, bridges, churches and public buildings required for their construction large numbers of labourers and he allowed assignment to proceed only on a small scale.

The practice of paying wages in kind grew up early in the settlement because there was no official currency or means of exchange. In rural districts even where free men were employed it became common practice to stipulate that employees draw stores from the employer's stock, but usually with an understanding in regard to prices. However, writing in 1821, Commissioner Bigge, in his report on the condition of the colony, estimated that the cost of a convict servant whether skilful or unskilful was £25/12/–a year, of which £9/2/–was the cost of the ration of meat; £6/10/–the cost of the ration for wheat and £10 money wages. By the end of the Macquarie era, the number of arriving convicts far exceeded the requirements of the country and neither was the government able to find employment for them on public works nor private employers to receive them on assignment. At certain times the numbers were so great that the accommodation available in the barracks and gaols was too small and the practice arose of allowing men whose services were not required particularly tradesmen such as tailors, shoemakers and the like, to be at large and at their own disposal. Many set up cottage industries especially for the barter of food and other sustenance for their wares.

Various estimates have been made of the value of assigned labour in NSW as compared with free labour in England. These estimates place the value of free labour as from 2 to 3 times that of a convict. Officially the cost of a convict was £36 being £26 for food and lodging and £10 per year for work after 3 PM. According to Bigge it was £25/12/-. Coghlan opines (page 64) that both figures are probably correct, with the Bigge figure being for the period before his arrival in 1819, and the higher for the period following Macquarie's departure. This post-Macquarie period was marked by the commencement of the struggle between emancipists and free immigrants. Emancipists who had attained a position of wealth and importance had inflicted upon them all the social indignities and disabilities available. This struggle impacted on industrial relations and slowed economic progress.

At the beginning of 1851 the industrial condition of NSW was rather better than at any time since the crisis of 1842-3 but wages were low and employment hard to obtain. Before the discovery of gold the ordinary wage of a mechanic engaged in the building trade was 4s 6d per day. Within a short time of the discovery of gold, those rates had almost doubled to between 6s 9d and 8s 3p. The same trades when working in the rural areas would receive £45 to £55 with rations and hut accommodation as compared to £30 previously. The discovery of gold in Victoria emptied the work areas of NSW and the governor of NSW gave directions that assisted migration from Britain should be revived and expanded. This further increased wage rates and in the year 1852 day rates for tradesmen increased from 7s 0d to 11s 6d. By 1854, the *Sydney Herald* was reporting that the day rate for tradesmen ranged between 8s and 30s.

Many circumstances encouraged the rise of entrepreneurship–the arrival of too many convicts, the artificially low wages for much of the period, the encouragement for convicts to work for themselves out of official hours and the impost of resourcefulness by rogue employers or masters, who created substandard conditions for assigned convicts. Arriving immigrants probably found the low wages were a direct encouragement to 'go out on their own', and use their skills for their own benefit.

CHAPTER 6

LIMITATIONS ON INDUSTRY & CONSTRAINTS ON GROWTH

PART A–IMMIGRATION POLICIES AND DEVELOPMENT

Free Immigration into the Colony

The need for education in the colony is an interesting pre-emptive to the need for free immigrants. Immigration would help solve numerous gaps in the colony–capital and labour, societal demands and the imbalance of men and women, the demand for a free enterprise economy and 'foreign' investment. The direct association then as now, between education and investment, knowledge and growth is unmistakeable. It was largely left to Macquarie to juggle the need for balance in the penal colony, but this was not a high priority and it was passed to Brisbane and then Bourke. Before migration could be practiced, thought Macquarie, I need to rid the streets of the waifs, orphans and unwanted children of a largely immoral society. Bligh had first drawn official attention to the deteriorating social fabric with 3 times as many 'kept' as married women, the dazzling count of illegitimate children compared with those that numbered in the legitimate category. Education would help not only with this social dilemma but also with the illiteracy that was rampant in the colony. The three Rs were down to one R and 'riting was largely limited to an X on the spot.

Education, a construction program, local discretionary revenue raising and elimination of spirits as the currency of the day, were Macquarie's top priorities—only then could free immigrants be welcomed. Of course a bank would be helpful in cementing the colony as a land of opportunity. The English thought in terms of symbols even if they were thin.

So, in this review on free immigration, an understanding of the needs for education as a precursor to establishing a migration policy will set the scene. The economy was at the top of the triangle pointing the way ahead. That 'the colony has no treasury' was a disincentive to migration, and Macquarie believed in balancing finely the needs of a despotic governor and the daily demands on government with the desire for free enterprise. Macquarie had decided that government had the need and responsibility to encourage and sponsor exploration, and it was the crossing of the mountain range west of Sydney town that inspired and commenced the first sustained economic expansion in the colony. The pastoral movement led the way for encouraging migration. The financing mechanism for the new policy was the sale of crown or 'waste' lands. The boom and bust syndrome was set in place by speculators in both land and livestock. The market economy would be in tatters within 20 years of Macquarie's exit.

This is the story of the need for education and a sound economy leading to migration as a catalyst for growth in the 'new' economy.

The early days of Education

A.G. Austin in Australian Education 1788-1900 offers an explanation as to the lack of interest in educating the lower classes.

> 'Nowhere in Phillip's Commissions or instructions was any mention made of the children accompanying the First Fleet, or of the child convicts whom the British Government saw fit to transport, for it was alien to the official mind of the late 18th century to feel any interest in the welfare of these children. By 1809 the War Office had been persuaded to appoint regimental schoolmasters, but in 1788 the education of these children formed no part of the business of any department of state.

> *The conservative opinion in Britain was convinced that education was exactly the wrong remedy and agreed with the Bishop of London's conviction that it was 'safest for both the Government and the religion of the country to let the lower classes remain in that state of ignorance in which nature has originally placed them'. In this atmosphere anyone who undertook the education of the poor became an object of suspicion. Even the devout Hannah Moore had to defend her schools against charges of Methodism, Calvinism and subversion. Ms. Moore wrote: 'they learn such coarse work as may fit them as servants. I allow no writing for the poor. My object is to train up the lower classes in habits of industry and piety'. Nearly a century later John Stuart Mill still thought it necessary to warn his readers that 'a general state education . . . established a despotism over the mind'.*

The Pitt Tory Government resisted those favouring State intervention in education. They saw no reason to meddle in the upbringing of other people's children, and no reason to suppose that the new Governor of NSW would presume to dispute their opinion.

The early governors of NSW soon found it necessary to change their adoption of British policies, especially regarding education in the colony, since Britain was not a fragment of English society transplanted, but a military and penal garrison in which the governors were responsible for every detail of daily life. In a settlement where the maintenance of discipline, the regulation of food production, the rationing of supplies, the employment of labour, and the administration of justice were necessarily committed into one man's hands, there was no room for that laissez-faire indifference which characterized the conduct of public affairs in Britain.

Not only were the governors moved by the misery of the convicts' children but also they realized that the future of the colony had to be built upon these children. In a colony where there was three times the number of men as there were women, a deplorably high proportion of illegitimate and abandoned children required some measure of protection and supervision. In 1807 on Bligh's testimony, there were 387 married women in the colony, 1,035 concubines, 807 legitimate children and 1,024 illegitimate children.

Phillip had set aside, near every town, an allotment for a church and 400 acres adjacent for the maintenance of a minister and 200 Acres for the schoolmaster. However the governors were not really concerned to assert the supremacy of either Church or State. All their actions were matters of expediency. To finance schools, they made direct grants of land, assigned convicts and issued rations. To staff schools they had used soldiers, convicts, missionaries and other literate person they could find. To accommodate the schools, they used churches, barracks, storehouses and private buildings. It was Macquarie who first set down the staging order of divinity. All clerics would be, for the first time, from 1810, responsible to the principal chaplain.

By the end of the Macquarie era, many changes had been made to the social order in the colony, including education, and most of these changes were in principal accepted by J. T. Bigge in his reports to the British Commissioners. Bigge's reported that 'the flow of immigrants and the increasing number of emancipated convicts has so increased the population of free settlers that the prosperity of the settlement as a colony has proportionately advanced, and hopes may reasonably be entertained of its becoming perhaps at no distant period a valuable possession of the crown. This makes me think that it is no longer fit for its original purpose'.

For public education to be considered as a government responsibility and controlled by a cleric meant that part of the cost could be defrayed by public revenue. The suggestions made by the new Archdeacon (Hassall–Marsden's future son-in-law) of the colony were that public education be controlled by a cleric who was also placed at the head of the Church Establishment. The costs could be defrayed, was the suggestion, by the parents contributing, annually, a 'bushel of good clean sound wheat, or equivalent value in meat, or $1/8^{th}$ of the colonial import duty could be diverted to education; governments could subdivide its land at Grose Farm, Emu Plains, Rooty Hill and Cabramatta into small farms and apply their rents to the endowment of schools in general'. The last suggestion and the one that attracted Lord Bathurst's ear was that a 'new land reserve of some 25,000 acres should be established near Bathurst or Newcastle'.

The British Government ultimately decided in 1825 to direct Governor Brisbane to form a 'corporation and invest it with clergy and school estates, and from the proceeds it should support the Anglican Church and schools and school masters in connection with the established church' The territory of NSW was to be divided into counties, hundreds, and parishes as a result of a survey of the whole colony. The Corporation was not a success largely because it was never properly funded the way it was expected, nor did it enjoy the high enthusiasm or interest of the governor.

Macquarie 'reported' to Viscount Castlereagh on 30th April 1810 on the progress in carrying out British instructions

'In pursuance to your Lordship's instructions, I lost no time in directing my attention to the principal object pointed out in them, namely, to improve the morals of the colonists, to encourage marriage, to provide for education, to prohibit the use of spirituous liquors, and to increase the agriculture and livestock so as to ensure a certainty of supply to the inhabitants under all circumstances'. In his next dispatch Macquarie reported that 'with a view to the decent education and improvement of the rising generation, I have established several schools at head quarters and the subordinate settlements, which I trust will not fail of being attended with very desirable effects'. He also requested 'a few more chaplains and some additional schoolmasters which are very much required, and it would be very desirable if some should be sent out as soon as possible'.

Alan Barcan in his imaginative work 'History of Australian Education' notes that, in line with regular military policy the NSW Corps brought their own tutor with them for teaching the children of military personnel. No such luxury was available for the residents of Norfolk Island. In 1793, Lieutenant King (Governor of the island) established an import duty on liquor in order to raise funds for education. King built the first stone schoolhouse in 1794 and a second in 1795. Collins records ('An Account of the English Colony in NSW') that 'the first school was for young children, who were instructed by a woman of good character; the second was kept by a man, who taught reading, writing, and arithmetic, for which he was well qualified, and was very attentive'.

In Sydney Governor Hunter met with the school children each year, and as David Collins records, in 1797, Hunter inspected the children from three schools and 'was gratified with the sight of 102 clean and decently–dressed children, who came with their several masters and mistresses'.

In 1798, the Rev'd Richard Johnson (the first cleric in the colony, who had arrived with the First Fleet) amalgamated the three schools in Sydney and the three joint teachers held classes in the church. They had 150 to 200 children enrolled of 'all descriptions of persons, whether soldiers, settlers, or convicts' (/Johnson's Rules). After the Church was burnt down on 1ˢᵗ October 1798, it moved to the courthouse and then to a disused warehouse, but enrolments halved.

King, as a subordinate and assistant to Hunter, also opened an Orphan Institution in 1795 when by this time there were 75 destitute children. These children were taught, fed, clothed, and given vocational training.

When King arrived to take over as Governor in 1800, he continued his deep interest in education and 'education expanded significantly'. (Barcan). There were three main reasons for this expansion.

a. King himself took a deep interest in education and brought with him the experience gained from his Norfolk Island success

b. Increased colonial prosperity and better financial provision. King imposed an import duty on goods to establish a fund for education. When the Female Orphan Fund opened in August 1801, there were 54 girls aged from 7 to 14 in the school. In August 1804, King gave it an endowment of 13 000 acres to secure its economic stability. Samuel Marsden, its Treasurer and religious guardian commented that the Orphan School is 'the foundation of religion and morality in this colony'

c. The growth of population, which produced both the need for and the ability to sustain schools. By 1800 Sydney was a town of 2 000 and the colony had some 5 000 inhabitants. Significance could be seen in the growth of a small commercial middle class, the publication of the Sydney Gazette, which offered an avenue for expression of opinion, a 'distinction' between state-aided 'public schools' and 'private' education. Vocational training was possibly the most important challenge and target of the education system. In 1798, Hunter reported that young male convicts had been assigned to an 'artificer's gang in order that they may be useful mechanics'. In 1805, King developed a system of apprenticeships for boys. In the same year advertisements appeared in the Sydney Gazette for apprentice seamen. The Female Orphan School developed some vocational training for the girls by offering 'needlework, reading, spinning and some few writing'. A few of the girls became servants with them being 'bound as apprentices to officer's wives'.

The overall shortage of labour in the colony caused vocational training to make only slow progress.

Immigrants and Free Settlers

Collins records that on the 15th January 1793, the *Bellona* transport ship, arrived in Sydney Harbour with a cargo of stores and provisions, 17 female convicts and five settlers one of whom was a master wheel-wright employed by the governor at a salary of £100 per annum. A second was a returning skilled tradesman who had been previously employed as a master blacksmith. All five settlers had brought their families.

Collins conjectures that these first five settlers had received free passage, a promise of a land grant and assistance with farming, as the incentive for becoming the free settlers,

Manning Clark (A History of Australia) records that in 1806, 'a dozen families from the Scottish border area arrived as free emigrants and each received 100 acres of land on the banks of the Hawkesbury River in a place they called Ebenezer. They were devout Presbyterians, and were allowed to worship in the colony according to their own lights'. However the authorities were not prepared to tolerate the practice of the catholic religion, because they saw it 'as an instrument of mental slavery, a threat to higher civilization, and a threat to liberty' (Clark Vol 1)

Developing Immigration

Even by the census of 1828, NSW had fewer than 5,000 people who had come out voluntarily, in a population of 36 598. The colony had the attractions unavailable in the USA, free land and convict labour. Settlers were given land for agriculture and pasture usage. This meant freehold land, and it only applied to men who had immigrated as private citizens, to military officers who had decided to stay and to pardoned convicts who had been granted land.

In 1831, the British Government, against the opposition of many in the colony decided to stop giving away land grants to settlers and chose instead to 'sell' the land and use some of the proceeds to sponsor migrants to the colony. The initial sales price was 5 shillings an acre. It was a way of inducing poor families to leave the country, but as well of relieving the labour shortage. Between 1831 and 1840 about 50,000 prisoners were transported and about 65,000 free men and women chose to emigrate

The balance of the sexes was more equal amongst emigrants than among convicts: but even South Australia, which was wholly an emigrant's colony, had only 8 females for every 10 males by 1850, and in Australia as a whole there was fewer than 7 for every ten. The resulting challenge was only partially met by Caroline Chisholm who met every convict and emigrant ship to stress the dangers to young unmarried women. Her main accomplishment was to convince the Colonial Office, in 1846, to offer free passage to all families of convicts resident in the colony. Her detractors suggested that the result of her efforts towards convict families and emigrating poor families would be to create an imbalance of Catholics in the colony, who were already twice the proportion of the Australian population as they were in England.

'Populate or Perish'

The history of Australia is bound tightly into two aspects—the economics of colonization and the story of immigration.

The first free immigrants came out on the Bellona, and were given small land grants on Liberty Plains (the Strathfield-Homebush area). The first family to arrive included a millwright who had been on the hulks in Britain for a minor crime and been released. It was Major Grose, acting as the Administrator after the departure of Phillip, who observed 'from some dirty tricks he has already attempted, I fear he has not forgotten all he learned as a former prisoner. He is evidently one of those that his country could well do without'.

Governor King wrote in his report—The State of the Colony in 1801—on the subject of free immigrants:

"Settlers are of two classes i.e. those who come free from England and those who were convicts and whose terms of transportation are expired, or who are emancipated. Of the first class, I am sorry their industry and exertions by no means answer the professions they made in England, several of whom are so useless to themselves and everyone about them that they were not only a burden to the public but a very bad example to the industrious. As they brought no other property than their large families, many have been and will continue an expensive burden on the public, or starve. The settlers are maintained by the crown for eighteen months and have two convicts assigned to each, which is very sufficient to provide against the time of doing for themselves, but that period too often discovers their idleness and incapacity to raise the least article from a fertile and favourable climate, after having occasioned an expense of upwards of 250 pound for each family, exclusive of their passage out The desirable people to be sent here are sober, industrious farmers, carpenters, wheel and mill wrights, who having been used to draw their food from the earth, secure sand manufacture it, would here find how bountifully their labour would be rewarded".

It appears that King did not have a very high opinion of the potential for free migration to the colony.

Phillip's successor—Governor Hunter—was instructed by the Colonial Office to 'encourage free settlers without subjecting the public to expense'. They were to be given larger land grants than the emancipists and as much convict labour as they wanted. Hunter observed in one of his submissions to the Secretary of the colonies that 'free immigrants would not come to the country whilst the needs of the colony were supplied from Government farms'.

The economic factors hit the immigration concept in 1801 when Governor King, as Hunters successor wrote to the Duke of Portland, as Colonial Secretary and suggested family immigration. It was turned down on the basis that transporting a family would cost 150 pound and annual maintenance until they were self-supporting would cost 250 pound (HRNSW)

In 1802, the HRNSW records that free settlers (28 in one group) arrived by the *Perseus* and Coromandel. More came in the Navy ship *Glatton*, including a person supposedly bearing 'perfect knowledge of Agriculture, having held a very considerable farm in his hands, but which through youthful indiscretion, he found it necessary to relinquish'. The governor was asked to place him 'above the common class of settlers'. The government, Governor King wrote 'was much imposed on' by these free settlers. The *Glatton* settlers were sent to the Nepean, where they were wrote King 'going on with great spirit and well applied industry'

King reported to Lord Hobart in 1804 that 'there were 543 free settlers supporting 351 wives and 589 children and utilising 463 convicts'. Further free settlers are recorded as being in the William Pitt in 1805, mainly because land and subsistence was being replaced by the lure of wealth coming from the fine wool being promoted by John Macarthur. This endeavour and attraction of wealth brought a different and probably better class of free settler—the Blaxland brothers arrived on a charter vessel with their families, servants and capital of over 6,000 pound. Again the governor received instructions. 'They are to be allowed 8,000 acres of land and the services of up to 80 convicts for 18 months at the commissary store's expense. Governor Bligh was given similar instructions in reference to a 'lady of quality'—a Mrs Chapman, a widow, Governess and teacher. Bligh was directed to 'afford her due encouragement and assistance'. The next governor, Lachlan Macquarie took a different stance—he discouraged free immigration, probably because the flow of convicts was almost overwhelming his administration. His position is not readily understandable. As a quasi social reformer and developer of free enterprise in the colony, one would have expected Macquarie to welcome free settlers for what social and economic values they could contribute. When the Bigge report was published in London, it raised the interest of men of wealth in the colony and a Lieutenant Vickers, an officer of the East India Company, volunteered to emigrate with 10,000 pound of capital, an unblemished reputation and a purity of private life 'not previously known in any class of society', and in return demanded privileges by way of land grants, livestock and a regular seat at the governor's table. Brisbane, as governor, was directed by Lord Bathurst as Colonial secretary to give Vickers 2,000 acres of land and a house allotment near Newcastle. Brisbane investigated Vickers and found him to be little more than 'an adventurer, a bird of passage, and boycotted by his fellow officers'. Marjorie Barnard concluded, 'Only distance made his deception possible'. Opportunities followed good publicity, and the floating of the Australian Agricultural Company in London in 1823 did much to promote the colony in Britain, and brought another spate of free settlers to the colony.

This then is the early trend in the free settler movement—it had not been seen yet as a government opportunity. But that was about to change. Lord Bathurst came along with an idea, urged by the Wakefield supporters and the rash of economists waging war on the increasing unemployment, poverty and lack of investment opportunities in Britain.

A privately sponsored scheme was funded by a loan to Dr. J.D. Lang by the governor in the amount of 1,500 pound, which brought out 100 selected 'mechanics' (semi-skilled labourers) and their families. Lang used a charter vessel to transport these immigrants, and the understanding was that the immigrants would repay their expenses from future wages. In 1831 this was an inspiring move to privatising a government policy.

Three factors were set to establish an on-going immigration policy. The three factors were bad times in England; shortages of skilled labour of both men and women in the colony; and the cessation of the assignment system.

A commission on Emigration was established in England to select and despatch suitable agricultural labourers. A plan to tax landowners of assigned convicts failed when the difficulty of collection was recognised. There were still 13,400 convicts on assignment in 1831.

The governor agreed that official funds would contribute 20 pound towards each immigrant family and try to recover it after the family settled. The collections were rarely made.

It was left to Governor Bourke to formulate a workable plan. The 'bounty system' relied on sponsored workers funded by government. The government paid 12 pound out of the 17 pound passage money. The Emigrants Friendly Society existed in Sydney to help and protect these sponsored migrants.

A more refined method was needed to select and sponsor these migrants. Glenelg reformed the financial side in 1837. He allocated the revenue from land sales in the colony as a means of affording immigration. The land as well as any revenue derived from its sale, lease or rental, had remained the property of the crown, not the colonial administration. Two-thirds of these funds were to be allocated to migrants by way of grants—£30 for a married couple, £15 for an unmarried daughter, £5 and £10 for children depending on age.

The zenith of immigration success could be seen in the 1830s under Governor Gipps. Land revenue was high, the colony was prosperous and plenty of migrants were on offer and the colony could successfully absorb them. The severe drought at the end of decade (1838) cause land revenue to fall sharply. Gipps proposed a loan to the Land Fund in order to continue the immigration program. He requested of the British Treasury a loan of 1 million pound. The intention of floating the loan would ensure the repayment of the loan. English interest still dwelt on the export of her paupers and her unemployed. The response by Gipps to Lord John Russell's criticism of the Gipps approach to immigration was that the bounty system had caused the depression of the 1842-44 periods and not the reverse.

The Report of the 1837 'Committee on Immigration' opened up for opposition to the traditional White Australia policy.

'This committee was appointed to consider and report their opinion made to the government of New South Wales, for introducing into the colony certain of the Hill Labourers of India; and to consider the terms under which Mechanics and Labourers are now brought from Europe'.

Summary

The British trait of pomposity came to the fore during the days of early migration to the colony. 'We are British, we are free, we are pure of spirit and more worthy than the prisoners already shipped' they thought' but we will take or families, our servants, our capital and relocate to the new colony, provided we are treated as privileged persons and given land, livestock and a seat at the governor's table'.

But establishing a class structure was not on the list of plans for Brisbane, Bourke Darling or Gipps. They hands their hands full keeping the economy moving forward and keeping the economy afloat. Although they were guided by an appointed Legislative Council, the governors' role was an onerous one–balancing the ever-changing political scene in Britain with the ever-diminishing financial support coming from the British Treasury for colonial operations, and the growing relaxing of isolation of the colony in world events. Trading ships of many nations were daily arrivals into the splendid harbour. The other settlement under the governor's watchful eye was taking more and more time. It was fortunate that Port Phillip settlement was a net contributor to the New South Wales coffers, whilst Morton Bay and VDL were still being supported out of Sydney. The huge influx of convicts made life difficult in the settlements. Finding places to put these people to gainful employment at little (if any) cost to the Treasury was growing more and more difficult. It was largely 'out of sight, out of mind'. Until they engaged in crime or the landowners ran into hard times and suddenly the convicts were unwanted and thrown back onto the charity of the government. Free settlers were fine in theory but their growing influence in the political and financial arena of the colony, made both political and economic decisions difficult. The constant pressure to open up new land, build new roads, carry out surveys, and create new settlements–was a continuing problem for the governor who kept demanding more and more money to run the colony. That placed pressure on raising more and more revenue, especially for public works, education, migration and government services.

Migrations soon became the life-blood of the colony. They brought their capital, their worldly goods, their ways of life, and over all made a valuable contribution to their new land. They were the basis of attracting new investment from the motherland. But migrants down through the years were always to be attractive in the Australian physic. This was to be a nation of immigrants, but society had to be built around the needs of this new world.

The impact of both education and immigration, from the standpoint of the economy, the social framework, the political structure and look at the rocky road that was created by religious bigotry and factions within the colony, must now be reviewed. Naturally as a bi-product of the immigration policies, the transportation (of convicts) program was its first and most significant contributor. Education was a significant economic tool, as the rate of illiteracy within the colony fell from 75% before 1800 to 25% by 1830. The development of local industry was most dependent then, as it is still today, on a literate and educated workforce. Immigration of free settlers hastened the end of the transportation program and although the mass of people supported and approved of its cessation, the pastoralists, traders and merchants bemoaned the shortage of labour and the high price of skilled labourers arriving from Britain. Naturally the discovery of gold in the early 1850s drove those same prices and shortages even higher, since many in the population looked to find their fortune on the goldfields and gave up regular employment in order to move to the goldfields.

Immigrants and Free Settlers

Collins records that on the 15th January 1793, the Bellona transport ship, arrived in Sydney Harbour with a cargo of stores and provisions, 17 female convicts and five settlers one of whom was a master wheel-wright employed by the governor at a salary of 100 pound per annum. A second was a returning skilled tradesman who had been previously employed as a master blacksmith. All five settlers had brought their families.

Collins conjectures that these first three settlers had received free passage, a promise of a land grant and assistance with farming, as the incentive for becoming the free settlers,

Manning Clark (A History of Australia) records that in 1806, 'a dozen families from the Scottish border area arrived as free emigrants and each received 100 acres of land on the banks of the Hawkesbury River in a place they called Ebenezer. They were devout Presbyterians, and were allowed to worship in the colony according to their own lights'. However the authorities were not prepared to tolerate the practice of the catholic religion, because they saw it 'as an instrument of mental slavery, a threat to higher civilization, and a threat to liberty' (Clark Vol 1)

Free Immigrants 1788-1810

Developing Immigration

Even by the census of 1828, NSW had fewer than 5,000 people who had come out voluntarily, in a population of 36 598. The colony had the attractions unavailable in the USA, free land and convict labour. Settlers were given land for agriculture and pasture usage. This meant freehold land, and it only applied to men who had immigrated as private citizens, to military officers who had decided to stay and to pardoned convicts who had been granted land.

In 1831, the British Government, against the opposition of many in the colony decided to stop giving away land grants to settlers and chose instead to 'sell' the land and use some of the proceeds to sponsor migrants to the colony. The initial sales price was 5 shillings an acre. It was a way of inducing poor families to leave the country, but as well of relieving the labour shortage. Between 1831 and 1840 about 50,000 prisoners were transported and about 65,000 free men and women chose to emigrate

The battle of the sexes was more equal amongst emigrants than among convicts: but even South Australia, which was wholly an emigrant's colony, had only 8 females for every 10 males by 1850, and in Australia as a whole there was fewer than 7 in every ten. The resulting challenge was only partially met by Caroline Chisholm who met every convict and emigrant ship to stress the dangers to young unmarried women. Her main accomplishment was to convince the Colonial Office, in 1846, to offer free passage to all families of convicts resident in the colony. Her detractors suggested that the result of her efforts towards convict families and emigrating poor families would be to create an imbalance of Catholics in the colony, who were already twice the proportion of the Australian population as they were in England.

'Populate or Perish'

The history of Australia is bound tightly into two aspects—the economics of colonization and the story of immigration.

Governor King wrote in his report—The State of the Colony in 1801—on the subject of free immigrants:

"Settlers are of two classes i.e. those who come free from England and those who were convicts and whose terms of transportation are expired, or who are emancipated. Of the first class, I am sorry their industry and exertions by no means answer the professions they made in England, several of whom are so useless to themselves and everyone about them that they were not only a burden to the public but a very bad example to the industrious. As they brought no other property than their large families, many have been and will continue an expensive burden on the public, or starve. The settlers are maintained by the crown for eighteen months and have two convicts assigned to each, which is very sufficient to provide against the time of doing for themselves, but that period too often discovers their idleness and incapacity to raise the least article from a fertile and favourable climate, after having occasioned an expense of upwards of 250 pound for each family, exclusive of their passage out The desirable people to be sent here are sober, industrious farmers, carpenters, wheel and mill wrights, who having been used to draw their food from the earth, secure sand manufacture it, would here find how bountifully their labour would be rewarded".

It appears that King did not have a very high opinion of the potential for free migration to the colony.

Phillip's successor–Governor Hunter–was instructed by the Colonial Office to 'encourage free settlers without subjecting the public to expense'. They were to be given larger land grants than the emancipists and as much convict labour as they wanted. Hunter observed in one of his submissions to the Secretary of the colonies that 'free immigrants would not come to the country whilst the needs of the colony were supplied from Government farms'.

The economic factors hit the immigration concept in 1801 when Governor King, as Hunters successor wrote to the Duke of Portland, as Colonial Secretary and suggested family immigration. It was turned down on the basis that transporting a family would cost 150 pound and annual maintenance until they were self-supporting would cost 250 pound (HRNSW)

In 1802, the HRNSW records that free settlers (28 in one group) arrived by the Perseus and Coromandel. More came in the Navy ship Glatton, including a person supposedly bearing 'perfect knowledge of Agriculture, having held a very considerable farm in his hands, but which through youthful indiscretion, he found it necessary to relinquish'. The governor was asked to place him 'above the common class of settlers'. The government, Governor King wrote 'was much imposed on'by these free settlers. The Glatton settlers were sent to the Nepean, where they were wrote King 'going on with great spirit and well applied industry'

King reported to Lord Hobart in 1804 that 'there were 543 free settlers supporting 351 wives and 589 children and utilising 463 convicts'. Further free settlers are recorded as being in the William Pitt in 1805, mainly because land and subsistence was being replaced by the lure of wealth coming from the fine wool being promoted by John Macarthur. This endeavour and attraction of wealth brought a different and probably better class of free settler–the Blaxland brothers arrived on a charter vessel with their families, servants and capital of over 6,000 pound. Again the governor received instructions. 'They are to be allowed 8,000 acres of land and the services of up to 80 convicts for 18 months at the commissary store's expense. Governor Bligh was given similar instructions in reference to a 'lady of quality'–a Mrs Chapman, a widow, Governess and teacher. Bligh was directed to 'afford her due encouragement and assistance'. The next governor, Lachlan Macquarie took a different stance–he discouraged free immigration, probably because the flow of convicts was almost overwhelming his administration. His position is not readily understandable. As a quasi social reformer and developer of free enterprise in the colony, one would have expected Macquarie to welcome free settlers for what social and economic values they could contribute. When the Bigge report was published in London, it raised the interest of men of wealth in the colony and a Lieutenant Vickers, an officer of the East India Company, volunteered to emigrate with 10,000 pound of capital, an unblemished reputation and a purity of private life 'hitherto known in any class of society', and in return demanded privileges by way of land grants, livestock and a regular seat at the governor's table. Brisbane, as governor, was directed by Lord Bathurst as Colonial secretary to give Vickers 2,000 acres of land and a house allotment near Newcastle. Brisbane investigated Vickers and found him to be little more than 'an adventurer, a bird of passage, and boycotted by his fellow officers'. Marjorie Barnard concluded, 'Only distance made his deception possible'. Opportunities followed good publicity, and the floating of the Australian Agricultural Company in London in 1823 did much to promote the colony in Britain, and brought another spate of free settlers to the colony.

This then is the early trend in the free settler movement–it had not been seen yet as a government opportunity. But that was about to change. Lord Bathurst came along with an idea, urged by the Wakefield supporters and the rash of economists waging war on the increasing unemployment, poverty and lack of investment opportunities in Britain.

A privately sponsored scheme was funded by a loan to Dr. J.D. Lang by the governor in the amount of 1,500 pound, which brought out 100 selected 'mechanics' (semi-skilled labourers) and their families. Land used a charter vessel to transport these immigrants, and the understanding was that the immigrants would repay their expenses from future wages. In 1831 this was an inspiring move to privatising a government policy.

Three factors were set to establish an on-going immigration policy. The three factors were bad times in England; shortages of skilled labour of both men and women in the colony; and the cessation of the assignment system.

A commission on Emigration was established in England to select and despatch suitable agricultural labourers. A plan to tax landowners of assigned convicts failed when the difficulty of collection was recognised. There were still 13,400 convicts on assignment in 1831.

The governor agreed that official funds would contribute 20 pound towards each immigrant family and try to recover it after the family settled. The collections were rarely made.

It was left to Governor Bourke to formulate a workable plan. The 'bounty system' relied on sponsored workers funded by government. The government paid 12 pound out of the 17 pound passage money. The Emigrants Friendly Society existed in Sydney to help and protect these sponsored migrants.

A more refined method was needed to select and sponsor these migrants. Glenelg reformed the financial side in 1837. He allocated the revenue from land sales in the colony as a means of affording immigration. The land as well as any revenue derived from its sale, lease or rental, had remained the property of the crown, not the colonial administration. Two-thirds of these funds were to be allocated to migrants by way of grants—£30 for a married couple, £15 for an unmarried daughter, £5 and £10 for children depending on age.

The zenith of immigration success could be seen in the 1830s under Governor Gipps. Land revenue was high, the colony was prosperous and plenty of migrants were on offer and the colony could successfully absorb them. The severe drought at the end of decade (1838) caused land revenue to fall sharply. Gipps proposed a loan to the Land Fund in order to continue the immigration program. He requested of the British Treasury a loan of 1 million pound. The intention of floating the loan would ensure the repayment of the loan. English interest still dwelt on the export of her paupers and her unemployed. The response by Gipps to

Lord John Russell's criticism of the Gipps approach to immigration was that the bounty system had caused the depression of the 1842-44 periods and not the reverse.

The Report of the 1837 'Committee on Immigration' opened up for opposition to the traditional White Australia policy.

"This committee was appointed to consider and report their opinion made to the government of New South Wales, for introducing into the colony certain of the Hill Labourers of India; and to consider the terms under which Mechanics and Labourers are now brought from Europe".

CHAPTER 7

ENTREPRENEURS

Colonial Entrepreneurs'

The purpose of this section is to follow the discourse of economic events by an understanding of some of the key people that contributed to these events.

The chosen entrepreneurs are

John Palmer
Robert Brookes
Thomas Sutcliffe Mort
Thomas Coghlan
Robert Campbell
Lachlan Macquarie
Samuel Marsden
Simeon Lord
Francis Greenway
John Oxley

Lists prepared by others often include John and Gregory Blaxland and George Howe

These men in the above list cover a whole range of economic activities and industries

Pastoral–cattle and sheep

- Industry–shipbuilding to refrigeration
- Newspaper editing and writing
- Politics and policy
- Free trade
- Statistical gathering and analysis to Federation
- Gold discovery
- Building & construction
- Exploration
- Commissariat operations, purchasing, trading
- Financing, consignment, auctioneering

This selection of entrepreneurs includes some fascinating backgrounds and specialties.

- A preacher turned pastoralist
- An industrialist
- A public servant turned landowner and ship owner
- An explorer
- Two former convicts–one an architect and the other a successful trader
- An aristocratic merchant
- A statistician turned author
- A free settler and successful merchant

These nine men together changed the face of the colony. They made a difference by being in this world. Although not the traditional entrepreneur as we think of that term today, but in their day, the colony would not have been as successful as it was without the contribution from these unique personages.

It was fortunate that the colony was successful for not all of these men ended up with the riches they might have deserved in better or other circumstances . . .

Many survived over adversity and demonstrated major courage. These were the men of the 18th and 19th century, without whom Australia would not be free economy.

Was there a common thread amongst these men? Their will to succeed, their willingness to take risks and their aptitude to use their innate skills and judgement brought them to the fore. The two who were convicts did not indulge in self-pity but strove too release themselves from bondage and make a new life for themselves.

Our selection of entrepreneurs includes some fascinating backgrounds and specialties.

- A preacher turned pastoralist (Marsden)
- An industrialist (Mort)
- A public servant turned landowner and ship owner (Palmer)
- An explorer (John Oxley)
- Two former convicts—one an architect and the other a successful trader (Francis Greenway & Simeon Lord)
- An aristocratic merchant (Brooks)
- A statistician turned author
- A free settler and successful merchant

These nine men together changed the face of the colony. They made a difference by being in this world. Although not the traditional entrepreneur as we think of that term today, but in their day, the colony would not have been as successful as it was without the contribution from these unique personages.

It was fortunate that the colony was successful for not all of these men ended up with the riches they might have deserved in better or other circumstances . . .

Many survived over adversity and demonstrated major courage. These were the men of the 18th and 19th century, without whom Australia would not be free economy.

Was there a common thread amongst these men? Their will to succeed, their willingness to take risks and their aptitude to use their innate skills and judgement brought them to the fore. The two who were convicts did not indulge in self-pity but strove too release themselves from bondage and make a new life for themselves.

Francis Greenway

Greenway, on the surface, may appear as an unlikely entrepreneur, especially when compared to the likes of Mort and Palmer, or even Marsden, but we can show that he had the technical skills to make an impact, the brashness to force his opinions when necessary and the luck that is essential to successful entrepreneur. But we must then ask does an entrepreneur need to show sound financial results? We know that Greenway went bankrupt as a precursor to his imprisonment and transportation, and we know that he died in great poverty; but an entrepreneur leaves the results of his success in many forms, and Greenway left his in a series of outstanding colonial buildings, few of which have been allowed to survive the years.

Greenway's contribution as an entrepreneur is neither nebulous nor questionable. It is, without doubt, his designs, his watchful eye at a building site and his extensive choice of materials that make Macquarie the giant of Colonial times and led the colonial economy to forge the base, in so many respects, that allowed successive governors and legislatures to build on a firm base and make the colony of New South Wales a burgeoning triumph. Greenway's contribution was essential to all this. A convict, he may have been but his luck changed the day the convict carrier *General Hewitt* arrived at Sydney Cove in February 1814. He was given a ticket of leave, opened up in private practice, became an adviser to Governor Macquarie and even advertised his service in the *Sydney Gazette* of December 1814. He first drew attention to himself and created a stir with builders and workers by his evaluation of the, in progress, 'rum hospital' on Macquarie Street. His commission from Macquarie had been to 'report on the construction of the hospital then underway for the Government by private contractors and developers. His report was devastating. The builders had to make costly alterations to the work completed and Greenway made the first of a long line of enemies who were to make his life difficult thereafter.

His list of buildings designed and commissions (refer attached) is formidable and impressive. Technically he made two and three story buildings stand erect for the first time in the colony. His key blocks for arches caused much dispute amongst builders and the other occasional designers in the town, but he persisted and won, and his arches stayed in place denying the critics the pleasure of having correctly predicted an impending disaster. By March 1816, only two years after his arrival in the colony on a fourteen year sentence, Greenway, by now married with seven children, had been appointed 'Civil Architect and Assistant Engineer' on 3 shillings per day. He immediately began to plan a large number of buildings that Macquarie had for years been hoping to build. His first official work was the lighthouse on South Head.

Macquarie was so pleased with this '*Macquarie Lighthouse*' that he fully emancipated Greenway and restored him to full citizenship. Then followed a new Government house and a stable block, the female factory at Parramatta, a large barracks and compound for male convicts–*he Hyde Park Convict Barracks*–, St. Matthew's Church at Windsor and St. Luke's Church at Liverpool, and St. James's Church in King Street, Sydney. This impressive list of valuable gems of Early Australian Colonial architecture stands as a standard for other buildings of that period and became the foundation stone of a thriving economy, and entrepreneurship that led to generations of trading, pastoral growth, inland exploration, gold discoveries, free immigration and the advent of rail transportation and telegraphic communications. The Macquarie building period was underpinned by Greenway's technical abilities and led to the development of new building techniques–the use of stone, high rise brick structures, the correct use of local timbers, the local manufacture of imported materials, the use of better lime for bonding and plaster works and moulding hitherto unknown in the colony.

Although Commissioner Bigge, in his 1823 report to the House of Commons, commented favourably on Greenway's abilities and sought to put the blame for the extravagant building program on Macquarie rather than on the architect, Greenway, not politically astute, was concerned only with the spoiling of his designs by both Bigge and Macquarie (with whom he had by now had a very public falling out).

Greenway's loss of political patronage and the Bigge cancellation of many of Greenway's projects, led to further effrontery to the Governor and Bigge when he presented (as a salaried employee) a bill for 11,000 pound for services performed based on a 5% fee on work completed. The bill was never withdrawn and finally settled by a grant of 800 acres in swampland on the right bank of the Hunter River

His association with Macquarie's successor (Sir Thomas Brisbane) was brief and resulted only in the Supreme Court building in King Street the Liverpool Hospital, a Government Store in Parramatta and a police office in York Street, Sydney.

Greenway's return to private practice in 1823 (he was dismissed from public service in November 1822) resulted in only one considerable commission–a house, stables and 'appurtenances' for trader Robert Campbell in Bligh Street. A number of small jobs came his way (the mausoleum for George Howe) but his professional life seemed to have ended with the completion of the Campbell house in 1828.

He retired to his grant on the Hunter River and completed some writing for the press.

His legacy is in the 73 buildings he designed and of those whose construction he supervised. The estimated cost (by this author) of those buildings is close to One million pound of which local materials accounted for nearly 450,000 pound. This contribution to the local economy was an amazing boost to the demand for labour in every sector of life. Free immigration was encouraged, traders brought in boatloads of goods from England on which the Government raised substantial duties for the state revenues, and returned to their homeports laden with wool, whale oil, fur seals, timber and coal. The government put the revenue to good use and encouraged new agricultural and farming ventures; built roads, created improved port facilities and underwrote 'cottage' industries such as boat-building, timber harvesting, and processing, a slaughterhouse and cloth making.

Greenway was indeed an early colonial entrepreneur and produced some of the finest buildings Australia ever had but like so many was failed by his awkward temperament. He could not have produced them alone but then an entrepreneur relies very largely on his personal skills and the support of an assembled team Macquarie's patronage and protection provided the atmosphere in which the architect could give rein to his genius. Alone, he may have crumbled away the attacks of less competent men or remained a convict for his fourteen-year sentence. Technical success, luck and brashness were his brilliant star and *bete* noir

John Palmer

John Palmer makes another interesting character in our choice of entrepreneurs. A very early start as a seaman at the tender age of only nine, stole his chance of learning the way of the world on dry land but set him, at a very young age, to the ways of survival, travel and learning the ways of a singular way of life—a seaman, naval cadet and adventurer. At the time of entering the navy, he served in the War of American Independence, during which time he was captured.

In 1786 he joined the HMS *Sirius* as purser, and voyaged to New South Wales with the first fleet, and continued to serve until that ship was wrecked on a voyage to open up Norfolk Island. Governor Phillip appointed him Commissary-General for the colony in 1790.

Palmer's entrepreneurial prowess and skills commenced from that time. The military corps was cornering the local market as 'traders'. Palmer at first resisted the beckoned association to throw his lot in with this bunch, but shortly saw the way to have the best of both worlds. As commissary, Palmer was subject to patronage by the military officers and, in turn, could bestow patronage as the buyer of produce and goods for the commissary. He successfully played both sides, and was granted 100 acres of land on the shores of Woolloomooloo Bay. For a 'poor' man, he built a luxurious house for his extended family (his wife and first child had arrived in 1800, together with his two sisters). By 1805 Palmer's pay had increased to One pound per day, whilst his deputy (William Broughton) remained at 5 shillings per day

Palmer's abilities had resulted in his first accumulation of wealth and besides his 'public' duties he engaged in timber milling and coastal trading.

By 1804, he owned three vessels voyaging as far south as Bass Strait and north to the Hawkesbury River. By 1807 he also owned farms totalling 2,500 acres–not a bad result for a boy seaman and a poor government servant.

Although he backed the wrong side during the Bligh overthrow, Macquarie re-instated Palmer to his office as Commissary-General, but in 1819 Macquarie became dissatisfied with the whole commissary operation and retired Palmer to half-pay. Bad investments and poor associations had stripped Palmer of all his lands and livestock, and he retired to his Parramatta and Rouse Hill holdings and was appointed a local magistrate. He became one of the Macarthur-Marsden-Blaxland circle, but died in 1833 at the age of 73.

His major contribution to the colony was the buying system for the commissary food holdings from local producers, the encouragement of local industries especially in the timber, metals and grain storing/milling operations. His keeping of essentially accurate accounts for the British Commissary is notable for its balancing and clarity. Even Commissioner Bigge in his report to the House of Commons in 1823 found the Palmer system of store receipts to be a sound system.

Palmer's beneficial associations continued especially after his sister, Sophia, married Robert Campbell who at one stage was the colony's largest landowner and livestock owner. One of the Palmer daughters, Sophia Susannah, married Edward Close, settler and Churchman in 1821. Close was a pastoralist with a 2,560 acre land grant at Morpeth on the Hunter River) and a magistrate appointed by Brisbane. Although removed from his position as magistrate in the case of Lt Lowe's murder of four aboriginals in custody, Brisbane's successor, Governor Darling, appointed Close to the NSW Legislative Council in 1829.

The Close daughter, married Robert Campbell's son George, and thus linked three main families in the colony–the Palmers, the Campbells, and the Closes.

Any man in Palmer's position was open to compromise, and Palmer accepted a role, on occasions, as the recipient of bitter complaints–especially about favouritism towards the local 'nobility' (the Macarthur family) who had been accused of misusing government livestock–a claim which probably had some merit since both Macarthur's livestock and the government livestock often shared the same pastures near Parramatta for grazing. Other areas of favouritism complained of included decisions about how much grain was to be purchased by the Commissary from various farmers and where it was to be delivered. The more influential farmers got the largest orders and could deliver to their local commissary store, whereas the disadvantaged farmers would have a smaller percentage accepted and would be required to deliver their grain to the Sydney store–usually a much greater distance to travel and a much higher cost. But as an entrepreneur Palmer carried out the governor's directions on rationing for all, fairly and equitably and without discrimination or rancour. He bought supplies fairly, engaged in enterprise of timber milling (again supplying the government lumber yard–a conflict of interest which should be overlooked because the quality of timber of higher than other suppliers could provide, and it had been air dried successfully for an average of two years. His boat building and shipping operations created supplies for export and again assisted the growth and development of the colony at a time when government revenue was flagging. Exports allowed a matching value of imports to be made, on which the naval officer could impose duties and tariffs. His agricultural pursuits were short-lived but his son George carried on with the large holdings near Queanbeyan (at Jerrabomberra NSW), Gungahlin (near the Campbell holding of Duntroon in the Monaro).

We know that Woolloomooloo was Sydney's first suburb, being settled in 1793 when Palmer was granted 100 acres and established a farm there. It remained largely undeveloped until 1840 when it was subdivided to satisfy the need for housing close to the rapidly expanding city. Reclamation of the Woolloomooloo Bay began in 1852 and the following decade saw a rapidly expanding population and the establishment of small worker's houses over much of the area. The Plunkett Street Primary School (the first school in the area) was opened in 1878 and named after John Plunkett a Legislative Councillor, Attorney-General and President of the Board of National Education from 1848 to 1858. When Greenway (q.v) designed and built the government house stables for Macquarie, the land used had previously been leased to Palmer who had constructed a bake house and a windmill (for grinding flour) on the site. Macquarie, when he wanted the site for his own use as the 4th government house and domain, considered these buildings inappropriate and resumed the land.

Palmer, as reported by Timothy Coghlan (*q.v.*) gave evidence to the House of Commons Select Committee on Transportation in 1812 that the lowest weekly wage for which a labourer could be obtained in the colony was 24 shillings. The commonest labourer earned from 5s to 7s per day.

Marjorie Barnard in 'A History of Australia' writes that the Commissary, under Palmer, was the proto-treasury, and when the colonial treasury was established the commissariat returned to being the sole provisioner for the convicts and military but 'withered away at the end of transportation'. The commissary had been regularly reformed–by Macquarie, Darling and Brisbane, although Palmer maintained the greatest amount of services through the commissary whilst in charge and probably maintained the best set of financial and stock records during commissary operations of over 60 years.

Barnard also observes that the Palmer manorial home set on 100 acres at Woolloomooloo Bay had a triple barricade of wall, ditch, and sweetbriar hedge inside of which he set gardens, workshops, orchards and a family vault.

Palmer once again felt no conflict of interest when he sat as magistrate in a case brought by Macarthur against Robert Campbell (Palmer's brother-in-law). On the other hand, Palmer sided with Macarthur in a matter concerning Samuel Marsden's refusal to marry a female convict at the Female Factory at Parramatta to a male convict. The case resulted in Brisbane dismissing the three magistrates (Palmer. Macarthur and Blaxland)

It was Palmer (writes Dr H.V. Evatt in *the Rum Rebellion*) who advised the House of Commons Committee in 1812 of the evils resulting from the traffic of spirits in the colony. Palmer had been entirely loyal to Governor Bligh who (Palmer believed) had been remarkably successful in suppressing the traffic in spirits. This action by Bligh led to the *Rum Rebellion*

Palmer may not been the great entrepreneur that his brother-in-law Robert Campbell became as a trader, but still his contribution is to be acknowledged as a formidable contributor to the colony and without whom the colony may not have prospered and grown as brightly as it did.

Robert Brooks

Brooks is relatively unknown in the Australian context and that is mainly because, in spite of his contribution to the Australian economic scene, he remained a resident of England and saw this country as he was but passing by (usually in one of his fleet of ships). He passed but once on his own ship *Elizabeth* in 1823-24. He invariably conducted his commercial and financial interests from the *City*, whilst his overseas operations were left largely in the hands of ships' masters, agents and other connections. His London office was kept simple—he never employed more than a few clerks in his office, in spite of the large trading business carried out

Frank Broeze, the Professor of History at the University of Western Australia, brought us the life story of Brooks in his competent 1993 work—'**Mr. Brooks and the Australian Trade**—*Imperial Business in the 19th Century*'.

Broeze describes Brooks as "One of the leaders of mid-19th century trade between London and Australia. Brooks' career can stand as a paradigm of the rise of that trade and of the City (of London) itself.

The white British-sponsored settlements (colonies) of Australia and New Zealand remained economically very closely tied to Britain Until 1850 (and the giant step of self-government) their location and the provisions of the British Navigation Acts ensured that virtually no other than British business could operate in Australia and New Zealand. In fact, under well after World War II, Britain was to remain these nations' most important trading partner and provider of shipping and other services".

During the 19th century Britain received virtually all cargoes from the South Seas, mainly because British investment owned or controlled the shipping and much of the large pastoral and manufacturing capability of the colony. Brooks was one of the more significant personages who contributed to this 19th century dominance. Brooks excelled in and extensively supported the concept of 'private merchant financing' (we see the same thoughts being pursued by another of our entrepreneurs–Thomas Mort). Research on this topic, since it is not a traditional or mainstream banking practice has remained relatively obscure–a delving into this subject would involve a close examination between the London-Australia axis and an understanding of the elements of the Australian trade and its dynamic core (the common players; the control, through investment, by London Boards of Australian industry; the control of shipping and ships; and the merchant banking that financed and funded so much of the exports being moved to London. Brooks' career spanned the turbulent times in the growth of each of these factors and in many ways owned and controlled main aspects of each sector.

Using the classic definition of 'entrepreneurial' aims as a basis for comparison, Brooks followed a business strategy of building a complex structure around ac range of mutually supportive operations, 'as well as a combination of personal, entrepreneurial and environmental elements through a mixed chronological and thematic approach.

A remarkable closeness can be traced between the evolution of the Brooks business and the development of the Australian trade in general.

Brookes participated in many ventures. He owned ships. He bought cargo to sale in those ships. He sold that cargo at the point of destination at a profit. For the return voyage, he bought wool or other products on his own account, brought it to London and marketed that product, and then started the cycle all over again. His fleet grew and grew, and his services were much in demand. He reluctantly took product on consignment or as paid cargo to fill his growing fleet. He was invited onto the Board of a number of significant trading and financial institutions in the City. He was active in the United Bank of Australia in its halcyon days. He contracted with the authorities to carry assisted passage settlers from England to Australia.

And like most entrepreneurs he had his times of crisis and despair but enjoyed the challenge of a recovery.

On many occasions, Brooks acted as both a commission agent as well as financier. For instance Broeze in his contribution to *Australian Financiers* records that on an 1827 order from a John Rickards of Sydney, Brooks charged 2 ½% commission and advanced, short-term, the funds at a rate of 5% p.a. At this time Brooks was particularly interested in whaling and a leading Australian based trader, Robert Campbell (another selected entrepreneur) consigned all his colonial exports to Brooks. By late 1832 Campbell owned brooks over 10,000 pound for advances on goods consigned.

It was in 1827 that Brooks introduced the greatest attraction for pastoralists based in Australia but wanting to benefit from the English wool sales. Brooks commenced advancing funds to exporters against shipments of produce. Following his first wool consignments in 1827, pastoralists and merchants, keen to turn their produce as quickly as possible into ready cash, responded actively to the new approach by Brooks which involved agents of London merchants making credits available. Brooks ran the biggest book of the lot. However for Brooks, the most important factor was his role in the founding (in 1837) and working of the Union Bank of Australia.

In 1838-39 Brooks and some associates attempted to gain control of the UBA in London, but these attempts failed. Although this attempt had failed it was the Brook policies that were adopted by the Bank's London (and controlling) Board . . . These policies included

- Refusing to discount bills drawn against exports to the colonies
- Declining to take mortgages on pastoral land
- The Bank Board also agreed to offer broad discounting facilities to directors and their connections.

Brooks benefited greatly from his privileged position and gained great advantage over his competitors, and used his position to assist friends in London and Australia.

In the colony, Brooks' associates used their access to the UBA to discount drafts drawn on Brooks as an almost unlimited line of credit for investment purposes. "The fact is (wrote Brooks to his agent in Sydney) that money is so valuable to people engaged in trade in this place, whether settlers, ship-owners, or other, that anything in the shape of produce must be turned into money or its equivalent as soon as possible".

By 1841-42 the boom of the previous decade was over. Overstocking of colonial markets, collapse of the land and livestock sectors, and the dramatic end of assisted migration, all made a downturn inevitable. Speculation was entrenched as well as greed by the country agents. They had begun the risky practice of advancing money not only against known bales of wool, but also against wool still on the sheep's back. Similarly with whale oil, advances were being made on the future catches of two ships still tied up at the fisheries. Brooks condemned these practices but his Sydney agents had speculated (with Brooks' funds) too heavily and the UBA called in the advances against Brooks as well as the agent (Robert Dacre). Robert Campbell and virtually all major traders (also making advances unwisely) had failed. Brooks survived by retiring from the trade but by taking over consignments from agents who had failed benefited significantly and kept his fleet operating successfully and profitably. Robert Campbell was also making a strong comeback after bankruptcy. With the UBA changing its risky policies, Brooks was partially shut out from his former influential role and took his Sydney banking business to the Bank of New South Wales.

Brooks had survived the colonial downturn and revamped his global operations. He brought his three sons into the business, assigned them control and in 1872 retired to his country estate.

Brooks had diversified his interests during the 1850s by investing in a fleet of 14 whalers The Brooks plantation on the Logan River near Brisbane successfully grew cotton at a time when the American colonies refused to send their cotton to England for processing, and the Brooks product received a British government bounty. He was offered a directorship of the London Dock Company, as a means of their ensuring his trade would be handled through those London docks rather than Hull, Bristol or Liverpool. Brooks also became a trustee of the Australasian Gold Mining

Company, and arranged for the UBA to extend credit facilities to the company at Bathurst.

The Robert Brooks & Co. firm was finally liquidated in Australia in 1967, after over 125 years of service to the London-Australia trade, numerous investments in the colonies and great success as an entrepreneur.

Robert Campbell

Of all the entrepreneurs analyzed in this section of the 'Colonial Economy', surely Robert Campbell, if not Thomas Mort, compete for the title of best entrepreneur. Their accomplishments are considerable and both men are well deserving of such a mantle. It is not surprising that in a small and closed community like the colony of New South Wales, an association can be found between the prominent citizens of the town. For instance, Palmer's sister married Robert Campbell; Greenway designed Campbell's house and outbuildings; Campbell was the largest trader in the colony and supplied large quantities of goods to the Commissary store of the colony. Palmer was the Commissary-General. Palmer's interest was in timber and sealskin and Campbell wanted to export such commodities to his markets in England.

Campbell left Calcutta in his ship *The Hunter* in 1798 with a full cargo and headed for New South Wales in an attempt to develop a trading connection between his firm Campbell & Co (a successor to Clarke, Campbell & Co)

Apparently it was a successful commission because upon his return with a second cargo in 1800, Campbell received the governor's permission to take up residence on Dawes' Point (on land that he had bought in 1798), where he began to build warehouses and a private wharf. By 1810 another wharf had been built, behind which stood the Campbell house 'furnished in an elegant manner with colonnades and two fronts'.

Campbell was soon heavily engaged in the Australian trade, at one time (in 1804) having over 50,000 pounds worth of goods in the warehouses. Trade became a two way street. Campbell returning to India with cargoes of timber, wool and coal, whilst coming home with cotton, fabrics, Bric-a-brac and many items badly needed in the colony by the growing numbers of free settlers, military personnel and of course, the many civil list employees. Governor King calculated that Campbell had imported over 16,000 of livestock into the colony between 1800 and 1804. Although Campbell imported 'excessive' quantities of spirits against the spirit of the governor's attempts to limit the trading and consumption of spirits in the colony (to the ultimate exploitation of convicts, farmers, workers and the government) his name was synonymous with fair trading, reduced prices and generous credit and was publicly acknowledged by the small settlers, officers and governor alike. Campbell largely initiated the sealing industry and won his challenge (albeit at some extensive personal cost) to the East India Company's sole right to southern oceans trading with England.

Under Bligh, Campbell quickly became involved with public administration, having an intimate knowledge of the colonial economy. In 1807, he was appointed a magistrate and the Naval Officer (the collector of customs revenues, harbour dues and wharfage charges). As Naval Officer Campbell moved to confiscate a still illegally imported by Macarthur, which move ultimately fused the rebellion against Bligh and the disposition of Bligh as Governor. As a fellow diner at government house on the evening of the rebellion, Campbell was arrested by Johnson and dismissed as treasurer, naval officer and collector of taxes. Following the marriage of Palmer's sister, Sophia, to Campbell, Palmer and Campbell had become limited business partners. In 1810 Campbell was reinstated to his former offices by Macquarie.

During his time in London in support of Bligh, his business ventures failed for lack of experienced management and upon his return to the colony Campbell faced some years of bleak operations and frugal living. He continued to pursue public duties and sat on the Court of Civil Jurisdiction, and assisted in establishing the Bank of New South Wales and became an original shareholder. Macquarie made him a grant of 1500 acres in the Bathurst district. Having assisted Macquarie form the Savings Bank in 1819, Campbell's close association with this institution led to it becoming commonly known as 'Campbell's Bank'. By 1820 Campbell's fortunes had begun to revive. He began handling wool to London, wheat shipments from the Derwent market and commissions from the growing

Newcastle settlement. By 1825, Campbell was a shipowner again and sent fully laden to Calcutta. In 1826 Campbell's wharf at Sydney Cove became a private concern and the two Campbell sons were admitted to a new Campbell & Co partnership. The entrepreneur was back on his feet. It is not surprising that the personalities of two key colonial governors wrought such different results on the colony and its people. Bligh reigned in a state of terror and brought disrespect to himself and many of his principal associates. His trial in London took key citizens away from the colony for extended periods and placed many at economic risk–Marsden, Macarthur, Campbell, Palmer and Close. Macquarie took a very different approach to his duties and restored the citizens to economic health, and encouraged rather than discouraged free enterprise and entrepreneurship. The economy benefited from his judgments and even England faired well.

If we take our starting point as the middle of the eighteenth century, then we begin with pre-industrial Britain, though it is evident that the process of industrialisation had already begun. This conjecture raises the question of a further motive in the decision to transfer British prisoners from England to the new planned penal settlement of New South Wales. Did some clever analysts foresee the need for new or additional raw materials for post-industrial Britain and saw that possibility coming from the penal colony and the associated availability of unskilled labour, being the British prisoners whose labour was available to service the needs of Britain, in the penal colony.

A comparison of certain common elements within both economies can assist in determining the impact of the British economic cycles on the colonial economy.

Poverty

Professor Deane points out that in pre-industrial revolution Britain, average wages were between £8 and £9 per annum per head of population, whereas by the end of the 1750s the average had reached to between £12 and £13, per head of the population. As the revolution took shape in Britain, wages rose, based largely on skills, age and mobility, so, how was poverty, even if common to most economic societies, a factor in the economic cycles relative to the industrial revolution? In Britain, unemployment was relatively high. Even so, the average per head, per annum wage levels may not suggest a high standard of material well-being but they do indicate the existence of a national economic surplus, 'even if this was distributed through socially undesirable channels.[133] Professor Deane goes on to point out[134] that there is a famous controversy concerning the worker's standard of living during the industrial revolution, but at this stage the point to notice is that although the standard of life was simple, and sometimes disastrously vulnerable to climatic extremes in the mid-18th century, there was some economic surplus–some slack in the economy. However it is obvious that the English were better off that most of their contemporaries in other countries–the three richest countries in the world were Holland, England and France. Dorothy Marshall writing in her 1956 study of *English People in the 18th Century* concluded 'there is little evidence to show that the average member of the labouring poor was filled with bitter resentment or economic despair.

2. Stagnation

"Another characteristic of a pre-industrial community which distinguishes it from an industrial one is that its standard of living and of productivity is relatively stagnant. This is not to say that there is no economic change, no economic growth even, in a pre-industrial economy, but that such growth as does occur is either painfully slow or spasmodic, or is readily reversible. However, the ordinary man saw little evidence of economic growth within his own lifetime and no improvement that could not be eliminated within a single year by the incidence of a bad harvest or a war or an epidemic. In Britain the normal long-term rate of growth (before 1750) was.5 of a percent in real incomes and it was almost as common for the economy to slide into decline as it was for it to grow."[135]

---

[133] Deane, P. *Ibid* P7
[134] Deane, P. *ibid* P10
[135] Deane, P. *ibid* P11

3. Dependence on agriculture

A pre-industrial economy is obviously one in which the principal economic activity is agricultural production. This was the case in Britain before 1750 and was certainly the case in the colony of NSW before 1810. 'An underdeveloped country may be defined as a country with 80 percent of its people in agriculture and a developed country as one with 15 per cent of its employment in agriculture, in both cases giving or taking a little according to foreign trade."[136] Primarily agricultural families accounted for about 68 percent of the English population in 1750[137]. Most inhabitants of 18th century Britain lived in rural areas, though the towns were already beginning to expand.

4. Lack of occupational specialization

Another obvious conclusion must be that a pre-industrial economy has little need of or planning for labour specialisation, whereas the industrialised economy has the need and use for specialised labour. Pre-industrial Britain was essentially unspecialised and the major industries were domestic industries subordinate to agriculture. There was mobility of labour and many mining employees moved from extractive industries to agriculture during harvest or planting time. It was at this time that Adam Smith urged the concept of 'division of labour'[138] and in essence the specialisation of labour. Adam Smith also concluded that in an industrialised economy the share of national income attributed to employees is generally over 50 percent, whereas in a pre-industrial economy this percentage will be generally less than 10 percent.

The low degree of geographical integration

Obviously a by-product of an agricultural economy and the low level of specialisation is the lack of integration among its regions. The general lack

---

[136] Singer, H *The Concept of Economic Growth in Economic development (1960)*
[137] Deane, P *Ibid* Page 13
[138] Adam Smith *The Wealth of Nations (1950)*

of mobility of labour is based on regionally based agricultural output as well as the lack of decentralised manufacturing activity.

'It is evident that the British economy of the mid-18th century displayed a number of features which can be recognised as characteristics of a pre-industrial economy'[139] In addition to any common elements there were certainly sub-elements of the main Industrial revolution. Gains and benefits achieved under and during the industrial revolution in Britain flowed to many countries and were widespread in the impact.

The demographic revolution

One of the features of an emerging industrial economy from its predecessors in the chain of economic development is that it enjoys sustained long-term growth of both population *and* output. The rate of growth of population depends largely on the rate of natural increase (the difference between the birth rate and the death rate). It was obvious in Britain that by the end of the 18th century the changes in both the birth rate and the death rate were such as to constitute a demographic revolution. Poverty, land enclosures and a brutal system of legal enactments in England tended to obscure the reality that a sizeable portion of the convicts were professional thieves hardened by repeated criminality. 'In the main they were working class, unskilled, town dwellers to whom law breaking had become a way of life.'[140]

Professor Deane concludes that there was a complex two-way relationship of cause and effect shaping trends of population growth and output. In the case of population, it was largely non-economic factors, which helped reduce the long-term death rate or raise the long-term birth rate. In the case of output, such factors as the growth of foreign markets and the widening of the technological horizon.[141] But there were other factors to be considered; such as the fact that new technology was introduced into a country that had labour, land and capital resources in reserve. If this was

---

[139] Dean, P *ibid Page 19*

[140] John Malony *Penguin Bicentennial History of Australia* p.16

[141] Deane, P *ibid* P.34

the case in 18ᵗʰ century Britain, it was slanted in a similar direction in the colony of NSW

Malthus observed

> *During the last 40 years of the 17ᵗʰ century and the first 20 of the 18ᵗʰ, the average price of corn was such as, compared with the wages of labour, would enable the labourer to purchase with a day's earnings, two-thirds of a peck of wheat. From 1720 to 1750 the price of wheat had so fallen, while wages had risen, that instead of two-thirds the labourer could now purchase the whole of a peck of wheat with a day's labour*

The Agricultural revolution

There were four unique features of the British agrarian revolution.

Firstly, it involved farming in large-scale consolidated units in place of the medieval open fields cultivated in strips by serfs with rights of pasture, fuel (cut timber) and game on the overstocked common.

Secondly, it involved the extension of arable farming over heaths and commons and the adoption of intensive livestock husbandry

Thirdly, it involved the transformation of the village community of (largely) self-subsistent peasants into a community of agricultural labourers whose basic standards of living came to depend more on the conditions of national and international markets than on the state of the weather.

Fourthly, it involved a large increase in agricultural productivity. That is the volume of output produced by the full-time labour force in agriculture grew significantly.[142]

---

[142] R. Nurske *Problems of Capital Formation in underdeveloped countries* (1953) (1953)

In Britain, the agricultural revolution took place when three related developments occurred. (1) The adoption of new techniques of production (2) enclosure, and (3) changes in entrepreneurial attitudes.

The agricultural revolution, as a division of the industrial revolution, contributed in a number of ways to the effectiveness of the primary transformation. (1) By feeding the growing population and in particular the population of the industrial centres; (2) by inflating purchasing power for the products of British industry, and (3) by providing a substantial part of the capital required to finance industrialisation and keep it going even through a period of major war.[143]

Ralph Davis, analysing British trade statistics between 1660 and 1700,[144] concluded that the commercial revolution 'for most of its pre-industrial trading history, England came close to being a single export economy whereby wool or woollen cloth constituted almost the whole of English exports'. Even by the middle of the 18th century, woollen textiles accounted for well over half the value of English domestic exports.

Is it any wonder that the first signs of the new Botany Bay settlement being able to sustain sheep production at a low cost and thus become a replacement for Spanish or German imports was so warmly welcomed and encouraged? English–plantations in the West Indies also opened up re-export markets to Europe and had it 'not been for the tropical products[145] with their elastic demand and growing markets in temperate regions, it would have been difficult to expand British trade with Europe'.[146] G.D. Ramsey analyses that the 'significance of the re-export trade in contributing to British economic growth and industrialisation lay predominantly in its indirect effect on economic organisation and opportunity. It was a direct source of incomes to groups of merchants and seamen'[147], and British re-export significantly supported the new colony of New South

---

143 Deane, P *ibid* P.50
144 Ralph Davis *English Foreign Trade 1660-1700* p.150
145 Such products as 'spices, tea, sugar, tobacco, cotton, indigo and dyewoods'
146 Deane, P *ibid* P.53
147 G.D. Ramsey *English Overseas Trade during the Century of Emergence* (1957) P.237

Wales, by being called upon to service all colonial supply needs, until the timeframe for ordering and receiving from the colonial commissariat through British merchants encouraged 'import replacement industries' in the colony and brought a new twist to the local manufacturing and agricultural industries.

Trade statistics can turn around very quickly as will be recognised by the immediate impact of colonial wool on the British textile market and the huge demand for imports by the Mills, to the point where a collection of Mill owners, combined to submitting a proposal in 1824 to Earl Bathurst for a land grant in Van Diemen's Land for wool production for sole export to Britain[148]; In 1750 grain accounted for 20% of English exports, but by 1800, Britain was a net grain importer. In 1750 woollens accounted for 46% of exports whilst by 1800, due to scarce source of raw materials, their share had fallen to 28%.

There are at least six ways in which foreign trade can be said to have helped to precipitate the industrial revolution. (1) Foreign trade created a demand for the products of British industry; (2) International trade gave access to raw materials, which broadened the range of British products and cheapened British products in their destination market; (3) International trade provided poor and undeveloped countries with the purchasing power to buy British goods;

(4) It provided an economic surplus, which helped to finance industrial expansion and agricultural improvement; (5) It helped to create an institutional structure and a business ethic which was to prove effective in promoting home-trade; likewise, a more sophisticated set of attitudes to the role of government policy in promoting economic prosperity emerged (6) The expansion of trade in the 18th century was a prime cause of large towns and industrial centres.[149]

---

[148]   This was the beginning of the second land grant company–The Van Diemen's Land Company, formed by Royal Charter in 1826 and still in existence today. Refer Beckett, G 'The Economic History of the VDL Company 1826-1899'

[149]   Deane, P *ibid* P.68

The Transport Revolution

The cheapest way of transporting bulky, weighty, goods was by water and Britain scored heavily in this respect by being narrow and insular–no part of the British Isles is farther than seventy miles from the sea–and by having a considerable length of canal system which is either naturally navigable or can be made so. It was this inland system of water navigation that provided the most spectacular innovations of the period. The first Industrial revolution grew on the basis of coal and iron and so it became necessary to move these heavy and bulky raw materials and the finished products quickly and cheaply around the country.

The transport revolution was the crucial factor in facilitating the cost reducing innovations necessary to sustain the industrial revolution.

The Textile Industry revolution

The cotton and iron industries are generally considered to be at the heart of the industrial revolution, that is the growth of modern manufacturing industry and all that this implies–large-scale units of production, labour saving machinery, regimentation of labour, and specialisation of the labour-force We could also say that the demographic, agricultural, commercial and transport revolutions were the most important preconditions of successful industrialisation and the sustained economic growth that goes along with it The iron and cotton industries were two industries which first experienced the changes in technological and economic organisation that made Britain 'the workshop of the world'.[150] The term 'textile' industry is intended to cover both the cotton and woollen industries since both enjoyed similarities in machinery innovation, better quality and better-improved raw materials and indeed a growth of 'subcontractors' in 'cottage' industries able to prepare value adding to basic raw materials at a much lower cost. The invention that really laid the basis for the revolution in cotton was the water-frame, patented by Arkwright in 1769. This produced cotton yarn strong enough to serve as warp as well as waft and thus created a new product–a British cotton cloth that was

---

[150] Rostow, W.W. *Stages of economic growth* p.53

NOT a linen mixture. Then came the 'jenny' and the combined effects of the water-frame and the jenny show up in the statistics of imports during the 1770s but it was not until the 1790s, after the American War that major increases in imports took place. Between 1780 and 1800 there was a 8-fold increase in raw cotton imports, but since the spun yarn was stronger and thinner, the raw material imports understate the increase in yardage and real value.[151] By the 1780s the volume of exports was 3-4 times the rate of twenty years earlier. By 1815 it was thirty times the volume of 1780. At this same time, exports of cotton textiles accounted for 40% of the value of British domestic exports, whilst woollen goods accounted for only 18 %. This situation caught the imagination of both businessmen and government and provided a dramatic lesson on the profitability of mechanisation. The factories, however, only provided a part of the immense increase in output that put cotton at the head of the British manufacturing industry—most of it was produced by a multitude of 'outworkers'. The tens of thousands of little men who operated Jennies and looms in extensions to their cottages provided the industry with buildings and machinery which would have required hundreds of wealthy capitalists to set up on a factory basis. It was this situation more than any other that permitted the immediate expansion of capacity in response to technological opportunities and market demand. Thus the costs and risks of the new industry were more widely spread that they would otherwise have been and were more readily undertaken because of this.[152] Obviously the cotton industry's success depended largely on its various factors of production, which were within the capability of the British economy to meet. It was labour-intensive rather than capital intensive, and there was a relatively abundant supply of 'skilled' (e.g. weavers) labour. The mechanisation and industrialisation of an industry had another benefit as well. It related to quality, and in the majority of marketing, when a commodity produced by British manufacturers was of 'good' quality it found a ready-made market. Its improved quality made it competitive with silk and linens and thus the market widened to mass proportions.

Another characteristic of the 18th century cotton industry was the fact that it was highly localised, as was the woollen industry. The reason for

---

[151] W. Radcliffe *The origin of Power Loom Weaving* (1828) p.62
[152] Mann, Julia *The Cotton Trade & Industry* (1931)

these concentrations is unclear but it is likely the concept of 'clustering' (cluster industries) is older than we think. Probably the most important reason for the cotton industry's ability to maintain its profits and hence its rate of investment was the fact that it enjoyed an almost inexhaustible low-priced labour supply. This sustained economic growth of the cotton industry between 1780-1850 is due, in part, to an increasing proportion of the incomes that it generated went to the entrepreneurs, who in turn ploughed back a substantial portion of their earnings into more plant and equipment. This meant two things: (1) the industry went on expanding its capacity to produce and increasing its economies of scale arising from the development of specialised ancillary industries in merchanting, bleaching, dyeing etc; (2) the industry went on improving its equipment even though radical changes in technique were not as rapid as they could have been, given the accessible range of inventions

The Iron Industry

Changes in the iron industry's system of production, which were involved in the industrial revolution, were less radical than changes in the cotton industry. The textile industry had been changed in organisation as well as technology. The iron industry was already capitalistically organised.[153] Another feature of the industrial revolution in iron and steel, which distinguishes it from the cotton industry is that the former expanded on the strength of domestic raw materials, whilst the latter encouraged innovations which enabled British industries to turn from charcoal (a dwindling resource) to coal (abundantly available) and from imported to native ores. Whereas the cotton saved labour through mechanisation, the iron industry did so by economising in raw materials by using materials that were abundant in supply and cheap in place of materials that were scarce and expensive.

It was not until the middle of the 19th century that iron was used to construct railroads, locomotives, ships, machinery, gas and sanitation systems, which greatly expanded the range of its outlets. However, since

---

[153]   Professor Nef *Essays in Economic History*

prices fell steeply due to changes in production techniques, demand was too inelastic to permit a dramatic rise in sales.

Schumpeter[154], makes the case for a cluster of innovations during this period, which was decisive for three main reasons: (1) because they occurred at roughly the same period of time; (2) they came when Britain's naval superiority and contacts enabled her to take advantage of rising European and North American incomes, and (3) because they reinforced each other in certain important respects. The turning point in the industrial revolution took place in 1775 when James Watt's steam-engine made it possible to apply increased power for blowing the blast furnace and mechanical power for forging. 'There is no doubt of the immense importance of the steam engine to the iron industry.[155] The iron industry revolution gave value to British iron-ore resources, which had hitherto been so low grade that they were practically worthless. In addition to iron ore, the industry used large quantities of British limestone and British coal. The iron industry was the most important factor in the rising demand for coal in the first half of the 19th century, and also for transport facilities

Good cheap iron was required for implements, ploughshares to lathes, for military and naval purposes for hardware, for telegraphic wire, for building purposes and for industrial machinery. The basis had been laid for the engineering industry to serve all British industry and supply the world with machinery during the 19th century, but the biggest contribution during this period was to the railways industry.

However, the iron industry played a role in British industrialisation that was both pervasive and stimulating. It provided cheaply and abundantly the commodity, on which, more than any other single material except coal, modern industry was to depend for its essential equipment

If the industrial revolution can be given a definition, there should be attached to it a fairly precise political and social philosophy and economic circumstance as well as a fairly precise timeframe. Within the main industrial revolution, there must be subsidiary components such as

---

[154]   E. B. Shumpeter *British Overseas Trade Statistics (1697-1808)* (1960)

[155]   R.H. Campbell *Carron Company* (1961) P. 60

innovation, invention, entrepreneurship, speculation and development of private and government policies hitherto unknown–such as a new role of government, introduction of banking regulation, encouragement of capital creation, free trade, protection of patents, all of which created the environment to foster, encourage and prolong the industrial revolution. Some of these aspects will be considered in further detail.

A Chronology of Innovation

Key aspects of the timeframe include: (1) Changes in entrepreneurial attitudes to innovation (2) changes in the market environment (3) changes in the pace of invention

The period 1783-1802 is not unique as representing change during the industrial revolution. Population was in acceleration before reaching a later peak. The canal mania was preceded by an earlier unprecedented burst of construction activity and canal construction was followed a generation later by the more spectacular and important railway mania. The cotton and iron industries had begun to transform their techniques in earlier decades and by 1802 were still too small a part of total economic activity to carry the national economy along by their own weight. The upsurge in foreign trade, which characterised the period 1783-1802, was also important but not overly spectacular. It was a rebound from the abnormally low trade levels of the 1780s, caused by the American War

The Changing Role of Labour

An inevitable condition of successful economic development is the existence of an expanding, mobile and adaptable labour supply. As a factor of production, labour must be seen as a key ingredient in economic development together with natural resources, technical progress, accumulation of capital, and an increase in the labour supply.

In essence, the rate at which any economy can expand its output of food and services depends on four fundamentals: (1) The rate at which it can enlarge its stock of natural resources; (2) Technical progress also permits the production of larger output of goods and services with a given input of labour and capital; The third determinant of the rate of economic growth is the rate of new investment, and the fourth is the rate of expansion of the labour supply. The determinants are closely inter-related and it is usual not to be able to increase the national stock of natural resources or to introduce technical change without increasing the rate of investment. In the end, the capital required per unit of output may be smaller but at the outset the absolute amount of capital required for the productive process is almost invariably larger. The fact that British entrepreneurs in the late 418th century and early 19th century were able to increase industrial output and capacity without facing correspondingly increased costs due to a rise in the real wage-rate meant that the reward for successful innovation was largely shared between the investor and the consumer. Because in the early stages of the industrial revolution, the increasing population was largely due to the combined effects of a falling infantile death rate and a rising birth rate, the increment was largely composed of infants. Thereupon by about 1821 the active labour force was growing at a slower rate than the overall population. Another factor, which helped to increase the input of labour into the productive process, was the increase in the average number of hours worked per worker and per day. It was also fortunate for British industrialists that the demographic factors were operating in their favour throughout the crucial periods of the industrial revolution, and fortunate also that the technical progress took advantage of the demographic situation. It is not to be imagined that the pioneers of the industrial revolution found a factory labour force ready to use. The transition from agricultural or domestic industries with their seasonal routine, their variable pace and their family based organisation, to the monotonous, machine-driven, impersonal grind of factory work did not come easily to British workers. The early water-driven factories, generally situated in remote rural areas on the banks of streams, were constantly short of labour.

During the second phase of the factory age, within the industrial revolution, there was no cheap labour, but it was largely unskilled and relatively homogeneous and elastic in supply.

The Role of Capital

A second factor of production (the first being labour) whose development was crucial to the British industrial revolution was capital. What additions were made to the nation's capital in the 18th century? For example, the enclosure movement was associated with new investment in hedging, ditching, drainage and those sorts of works required bringing commons and wastelands into permanent cultivation. Urbanisation involved investment in buildings, street paving and lighting, water supply and sanitation. Improvements in communication entailed substantial capital expenditure on roads, bridges, river navigations and canals. These developments were taking place throughout the century though more extensively in the second half of the 18th century, and there was a marked acceleration over the last three decades in the pace of enclosures, of urbanisation and of canal building. But if the national capital grew faster between 1750 and 1799, so too did the national income and the population. If land is excluded from any calculation of the nation's capital, then man-made capital accounts for less than half of the remaining total–this consists mainly of industrial, commercial and financial capital (such as inventory or stock-in-trade, machinery, canals and foreign assets); additionally, public property accounted for about 33%, and farmer's capital for nearly 20% at the beginning of the 19th century. By the 1830s industrialists had been ploughing back profits at a higher than normal rate, or putting more savings into fertilizers, improved breeding stock, and farm machinery, than into enclosure of commons and waste. After the railway age, a very different picture emerges. New estimates put land in at 30%, but declining in relative importance, so that by 1885, land accounted for less than 20% of the total. Farm capital was also less important and declining in absolute terms by the fourth quarter of the 19th century

Railways were not initially a government instrumentality, but consigned to finance and development by private capital. As was the case for the railways, the bulk of the capital needed for the canal developments came from local businessmen who had a special interest in the success of the projected developments. There was much wastage of capital when speculators poured money into questionable projects. In addition to speculative losses, British capital was also being 'exported' and annual capital outflows represented between 3 and 4 percent of national product.

More than £500,000 million was invested abroad between 1850 and 1870.

Another way of financing capital formation was to use inflation as a means of generating 'forced savings'. Inflation, sometimes uncontrollable, was a feature of the industrialising economy. Where prices are rising faster than wages or profits grow more rapidly than either, and because prices (and profits) go on rising, industrialists are happy to plough this windfall back into capital formation.

The capital required for the industrial revolution was found not so much through national savings because the rate of demand for investment seems to have grown little, but from those who had resources to spare and had productive ideas for their use. In practice, the innovators used their own resources or those of friends and relatives. It was often possible for an industrious man to set up in business with very little capital and to build up his own resources until they were large enough to attract the interest of professional investors. Once the new enterprise was earning a steady profit it was usual to finance its continuance and its expansion by ploughing back the profits. Until the Joint Stock Company Act of 1856 established limited liability, incorporation was slow and expensive and required parliamentary sanction, and was rarely used except for schemes requiring abnormally large and unspeculative capital contributions–such as canals, docks, water supply, bridges, roads, gas supply and railways.

The Role of the Banks

The main determinant of the supply of money for the industrial revolution was the supply of gold, as the volume of coinage depended solely on the supply of gold, which in turn depended on the world supply and availability of gold and on the British balance of payments. If exports exceeded imports this generally implied an inflow of gold; conversely, if imports exceeded exports, the excess had to be financed by an export of gold. A system of credit, which depended so heavily on the state of confidence within the economy, caused instability in the economy when anything happened to disturb that confidence; though while the system was incompletely articulated it was still possible for a loss of confidence.

This is what happened in 1797 when it was decided to lift the strain by breaking the link between gold and the money supply. The main reason for this decision was the fact that gold was flowing out of the country and there was no immediate prospect of stopping the drain. Apart from the general situation there were also some special circumstances, which precipitated the crisis of confidence. The first of such circumstances was the bad harvest of 17895. Britain's growing population could no longer feed itself when the harvest was below normal, and heavy imports of corn were required in the season of 1795/96. Abroad, the heavy expenditure on British fleets and armies, the subsidies to allies, the loans raised by allies on the British market, all created fresh pressures on the balance of payments, fresh reasons why payments to foreigners should exceed the value of receipts from foreigners and so have to be met by the export of gold. In 1821, the wartime emergency monetary system came to an end and Britain went formally and legally on to the gold standard. English monetary institutions at that time included: (1) a central joint-stock central bank–The Bank of England–which acted also as the government's bank and custodian of the nation's gold reserve; (2) about 60 London private banks of great strength; (3) about 800 small private note-issuing country banks uncontrolled in all matters except the denominations of the notes issued. Probably the English banks have never been so ready to assist innovation or finance long-term investment in industry as they were in the period 1770-1830 when the industrial revolution took shape. However during the period 1809-1830 there were 311 bankruptcies of country banks of which 179 took place in the two periods of 1814-16 and 1824-26.

Adoption of Free Trade

An elaborate system of tariffs designed to protect domestic industry from foreign competition was the focal point of a static economy where the major task of commercial policy was to maintain the *status quo*. *Innovation* and successful *industrialisation* provided opportunities for expansion, and encouraged a less restrictive commercial policy. Even as late as 1850, agriculture was still the major British industry. Whatever affected the level of incomes in the agricultural sector, affected the standard of living of more than a third of the population of Britain, during the first half of the 19th century. A second reason for agriculture's dominance is due to an industry-wide increase in efficiency Farmers responded to extreme adversity by introducing cost-reducing innovations. The more inefficient farmer was forced off the land by a succession of crises from which there was insufficient time to recover and those that were left were the fittest to operate in the industry. This higher efficiency resulted from increased investment in agriculture, in improved methods, and hence higher productivity.

The Changing Role of Government

Between 1780 and 1860 a great many restrictions on economic enterprise were done away with. Was this due to the 'triumph of the invisible hand'[156] or did it reflect the deliberate self-effacement of government in favour of a policy of complete laissez-faire? Was the British government really a passive agent in the British Industrial revolution? It was only when government took a more positive and serious role in the economy that it began to streamline its administrative machinery, to remove regulations that it was unable top enforce, and to formulate a considered view on what form its interventions should take and to sharpen its powers in the areas where it wanted to exert most influence. The beginnings of purposeful government economic policy go back to Pitt the younger.

'The odd thing was that a revolution in government, which represented the beginning of collectivism and of the modern welfare state, should have taken place in a community whose articulate political prejudices were flatly in opposition to such a development. It happened because of the existence of strong underlying pressures, which proved irresistible in the end.[157]

Nor was it only the central government that was strengthening its power and its will to intervene in the conduct of private enterprise. Local government began to assume wider responsibilities, especially in those larger populated urban areas.

[156] Arnold Toynbe *The Industrial Revolution* (1884)
[157] Arnold Toynbe *The Industrial Revolution* (1884)

Economic Growth and Economic cycles

The crucial perception that the economic life of *man* was a continuous economic change came in the century 1750-1850 when the scale of the British economy began to expand perceptibly and without limit, and this led to a sustained growth in incomes per head. Somewhere in the middle of the 18th century there is evidence that total national output began to grow-faster than it had done over the previous 100 years. We also know that population and prices and certain kinds of production and incomes and overseas trade, were growing much stronger than ever before. Were prices growing faster than the benefit from improvement in incomes, or was population growing faster than any improvement in production? In trying to assess the national rate of economic growth, the first assumption is that foreign trade (the best source of statistics for the 18th century) was of considerable importance to the economy, whilst an early conclusion is that there was growth in the total national product, in national productivity and in the standard of living (that is, a growth in real incomes per head. After a period of stagnation in output, prices, population, incomes and standards of living between 1700-1750, there was an upward trend in total national output dating from 1750.[158] It seems likely that the national rate of growth was slowed by the French wars before accelerating again in the 1820s and 1830s. In a pre-industrial economy, seasonal fluctuations are more significant than in an industrialised economy, because so much of economic activity is concerned with agriculture, fishing, seafaring and building—all of which are heavily influenced by climatic conditions—and only partly because one of the forms which technical progress takes is the adoption of methods and equipment which permit a more even utilisation of capacity and labour and an even flow of transactions throughout the year.

Two characteristics identify a trade cycle (1) an upward surge in economic activity that creates a crisis of confidence and a down turn: (2) a chain of interaction, which carries this disturbance from one sector to another and into the heart of the economy. The more interdependent, the economy the longer and stronger is the chain of the interaction and the greater the

---

[158] National output in 1780-1799 was growing at the rate of 1.8% per annum, and output per head at a rate of.9% p.a.

impact of the initial disturbance on the total national economic activity. In 1772, the failure of an important banking house caused a severe panic, and the American War brought a deep trade depression, followed by another boom in 1783, followed by another panic. The next panics took place in 1793 at the outbreak of the French wars and in 1797 on the occasion of a naval mutiny. There were crop and weather cycles, which produced sympathetic commercial cycles in pre-industrial economies, when agriculture was the chief economic activity and both trade and industry were dependent on the fortunes of agriculture. There is considerable evidence about the influence of harvests on levels of economic activity, especially where agriculture was the major industry. For the whole period 1750-1850, agriculture was Britain's number one industry. It probably absorbed half of the labour force in 1750 and more than 20% in 1850; it provided most of the nation's food; and in 1750 it made an important contribution to export trade, while by 1850 the harvest was so significant that it impacted on the balance of payments, on the level of imports and on the state of credit in general.

When harvest conditions were such that there was a dearth of agricultural products, the results could be pervasive. (1) There was a rise in raw material costs for a large number of industries; (2) high food prices and unemployment for agriculture workers, and thus reduced purchasing power for industrial products; (3) budget deficits due to a decline in output of dutiable commodities (which were mainly agricultural), which reduced government revenues and an increase in the food bill of the military which increased government expenditures; and (4) an unfavourable balance of payments due to a reduction in exports or an increase in imports of foodstuffs. War was another powerful factor in fluctuations of overseas trade. When war was imminent, merchants hastened to move goods before the trade lanes were closed and overseas business interrupted.

An expansion of the demand for exports produced three effects. (1) A condition of full capacity in some sectors; (2) an expectation of continued increase in output, and (3) an increase in profits. Each of these tended to stimulate an expansion of domestic investment.

Growth in the British economy has been cyclical rather than steady. The three main types of cycles are: (1) the single year seasonal cycles (2) the trade cycles generally completed within a span of 9 years (3) and the long waves which stretch over a period of 50-60 years

TO BE COMPLETED

1. Introduction to the need for Industry
2. Benefits flowing to the colony from Industrial revolution in Britain
3. The role of the commissariat
4. Industries on the Rise
6. Limitations on industry & constraints on growth:
   Finding Capital
   Finding skilled labour
   Finding markets
   Finding raw materials
   A shortage of entrepreneurs
7. Entrepreneurs
8. Statistical Synopsis of manufacturing industries
9. Impact of the Industrial revolution on Colonial NSW
10. A time-line of new products
11. The Spread of Population

CHAPTER 8

TIME-LINE OF NEW PRODUCTS

Food & Drink	A	
clothing & textiles	B	
metal trades	C	1
building & construction industries	D	3
Agriculture	1	3
Minerals	2	3
Manufacturing& value adding	3	3
Retail	4	3
Import	5	3

Colonial Manufacturing Industries   1788-1821

A steam engine for saw-milling, grinding corn and other purposes

Agricultural equipment--1816   ploughs, harrows, threshing & cleaning equipment

Item	Material / notes	
blankets	wool	3
blocks	stone	3
boat-building	local timbers	3
boots, shoes	tanned leather 2/6-3/6 pair	3
brewing (spirits & beer)	grain (Indian) corn, barley	3
bricks & tiles	clay	3
candles	tannery of leather, candles	3
canvas	wool	

100,000 pairs pa (2 per convict)

4 coys x 6wkrs& 12,000gals pw

73rd reg contract for £500 pa

Item	Details	Raw material / source	Government
carts		timber	
casks		local timbers	
clothing	slops for convicts & 1819, 4000 articles made from local cloth		
cloth factories	3coys in 1820		
coal		Newcastle mining	
farm implements		imported iron & steel	
flannel		wool	
Flour-Mill-	1600 bu ground/wk @ 1/3d bu	grain	yield was 54.5 lbs ground meal from 56 lbs of wheat
gentlemen's clothing			
Gov't linen from local flax	In 1820 260-370 yds of cloth pw	wool	
Gov't woollen factory	In 1805, 3700 yds canvas+4600 fathoms of rope, lines, twine		
hats		wool	
leather		tannery/hides	
lime kilns for making lime		shells	
linen	3 coys pdcg woollens & hats	flax	
newspapers		imported materials	
rope		wool	
salt works		salt flats	
silversmithing		imported tinplate	
soap		tannery	
tannery for leather-making	3 coys in 1820 with 64,000 cattle in colony	hides	
timber		Pennant/Castle Hill	
tin		imported tinplate	
twine		wool	
wind mill			

wood screws iron & steel
woollen factory imported fabric and woven wool

Main Categories of MANUFACTURING BEFORE 1821

Food & Drink 1. industries processing local products for local consumption
clothing & textiles 2. industries that produced goods for import
metal trades
building & construction industries replacement or competing with imports
eg. Textiles, tanning & brewing

Labour Usage 1820 ## Capital Invested in Industry 1818

Manufacturing/construction 20% £50,000
Government 35%
Assigned 65%

Sydney Buildings in 1821

Population in 1821 was about over 1000 buildings
40,000, half living in Sydney 300 from brick
100 from stone inc public bldgs

Production By Government Business Enterprises

Early governors usually did everything in their power to stimulate agriculture in the settlement, Macquarie in NSW and Collins in VDL did not lose sight of the desirability of promoting other industries. Writing to Governor King, early in 1805, Collins emphasised the opportunities arising from developing both whaling and pastoral industries.

'The utility of these colonies can never be better evinced than by their natural productions becoming articles of commercial import to the Mother Country, and I consider myself fortunate in being placed in a situation which promises so early to be a national benefit'

Macquarie in NSW took much the same approach, except he balanced his encouragement of sealing and whaling with on shore industries such as boat building and repair, stevedoring and provisioning, and the export of seal and whale oil.

THE RISE OF MANUFACTURING IN COLONIAL NSW

The need for manufacturing in the colony was created by local demand for tools, materials and supplies, in large demand for meeting general construction and housing needs. Manufacturing in the colony was catered by the private sector and the government sector. The private sector was sponsored by a handful of entrepreneurs or skilled settlers, who wanted to satisfy local demand for their product by creating a 'cottage industry', due to generally limited demand and a constantly changing market. The public/government sector became involved through the commissariat operations In order to put convicts to productive work, reverse the long lead time for purchasing urgent materials from Britain, and more fully utilise the 'free' local resources such as timber and convict labour. Barnard observes[159] 'The colony was never wholly penal, like France's Devil Island, nor was it intended to be. It was, in due course, to be balanced by freed men, their children, and such other settlers, soldiers, seamen and the like who cared to take the reward for their services in land, of which the Crown had a superfluity. Actually, NSW suffered very little from being a penal settlement and was fortunate in that her first unpromising

---

[159] Barnard, Marjorie *A History of Australia* 1962 (Page 304)

colonizing material was early swamped by infusions of new blood, that wool, land grants and then gold attracted free colonists. There were no foreign elements to arouse Imperial suspicion, no subject race to put what might have been considered a necessary brake on progress'. This statement by Barnard is a rewriting of history, but would be an ideal policy, if it were true. The settlement was designed to be a penal one, and every move made was designed to be about the convicts—their work, protecting them from themselves, feeding, clothing and maintaining them, providing them with tools, equipment and supplies. Laissez-faire might have been in vogue in London during the Phillip Administration but the settlement struggled whilst awaiting food and other supplies, and convicts were held tightly accountable for all their activities. Until 1823, the entire responsibility for the settlement rested on the Governor. Upon him was bestowed a power to control lawlessness, which he effectively exercised.

The diversity of manufacturing within the colony by 1821, at the end of the Macquarie Administration was far more impressive than could reasonably be expected from a former penal colony transforming itself into a free market economy. Macquarie's enthusiasm for free enterprise and 'cost saving' led to great production sponsored by the commissariat. Convict labour was considered to be without 'cost' and therefore without 'value', as was local raw materials, so much of the output of the commissariat business enterprises left without recognition of value, which well-suited Macquarie's purposes. Ass early as 1812, he had been sternly warned by Colonial Secretary Liverpool [160] that 'the burden of the colony of NSW upon the Mother Country has been so much increased since the period of your assumption of the government of it, that it becomes necessary that you should transmit a more satisfactory explanation of the grounds upon which the unusual expenditure has been sanctioned by you'. Liverpool admitted he had misgivings of this attack when he continued his letter to Macquarie in terms of 'I can't point out what expenses have been unnecessarily incurred, and the only ground I have for forming a judgement is by comparison of the total amount of bills by your predecessors and yourself'. Naturally enough, absolute total were progressively higher, but in terms of bills drawn per head of convict on the store' the comparisons declined. Macquarie was actively creating an investment for the future,

---

[160]   HRA 1:7:476 Liverpool to Macquarie 4th May,1812

and at some future point the colony could easily be self-supporting and outside the need for treasury appropriations. However, in philosophical terms, why should the local revenues be used to support any form of a penal colony for Britain. Surely the free settlers could grow in conjunction with the transfer of convicts to the colony; whilst Britain supported the convicts and the colony supported its own operations. One of Macquarie's goals in having the government business enterprises so active in the colony was to quickly achieve this self-sufficiency and be out from the clutches of Whitehall. Macquarie's thinking was only half right. He was so preoccupied with the economic and fiscal arrangements in the colony that he lost sight of the overall plan. Local revenues were first raised in 1802 and were designed for 'discretionary' expenditure by the governor of the day. The reason for this loose arrangement was that the Treasury appropriated funds for specific purposes such as convict maintenance, and civil establishment salaries, but did not see the need for maintenance works, repairs, infrastructure development and the like, so the money for these essentials had to come from local sources and be reserved for deployment by the government. Whitehall soon caught onto this stream of revenue and although the Treasury officials new it was illegal revenue, they restricted its use by withholding British funds to the amount of revenue raised within the colony. Thus in Macquarie's administration, private enterprise figured as a means of both import replacement and cost saving for the colony. Manufacturing filled the joint roles of availability of key/essential merchandise and of putting convicts to productive work.

Barnard records[161] that even the 'boys–some as young as eleven–were kept in Sydney at Carter's Barracks near Brickfield Hill and were working as a carpenter, shoemaker, stone-cutter, blacksmith, and other trades to which the boys were apprenticed. The product of their labour went into the public store, and a pool of much needed mechanics was created'. This observation is rather unique, is unsourced and does not have the ring of accuracy about it. Barnard is implying that these trades were carried out at the Barracks, which means that materials and tools were brought daily to the barracks. With carts and bodies for hauling purposes being in very short supply, it seems unlikely that large lumps of stone or tree trunks would be hauled from Upper George Street (the Lumber Yard was

---

[161] Barnard, M *A History of Australia* Page 237

at the corner of George and Bridge) all the way to Brickfields Hill for young boys to play with. The carter barracks were used for confinement and punishment, and there was little space for practicing wood craft or stone masonry. It is much more likely that the boys were released on a weekly basis, under supervision, and taken to the raw materials source–for instance the stone-yard and the Timber Yard, which were both on George Street North. This is a rare unsourced apparent contradiction by Barnard. She is probably incorrect when she states the apprentices' output went to the public store–it probably went to the Lumber Yard store–from where all building materials, supplies and tools were inventoried. The public store kept only dry goods, fresh foods or grain.

The extent of private sector manufacturing ranged from clothing, castings and carts to soap, silver-smithing, tanneries and tin-smithing. In addition government manufacturing covered an equally broad range–from nails to timber framing, bricks tiles and stone blocks, forged items and boot making.

The broad intent, because of the small local population, which by itself would not have supported such a sector, was two-fold–to replace imports and the timeframe of a year or two between ordering and receipt of goods, and to create an export market of sorts.

According to Jackson[162], the population in the colony during 1820 was only 34,000 and too small to create sufficient demand for private sector output and to establish economic development.

The early entrepreneurs and their activities raise numerous questions which to-date has not been studied in the literature. Hainsworth records[163] 'Simeon Lord cannot be described as a typical emancipist trader for his operations were too large and diverse, but he was a member of a talented group. Another was Henry Kable, whose commercial beginnings are still more shadowy–an illiterate man transported in the first fleet, Kable was for several years a constable of Sydney and probably profitably plied with liquor the drunks he locked up'. What Hainsworth is by implication

---

[162] R.V. Jackson *Australian Economic Development in the 19th Century*
[163] H.R. Hainsworth *Sydney Traders* P.41

questioning, is how these two (of many) eventually became such successful traders? What was their source of start up monies? How did these emancipist traders get started? Hainsworth, later in his study concludes 'the capital they mobilised for shipbuilding and sealing in 1800 must have come from trading'[164] Other examples of early unexplained success include John Palmer and his associates, who as the third Commissary on 5/–per day, became the wealthiest man in the colony during the King Administration, and that was before his sister, Sophia, married the largest merchant in the colony, Robert Campbell. Palmer and his trading colleagues prospered in a colony whose commercial life was supposed to be monopolised by an officer clique.[165] Although the officer class is usually described by historians as having caste a large shadow in the early 1790s under Hunter, they could not stop an undertow of small dealers and emerging traders growing up around them. Rather the officers brought this about by allowing the retail trade to fall into the hands of 'ambitious and able (if uneducated) men with no gentility to lose'[166] In many cases because the wholesale market was officer controlled and these emancipist retailers wanted to continue to expand and grow, they moved into 'cottage' manufacturing–often working with the commissariat to supply finished goods or raw materials for further processing by the Lumber Yard or Female Factory (e.g. Tanned leather, scoured wool, and crushed grain). For many emerging entrepreneurs, this was the way they commenced their manufacturing activities–trader, marketer and then manufacturer. According to Hainsworth[167], Simeon Lord was typical of the early merchant traders. When a shortage of circulating notes occurred, Lord (amongst others) requested his creditor customers to liquidate their debts to him by any means possible. The result was that Lord accepted grain, (which he then put into the store on his own account), most of which he had bartered from his retail customers, payroll bills from military officers with whom he was dealing on a wholesale basis, individual 'notes or bills' payable, which were freely circulating and classed as petty banking. Lord would consolidate these bills and exchange them for one large bill drawn by the Commissariat on the Treasury in London.

---

[164] Hainsworth refers his readers, on this point, to his inserts in the ADB for Lord, Kable and Underwood Volumes 1 & 2

[165] ADB Volume 2–John Palmer (Hainsworth)

[166] Hainsworth *The Sydney Traders* Page 42

[167] Hainsworth *Sydney Traders* Page 83

This bill he would then release to his suppliers—usually visiting ship's captains, or transfer to his Indian or Macao (Hong Kong) suppliers. So obviously the greatest limitation to entrepreneurial activity in the colony was 'the medium of exchange: the lack of a mint and a Treasury, or even a private bank of issue. However with all its faults the system worked. It was the only system they had and the traders made the best use of it'.[168]

Thus private sector output was limited by government demand for food and materials.

The Jackson theory is that the sale of goods to the government store (commissariat) provided a major source of foreign exchange to the private sector because sale proceeds were made available in the form of Treasury Bills drawn on London.

Organisation of Government Business Enterprises

Under the guise of controlling the activities and rehabilitation of convicts, Macquarie decided that placing all convicts on assignment, thereby removing any financial obligation for their maintenance, a percentage could be put to work on behalf of the government. This would be accomplished in two ways. Firstly, direct convict labour, rather than the preferred contractor program, would be used for infrastructure development and the other public works program, specifically government building.

So there became a great concentration of convicts in Sydney, employed in two big workshops, the lumber-yard and the timber-yard. Both were located on George Street, together with the stone-yard (across from the lumber-yard) and the three-storey Commissary Store, wharf and Dockyard, fronting the western side of Sydney Cove. The convicts worked on a task, or piece system. In the Lumber Yard, surrounded by an 8 foot high brick wall, for security purposes, forges were used for making nail, hinges, wheel irons and other metal products. Other 'sections' were set aside around the outside walls of the factory, for boot-making, cabinet and furniture-making, coopers for barrel making, course wool and cotton for

---

[168]   Abbott & Nairn (*Growth*) Chapters 8 & 9

slops and hat making. In the centre of the large factory the two saw pits were manned by up to 25 men, who cut the timber taken from the kiln after its drying process. In the timber yards, beams and floor-boards were sawn and prepared from the timber drawn from the lumber-yard. The brick and tile yard was built around a huge kiln (22 feet long by 18 feet high producing 24,000 bricks at one raking. The Stone-yard not only produced large building blocks from stone but also flagstones, hearth-stones and mantelpieces. Within the lumber-yard, was stored all the tools required within the various business enterprises as well as on each work site. Each item was recorded going out and coming in. Equally carefully, all materials–both raw material and finished product–were recorded at the clerk's office located at the main gate. The Superintendent of Convicts, Major Ovens had set a piece work productivity rate. For instance, the shoemaker's gang of about eight me, were supposed to produce a pair of shoes each day, each man from leather tanned at the government factory at Cawdor; likewise, the brass-foundry and the tailors' gang each had their own production goals; the carpenter's gang which was usually of fifty men, was made up of cabinet-makers, turners and shinglers; the bricklayers' gang was generally between five and ten men who were expected to lay 4,500 bricks each week; the Sawyers gang was usually twenty-five men. Other gangs based in the lumber yard were also sent out to garden, cut grass, dig foundations, and carry grain. The lumber yard was responsible for over 2,000 men in all.

The government business enterprises were a comprehensive and massive undertaking, and Macquarie took pride in their output and accomplishments.

Manufacturing is only part of the story included in any study of economic development of the period. Economic development drove public finance in the same way that population growth, pastoral growth and growth of decentralisation and land utilisation impacted on the source and use of public funds. Other factors to be considered include:

1. The commissariat established multiple stores and supplied foodstuffs and materials (at government expense) not only for convicts but for civilian and military personnel as well. In the

early years, well over 50% of the entire population would have been victualled by the commissariat

2. The commissariat also established, work centres for convicts:

    i.   The Lumber Yard,
    ii.   The Timber Yard
    iii.   The Dockyard
    iv.   The Stone Quarry
    v.   The Boat Yard
    vi.   Timber-Cutting Camps
    vii.   Land Clearing Camps
    viii. The Government Farms
    ix.   The Government stores

These centres employed until 1820 over 50% of the convict population.

The output of these centres was directed at Agricultural output; Livestock supply;

Import Replacement manufactures; Materials required in the Construction and building industries; Materials required in the Public Works and Infrastructure Construction program, and Transport and storage requirements of the government.

Colin White[169] in has concluded that the colonial government controlled the local economic mechanism. There were three main elements to the mechanism:

(1)The government provided the social infrastructure to mitigate risk to individuals, and further, (2) guaranteed a market, at fixed prices, for output of the private sector. This government action also provided (3) grants of free land, inexpensive credit and cheap labour with the return of any redundant labour to government service when needed.

---

[169] *Mastering Risk–Environment, Markets and Politics in Australian Economic History* Page 52

Public Works

Public Investment in public works infrastructure was a major challenge. Britain essentially saw the settlement as little more than a tent town. These inhabitants were prisoners, under guard, transported 'out of sight and out of mind' and had no need of money or coins, public buildings or fancy housing or amenities. Early governors from Phillip to Bligh kept to the minimum work and therefore expense, and by the time of Macquarie's arrival, there was a deferred maintenance and construction schedule that dumped all of the expense and workload on his Administration. Commissioner Bigge recorded for his Enquiry that 76 buildings had been completed under Macquarie, some of which were extravagant for example the Governor's *Stables*, The Rum Hospital, and the toll booths on the Parramatta Road. Bigge directed they be revamped and put to alternate (less extravagant use). Bigge made no comment on the provision of water, sewer or drainage measures made for a town with a growing population. Macquarie had drained the marshes in the present Centennial Park as the water supply for the town—and outlawed the use of the Tank Stream for animal grazing, washing, and waste sewer.

Governor Darling, as part of his structuring of a public service for the colony, established in 1826 the first Office of Inspector of Roads and Bridges, with charge over the Engineer's office. From April 1827, his title was changed to Surveyor of Roads and Bridges, and the office remained active until 1830, when in an economy drive, Sir George Murray, Secretary of State for the Colony and War Departments passed these responsibilities to the Surveyor-General. In 1832 the Colonial Architect's Department was established in order to be responsible for the planning, repair and construction of public buildings. In 1833, in another economy drive, this department was also transferred to the Surveyor-General. Later the duties of colonial engineer for superintendence over roads, bridges, wharves and quays were added to those of the Colonial Architect and all planning came under the Surveyor-General. It was this concentration of work load in such few hands that led to an increasing public investment in public works.

Another effort by Governor Darling to centralise planning and control into a new public service bureaucracy, was the establishment of the Clergy and School Lands Department in 1826. The corporation was to receive a seventh in value and extent of all the lands in each county in the colony. Out of this land the corporation was to be responsible for the payment of salaries of clergy, schoolmasters, and for the building and maintenance of churches, school and minister's residences.

Governor Darling had centralised the planning for all public works into one department—the Land's Department which in turn employed the Surveyor-General and provided for the Lands Board. This balance assisted in prioritising and funding all public works and thus brought order to the former Macquarie chaos of building as he saw fit. A by-product of this new policy was that all convicts were now on assignment and 'off the stores', and a competitive contracting arrangement was used for tendering for all public works.

An Economic Model of the Colonial Economy GDP

The pre-1861 period has long been considered[170] too risky to assemble data for creating an economic model of the times. However certain elements of such a model can be identified and used for, in the least, a good indicative assessment of the economic growth between 1788 and 1860.

A practical example of an economic model which could be adapted for the period was found in McTaggart, Findlay and Parkin *Macroeconomics*.

The basis for the model is that 'aggregate expenditure equals aggregate income i.e. $Y-C + I$, where aggregate income (Y) equals aggregate expenditure $(C +I)$'. A corollary will be that aggregate production or GDP = aggregate expenditure= aggregate income'.

There is a circular flow which equates *inputs* and *outputs*

Inputs	Outputs
Labour	Agricultural Production & Natural resource extraction

---

[170] N.G. Butlin and T.A. Coghlan write of the inaccurate statistics and other data for this period.

Public Capital	Public Infrastructure
Private sector subsidies by government	Manufacturing
Imports	Exports
Civilian/military payroll	Entrepreneurial Profits
Foreign Investment	Growth of Inventories
Local Natural Material	Foreign Ownership of Land & Capital
Trees Import	Replacement
Lime	Import Replacement
Clay	Import Replacement

Aggregate expenditure equals aggregate income.
Where:
Consumption expenditure is (C)
Investment is (I)
Government Expenditure on goods/services is (G)
Net Exports is (NX)

GDP = C + I + G + NX (where, NX =EX-IM)

Investment is financed by national saving & overseas borrowing

Disposable Income (consumption expenditure + savings) = Aggregate Income–Net Taxes

Colonial GDP	**Gross Domestic Product**	
Circular Approach		
Aggregate Expenditures **equals**	Aggregate Incomes	£
Consumption expenditures(C) £	Aggregate Income-Taxes = Disposable Income =	
Investment (I) £	Consumption exp +	Savings
Government expenditures (G) £		

Net Exports (NX)

£

GDP = C+I+G+NX   £

Investment is financed by
National Saving AND Borrowing
    Overseas

Colonial GDP
THE PRODUCTION APPROACH

                                              1820
                                              £

Agriculture, Fishery & Forestry
Mining
Water, lighting & heating
Construction
Wholesale Trade
Retail Trade
Hotels, Cafes
Transport & Storage
Communication services
finance & insurance
Gov't admin & defence
education
health & social services
cultural & recreation
taxes on products

                                         Total
                                         £

The rise of manufacturing was a significant part of the economic growth in the early colony. Of all the sectors, agriculture (including whaling, sealing and wool) gave the most significant results in terms of manpower used, capital invested, export returns, and GDP. In second place would be the development of local natural resources followed closely by manufacturing outcomes. These observations can be made from individual statistics of employment, exports, convict work organisation and data about immigrants and their assets. However, the more reliable statistics will come from the assembly of a model using either the production approach, or the aggregate income/expenditure approach. Both methods will be attempted and compared, but as can be seen an understanding and assessment of manufacturing is essential to either methodology.

Hainsworth in the prologue to *The Sydney Traders* writes 'To study the 'entrepreneur' is to study the central figure in modern economic history– the central figure in economics'. The years 1788 to 1821 are the seed-time of Australian government'.[171]

Although it is difficult to connect the growth of economic development in percentage of contribution terms for any one sector, we know that the more important sectors must be

1. Growth of population
2. Government immigration policy
3. Foreign capital
4. The need for Import replacement
5. The need for foreign exchange through exports.

In each of these the commissariat had a role and an important government need.

The government had to grow the economy at the lowest practical cost, but offer official services which would attract growth, trade and population. This it achieved, at least through 1821, by using the commissariat as the quasi-treasury, the manager of government business enterprises, and the employer of government-sponsored convict labour.

The point here is that the economic model had to incorporate each of these 'input' factors and reflect them. Here in brief is the methodology used.

---

[171] Hainsworth *Sydney Traders* prologue page 14

The commissariat influence over foreign exchange, imports and exports, and government-sponsored manufacturing and even over attracting foreign investment capital is without comparison, but measurable. The economic model for the period does not nor cannot parallel Butlin's measurement of post-1861 GDP, but does use basic ingredients like:

1. Computing working free population
2. Computing working convict population
3. Assuming a productivity adjustment for lower than expected convict output
4. Valuing productive labour at Coghlan suggested rates
5. Interpolating labour product to total output.
6. Comparing annual total production per head of population and per head of 'worker'
7. Estimating total output by industry and comparing this to underlying assumptions about labour output.
8. Extending the estimated GDP from 1800 to 1860 to ensure the recessions of 1810-1816, 1828-29 and 1842-45 as shown in the GDP figures were responsive to these downturns.
9. Comparing the growth of local revenues from 1801 and of trade, for the same period reflected changes to estimated GDP.
10. Announcing the adopted GDP figures for the period 1800-1860 and seeing how they blended in with the Butlin figures.

The results are assembled on a spreadsheet for each year, but a summary has been produced as an extract in order to evidence gains for each ten-year interval, and to show that the Beckett compilations and the Butlin compilations fit in with each other.

TABLE ESTIMATES OF GDP BETWEEN 1800 AND 1900

Year	GDP per head of popln	GDP per head of workforce
1801	13.61	35.1
1811	28.06	49.95
1821	33.54	59.70
1831	35.68	63.51
1841	39.66	70.60

1851	40.13	76.43
1861	46	85
1871	47	118
1877	57	139
1881	63	151
1889	67	158
1891	66	155
1900	57	132

Source: Beckett *Handbook of Colonial Statistics for period 1800-1860*
Butlin, N.G. *Investment in Australian Economic Development 1861-1900*

Certain conclusions can be reached about this table:

1. GDP in the colony grew in each ten year period because the components of that GDP grew eg population, manufacturing enterprises, convict numbers, exports and immigration. As the colony went through its transition from penal to free, especially a free market-based economy, so government investment in services and infrastructure also grew. Personal investment in housing increased and the individual wealth as well as the collective wealth of the colony grew. The down turn in 1900 was due to the recession in the mid-1890s, when many banks failed, unemployment increased and the previous land boom of the 1870-80s crashed, leaving many families and businesses in tough times.

However certain questions remain: This model relates to restricted sectors of the colonial economy, but only touches indirectly on important sectors such as the pastoral industry, the whaling and seal industry. These sectors are indirectly reflective of a growing export market. A more detailed model with declared sub-elements would express the importance of these natural resource or primary production industries including timber, shipping, coal, minerals as well as wool and wool by-products

There were some distractions from within the colony to Macquarie's aggressive enterprise policies. In a wave of perversion, William Charles Wentworth led an anti-Macquarie movement against local manufacturing in favour of importations.

In January of 1819, Macquarie gave permission for a group of clergy, merchants, settlers, and other gentlemen to convene a meeting in the court-room of the new General Hospital, to prepare a petition. The petition was for a redress of grievances and essentially was to try and expand rather than restrict imports into the colony. Macquarie by trying to match exports with imports (in value terms), was restricting the type of imports authorised.

Macquarie, in a despatch to Bathurst of 22nd March, 1819 notates[172] the resolution

'1. That a regular demand exists in the colony for British manufactures of nearly all descriptions, greater than the established mercantile houses here have supplied or are likely to supply regularly.
2. Restrictions prevent merchants from employing ships of less three hundred and fifty tons burthen (under the *Navigation Acts)*
3. That this meeting requests Gov Macquarie to try and expand shipping between Britain and Australia for transporting Manufactures and colonial produce.'

The sentiments were laudable but the request baseless. The commissariat with its huge buying opportunities could have achieved the desired result. Merchants' collaborating into a buying group could have achieved the same result but the obvious solution was to encourage the local production of all imported items at a lower cost.

Macquarie made no recommendations to Bathurst, which meant that he had strictly fulfilled his role to the petitioners, and had left Bathurst with the opinion that the colonial manufacturers and merchants were ill-prepared to fight British exports

In over 300 pages of text, John Ritchie[173] reviews the submissions made in the colony to Commissioner Bigge, but does not recite any submission made by merchants or manufacturers. However in the Bigge reports, we find details of evidence submitted by Simeon Lord about his manufacturing

---

[172] HRA1:10:52 Macquarie to Bathurst 22nd March, 1819
[173] Ritchie, John *Punishment and Profit–The Bigge Commission in to NSW'*

activities. At his factory at Botany Bay, he employed between 15 and 20 convicts in the making of:

Blankets	Stockings
Wool hats	Trousers
Kangaroo hats	Glass tumblers
Seal hats,	Kettles
Possum skin hats,	Thread
Boot leather	Shirts

Between 1810 and 1820 the number of sheep trebled in the colony, and many producers were finding it more profitable to sell carcasses instead of fleeces

Local manufactured items did not entirely replace imports. Items were still imported from India and China.

From India came

Sugar
Spirits
Soap
Cotton goods

From China came

Sugar candy
Silks
Wearing apparel

Colonial Exports included

Sandalwood
Pearl shells
Bache de mar
Whale oil and meat
Seal Oil

Trade exchange, on a barter basis, was made with a number of the Pacific Islands of 'coarse cotton' and ironware, for coconut and salt pork.

Among other evidence to the Bigge Enquiry were numerous complaints by manufacturers on the limited supply of materials, the high cost of buying from government business enterprises–for instance the cloth produced by workers at the government female factory was 2/5 1/4 d per yard, whereas at Mr Kenyon's private establishment it was only 11d. The Manager of the Robert Campbell merchant business complained to Commissioner Bigge about the duties on whale and seal oil from the colony, arriving in England. He also criticised the port regulations which required captains to give 10 day's notice of intention to sail–he claimed this resulted in high wharfage charges.

Ritchie (*Punishment & Profit*) concludes that although Bigge wanted to encourage trade and certain manufacturing, he was reconciled to the fact that their promotion would not provide an adequate or proper solution to the question of convict employment, punishment and reform. [174]

Observations on Industry & Commerce in NSW

By 1820 Simeon Lord had turned the profits of fishing in the south seas and trade in the Pacific Islands into a manufactory at Botany Bay where he employed convicts and from 15 to 20 colonial youths making blankets, stockings, wool hats, kangaroo hats, seal hats, possum skin hats, all of them shoddy but cheaper than English imports of hats, boots, leather, trousers, shirts, thread, kettles and glass tumblers. [175]

The heavy influx of immigrants during the Darling Administration brought its own difficulties, especially when drought and depression closed down on the colony at the end of the 1830s. This period led onto the sever economic depression of 1842, which had been fuelled by a reduction

---

[174] Evidence of sundry manufacturers to Commissioner Bigge Enquiry)

[175] An quote extracted from Clark, A History of Australia sourced by Clark from 'An account of Mr Lord's manufactures, submitted to Commissioner Bigge, 1ˢᵗ February 1821

of foreign investment, a cessation of the British speculators and absentee landlords, as well as local factors, partly sponsored by Sir George Gipps, the successor to Darling as Governor. Between 1831 and 1841, imports had increased by 518 percent to a total of over two and a half million pounds and exports by 1257 percent to a total of two million pounds.[176]

The severe drought of 1825-8 was unfairly blamed on Darling, as was the epidemic of 'hooping cough' which killed Darling's own son and of smallpox which afflicted the colony.

Between December 1831 and December 1832 325,549 gallons of spirits and 109,406 gallons of wine were imported and at least another 11,000 gallons of gin were distilled locally–all for a population of only 15,000.

As for prices, milk was 8 pence per quart, potatoes were fifteen shillings a hundredweight, beef had declined to one penny halfpenny a pound[177], mutton twopence halfpenny, veal five-pence, pork four-penny halfpenny. Fowls cost from 1/9d to 2/3d per pair, whilst butter varied from season to season between 1/–and 3/–per pound,; cheese sold at 4 pence per pound, Cape wine was 8d to ½ per pint and port was 1/45 to 2/–per quart. Respectable lodgings were a pound per week. And a horse could be hired for 10/–a day, and a gig for 15/–per day. Housing costs had risen to 530 pound for a six-roomed cottage

The depression that lasted from the late 1830s to 1842 but created a slow down in the colony until gold was discovered in 1852, caused an estimated 1638 bankruptcies. There was a glut of livestock such that sheep were selling for 6d per head. Land sales ceased and there was an oversupply of labour for the first time in 50 years. Almost a final blow to the struggling economy came with the discovery of gold in California, with estimates of 5757 houses being empty out of the 7100 houses in Sydney town.[178]

[176] Barnard, Marjorie *Sydney–A story of a City* P.18
[177] Beef during the Macquarie Administration was bought by the Commissariat at 5 pence per pound
[178] Barnard Marjorie *ibid*

The economy in the period up to 1800 was based upon the limited trade monopolised by military men like John Macarthur as well as a steady expansion of government-financed agriculture to feed the growing number of convicts. This expansion could only continue until the colony became self-sufficient in food. Then an alternative product, of sufficient value to be exported would be required to generate the hard currency that in turn would pay for the increasing imports demanded by the growing economy. Only by developing such a staple export could the colony become economically viable and thereby partially believe the treasury of the burden of supporting it. With such a staple export attracting additional population, the colonists would also have some hope of eventually claiming the continent's wide interior.

By 1802, Governor King could report to London that seal skins were the way ahead in terms of exports. More than 100,000 skins were landed in and shipped from Sydney between 1800 and 1806, In 1804, 11 Sydney-based ships were engaged in the Bass Strait sealing trade, in addition to the large number of ships in pursuit of whaling.

By the early 1800s there were four main types of economic activity in the colony. Agriculture and grazing was making the colony almost self-sufficient in this product, and large landowners were undermining the governor's attempts to encourage yeomen farmers. Many of these large landowners also engaged in mercantile activities. A growing number of emancipated convicts became traders on their own account, with speculation in trade marked by gluts and scarcities. Many merchants also operated their own vessels, engaging in sealing and whaling. The number of whalers operating out of Sydney rose from 5 in 1827 to 76 in 1835. Between 1826 and 1835 the value of fishery products passing through Sydney reached £950,000. In 1849, there were 37 boats based in Hobart employing 1000 seamen.[179]

Sealing and Whaling were followed by exports of wool. Although only 29 sheep had arrived with the First Fleet, successive convict fleets added to the flocks and herds and the numbers quickly expanded by natural

---

[179] Day, David *Claiming a Continent—A new History of Australia*. Pages 49,50,51

increase. By 1805, there were 500 horses, 4000 cattle, 5000 goats, 23000 pigs and 20000 sheep. The efforts of these large landowners, including John Macarthur resulted in a dramatic change in the export statistics, with the weight of wool being exported rising from just 167 pounds in 1811 to 175,433 pounds in 1821.[180]

By 1835, the supremacy of pastoralism was beyond dispute, with exports of fine wool dominating the trade figures. The success of the pastoral industry was at the expense of the British government's efforts to slow the invasion of the interior. The success was the result of a combination of factors—cheap land taken from the Aborigines; cheap labour in the form of convict and even cheap Aborigine labour from those able to supervise large flocks over extensive unfenced grasslands in the interior.[181]

Not surprisingly the Europeans found the same attractive places to settle, as the aborigines also found most desirable—water sources and native grasslands.

By 1850 over 4000 pastoralists with their 20 million sheep occupied 400 million hectares (1000 million acres) of inland Australia.

The growth of population contributed greatly to the rise of manufacturing and the general economic growth in the economy. NSW grew from 76845 Europeans in 1836 to 187243 in 1851. Growth in Port Phillip and South Australia was even more dramatic. By m1841 more than half the male population of NSW was colonial-born or immigrant rather than convict, while convicts and emancipists comprised just over 1/3rd of the total population. However males still outnumbered females roughly two to one.

One aspect of trade is generally overlooked when it comes to identifying special and important exports. Wool exports began to sour in the early 1820s, and most historians claim wool dominates agricultural exports and that opinion clouds the real truth.

---

[180] Day, David *Ibid pages 52,53*
[181] Day, David *ibid* page 74

In fact from 1788 to 1828, if a reliable set of export statistics is compiled, it will be surprising if Australian-owned whaling and sealing vessels are found to be less productive than sheep in those first 49 years. The figures do exist for the next six years from 1828 and for Australia as a whole; whaling narrowly exceeds wool for that period, whilst as late as 1833 whaling is New South Wales' main export industry. However, after that time, 'wool races away, yielding in the last three years of the 1830s almost double the export value of Australia's whale products[182]

A secondary importance of this industry is that each vessel whilst in port is estimated to have spent an average of £300, not counting the sovereigns the crew spent in the inns and elsewhere.[183] Then there was the work for the dockyards. Shipbuilding was probably the largest and most dynamic colonial manufacture before 1850, and Tasmania alone built 400 vessels from small cutters to ships of 500 tons burthen that joined the England-Australia run. Blainey also observes that the reluctance to put whaling into accurate perspective in importance to the colonial economy stems from apathy towards maritime history. He claims that 'except for ship-lovers, the sea and ships are still virtually banished from written history'.[184]

Bigge referred in his third report in 1823[185] to the high level of efficiency amongst the convicts assigned to 'task work' for the government manufactures. Commissioner Bigge discovered at the close of the Macquarie period that the significance of the Government Store as a market for colonial produce and a source of foreign exchange were greater than ever. The heavy increase in the number of convicts transported after the end of the Napoleonic wars had correspondingly increased the government's demand for foodstuffs. Thus Bigge reported, had retarded the growth of export industries by encouraging the growth of agriculture—farming as opposed to grazing. 'It is possible, given other circumstances the settlers

[182] Blainey, Geoffrey *The tyranny of Distance* Page 115
[183] Coughlin, T.A. *Labour & Industry in Australia* Volume 1, Page 367
[184] Blainey *ibid* Page 116-7
[185] Commissioner Bigge's Estimate of the value of convict labour in Sydney for 1822

might have turned their attention to the production of other objects than those that solely depended upon the demands of the Government'[186]

Bigge also refers to the high level of skills used in the Government Business Centre–the Lumber Yard–and to the benefit the colony derived from the local public sector manufacturing.

Summary

Of the nine economic drivers within the colonial economy, the role of manufacturing had the far reaching and desirable results.

The Macquarie Administration decided to centralise and highly regulate the labour and output of the more than 50% of the convicts, who having arrived in the colony were assigned to private or government work. For those assigned to government labour, the broad range of activities required a smarter government store than had hitherto been the case. The store was to have on hand sufficient tools and materials to keep these people fully utilised in their allotted task. Those convicts assigned to land and road clearing needed grubbing tools and axes. They required hauling equipment, and food supplies. Those allocated to public building projects and public infrastructure required tools, bricks, blocks, tiles and a large array of sawn timbers.

The Governor ordered the commissariat to create a central facility for assembling and distributing these materials. Most items could have been ordered in from Britain or elsewhere in Europe. The lengthy purchasing and requisition procedures required a lead time of between fifteen months and two years. Thus Macquarie's charge to the Commissariat to employ convict labour in the manufacturing locally of as many imported items as possible created an import replacement program that created employment, led to private sector entrepreneurs, and generated a program of transition in local manufacturing from the public to the private sector.

---

[186] Bigge, J.T. *Report on the Agriculture and Trade of NSW* 1823 Page 22

Commissioner Bigge reported on the extent of the trades utilised in the Lumber Yard and it makes an impressive list[187]. The trades carried on in this government business enterprise [in this case, the Lumber Yard] are also reported on by Major Ovens, the former Superintendent of Convicts[188]

'In the Lumber Yard are assembled all the indoor tradesmen who work in the shops such as blacksmiths, carpenters, sawyers, shoemakers, tailors etc. The workmen, carrying on their occupations under the immediate eye of the Chief Engineer are probably kept in a better state of discipline than those, who working more remote, are dependent on the good behaviour of an overseer for any work they may perform. Whatever is produced from the labour of these persons[189], which is not applied to any public work or fore any supply of authorised requisitions, is placed in a large store and kept to furnish the exigencies of future occasions'.

Growth in the colonial economy came in numerous guises, such as technological progress in industry and agriculture, transport and communication; the growth of population, and the accumulation of capital; the discovery of raw materials, and the spread of economic freedom.

The rise of a manufacturing sector relied on most of these areas, especially technological gains, supply of capital, immigration of skilled trades and Macquarie's sympathetic encouragement of entrepreneurs. Although not as vital as the agricultural sector, the manufacturing sector provided substantial employment, innovation, skills training, and the basis for potential decentralisation. Most importantly, during the Macquarie Administration, the manufacturing sector supported Macquarie's transition from a penal to free market economy. As the colonial economy stabilised, it became attractive for a large number of British based industries wanting

---

[187] Bigge, J.T. *Report on the Agriculture and Trade of NSW* 1823 Page 22

[188] Report by Major Ovens to Governor Brisbane on reorganisation for the Lumber Yard HRA 1:11:655-7

[189] Sawn timber for framing, roof battens, flooring, window frames, doors, nails, bolts, bellows, barrels, furniture–from Beckett *The Operations of the Commissariat of NSW 1788-1856*

to open branch offices in the colonies to invest in small scale activities, often transferring skilled labour from Britain to underpin their colonial operations.

Local industry also helped develop local resources, both human and capital. Both coal and timber became important exports for the colony, whilst the list of other natural resources being developed for both local use and exporting grew longer and longer.

New industry required new talents and skills. So a number of adjunct industries came into being–engineering design, equipment manufacturing and equipment maintenance. Not all new equipment was imported and particularly in agricultural equipment suitable for local conditions, local manufacture and assembly was the norm rather than the exception.

Employment in the sector grew to an important level, with the number of factories in NSW increasing from 37 in 1829 to 174 in 1850[190]. Exports increased during the same period from £79,000 per annum to over £8,000,000[191]. Boatbuilding peaked in 1843 at 46 vessels for the year, although the average size halved between 1841 and 1843. There were 102 vessels registered in the colony in 1841 disbursing 12,153 tons. By 1843, this number had declined to 77 and continued to decline until the 1900s.[192]

Even as late as 1827, the Colonial Office was still very suspicious about the expenses of the convict establishment. Lord Bathurst wrote of 'the difficulty I feel in reconciling the scarcity of assignable convicts . . . . with the enormous and increasing expense with which this country is still charged'[193] Every effort to trim convict maintenance expenses or expand the assignment system impacted on the Commissariat business operations. The Superintendent of Convicts would agree to the training of apprentices,

---

[190] Butlin, Ginswick & Statham *The Economy before 1850* (Australians: Historical statistics–p.108)

[191] Butlin et al *ibid*–P. 109

[192] Sourced by Beckett from original data in *Australians: Historical Statistics,* Coghlan and Butlin

[193] HRA 1:8:221

only to find them sent of 'on assignment' whilst the best workers in the Lumber Yard were always in demand by private manufacturers, and government building workers, were constantly in demand by the private contractors.

CHAPTER 9	

SUMMARY AND CONCLUSIONS

It is not a novel presumption to claim that many linkages lay behind the rise of the manufacturing industry in the colony.

For every key aspect, a link can be found to connect the growth of manufacturing to an event.

For example:

i. The fact that the settlement developed without any coinage or official means of exchange created the barter system

ii. The inability to rely on definite foodstuffs arriving into the colony from Britain or other trading countries imposed strains on local production

iii. Local production created a strong facilitator such as the commissariat

iv. The main bartering base was spirits, and numerous attempts were made to grow grains and other ingredients in order to make local spirits and ales. The huge profits made by the military importers also created efforts to produce alcohols locally. Distillation was one of the first local industries.

v. The commissariat facilitated the various convict work centres and the government business centres such as the Lumber-, Timber-, Stone-, and Naval Dock-Yards. Production from these facilities was often transferred from the government to the private sector, and began the private manufacturing sector as well as the first import replacement industries

vi. Governor Phillip encouraged the sealing, whaling, timber and coal exporting as a means of offsetting the growing imports into the settlement and balancing the foreign account balances for the small colony. In this way, soap, candles, coal for local heating were developed locally. Timber development met many requirements but bricks, tiles and building blocks were developed strictly for the local construction industry.

vii. The first trial production of wool led to the female gaol in Parramatta being used for cloth weaving and dying and the production of blankets, crude clothing garments, slops, hats, shoes. All this output was designed for local use and import replacement.

viii Salt works, leather tanning, twines tin-smithing all became important local industries and import replacers.

ix. The importation of flax plants generated the raw materials for linen weaving, followed by weaving machinery from Britain

x Even paper production, cask making, wheel-making, cart–making commenced before 1820 and added further to the benefits of having local industries–employment, attraction of foreign migrants and capital, attraction of entrepreneurs, servicing of imported capital goods

The key manufacturers in the colony before 1821 can be identified in three categories

1. Food & drink, metal trades
2. clothing & textiles
3. building & construction

Convict labour was used successfully in reach of these areas–Assignment took 65%; government accounted for 35%, whilst manufacturing and construction utilised the other 20%

Each chapter in this study is designed to account for the development or catalyst of new industries–The Introduction to developing industries; the status of the economy that could sustain new industry, training of labour and a new secondary sector suitable to support and sustain the key industries–agriculture, construction, exports, and shipping.

Entrepreneurs required foreign investment and migration to be encouraged by government and Macquarie catered well for this need. Thus the chapters on entrepreneurs, immigration and foreign investment were included. Reasoning shows that the benefits of the industrial revolution in Britain flowed onto the colony and a chapter is included on this relationship. Finally the spread of population led to decentralisation and created a demand for a new type of secondary industry, which flowed onto a demand for better education and training, a more focused financial industry and yet more foreign capital.

THE VAN DIEMEN'S LAND COMPANY 'A STUDY OF FAILED INTENTIONS'

CHAPTER 1

INTRODUCTION

- A well-thumbed book in my collection of Australiana is a volume by Henry Gullett, published in 1914, and with an introduction by Lord Chelmsford, Governor of Queensland (at that time) and then of NSW in the first decade of the 20th Century. Gullet writes in this volume, which he entitled *The Opportunity in Australia* 'When my memory begins, the worst of the pioneering was finished on the selection. Our block, like the rest of agricultural land in northern Victoria was taken up from the Crown at 20s an acre, payable in twenty years. That was in the early seventies.' There are remarkable similarities between Gullett's story and our story of the VDL Company.

Amongst the numerous writings in support of 'opportunities in VDL in the 1810-1820 period', is one was by an Edward Curr, who presented (as an opportunity) 'the great country of VDL' from which he had achieved wealth and land ownership. The text by Curr was written during his boat trip home to England, for a short visit, following his father's death, and as a means of protecting his interest in his Father's estate from a greedy brother. Little did Curr realise what fortuitous events would follow the text's publication in the London of 1824. It was used by a group of 'investors' (active in the wool industry and milling in England) as a means of establishing a reliable source of wool for their mills, as well as the means of becoming involved in the great speculative atmosphere of the day. That Curr would be accepted by this group of wool merchants, who were starry eyed about prospects for producing wool in the VDL, is indicative of both his persuasive abilities and his greed. But the similarities between Gullet's story and the story of the VDL Company diverge from that point. These profiteers led by Curr did not want to pay 20s per acre for their selection. They wanted to follow the Australian Agricultural Company who had applied for and received (from Lord Bathurst–Secretary for State of the Colonies) one million acres of land grant in NSW in exchange for agreeing to develop the land, grow wool (Bathurst demanded the growing of 'fine' wool), and take on as many convicts as required and thus relieve the government of the expense of holding and working these convicts. Another side benefit to Britain was the opening up and development of new farming country and settlements, thus diversifying peoples and towns far and wide in the new colony. The Curr group named themselves tentatively the VDL Company, because their plan was to compete with the AAC not in NSW but in the VDL) and they applied for 500,000 acres in the Van Diemen's Land Colony, and then offered to capitalise the company at half a million pound and grow fine wool–not so much for the general market, but for their own use within the woollen mills owned by the company promoters. These promoters were drawn from the ranks of woollen mill owners, merchants, bankers and investors.

Gullet resumes:

> '*I did not then know what it was to have missed the pioneering; to have come too late to see the selection covered with a green eucalyptus forest untouched by the axe, too late to ride in shadow over the 320 acres and choose the site for the homestead on the little sand hill in the north-east corner, or to set about the ring-barking and the clearing, and all the rest of the work which is the most satisfying in the world–the carving of a home out of wilderness.*'

Curr had faced these problems with his selection, 70 years before the pioneering Gullett wrote his tome, but Curr did not miss the tall trees, or the ringbarking or the sand. By 1824, he was ready to be a 'manager' and guide the fortunes of a well-capitalised company with access to lots of workers–even if they were going to be convicts–from behind a desk. Curr had had enough being poor and doing all the hard work. Lord Bathurst had restricted the land grant to 250,000 acres of wool growing land (not forest area, Curr argued), to be selected from the north-west corner of the Island—an unexplored and largely wilderness area, whose productive value was untested but Curr shrank away from forest land as being too costly to develop, but on the other hand he could not find sufficient open 'quality' land. Curr's associates held very different opinions of 'quality' land, which somewhat signalled the start of the failure of the VDL Company over the next 180 years.

The way Gullett spins his story is certainly an inducement or enticement for migrants from Britain to realise the opportunity awaiting them in colonial Australia. However, Curr's story is anything but the realisation of an opportunity. Rather it is the tale of wasted opportunities, of fiscal failure, poor management and ego-driven actions that brought disappointment to the London directors and the stockholders, and disrepute to the company within Van Diemen's Land itself. We do find an explanation, of sorts, for the eventual disinterest, by the English directors, in the company operations in the colony. Their reliance on European wool was over, and there was a virtual glut of colonial wool arriving in England, both from elsewhere in VDL and from the colony of NSW. Within 20 years of VDL Company finally selecting its land grants (which activity took almost five years), England was receiving half its wool imports from the Colony. No longer was their wool supply the by-product of a political will and the result of tenuous, if not temporary, peace negotiations in Europe.

In the early years, VDL (as a new Colony) enjoyed greater prosperity than NSW. Marjorie Barnard writes in *History of Australia* 'The mainland's need was her (VDL) opportunity. By 1820, sixteen years after the foundation, VDL was exporting wheat and salt meat to NSW. She had a population of about 5,500, of which 2,588 were convicts and 2880 free men, of whom all but 712 were ex-convicts.'

It is estimated that in 1820 there were 30,000 cattle and 180,000 sheep on the Island. The wool industry commenced when Governor Sorell (the third VDL Governor) imported merinos bought from Macarthur in NSW. Earlier, Governor King had already sent eight merinos to VDL to try to revert the breeding of sheep for meat to a breed more suitable for wool production. The early wool, if used at all, was restricted to the stuffing mattresses and it was this type of fleece that sold in NSW in 1820 for 4p per pound–for manufacturing of rough woollen clothing for convicts, if not entirely satisfactory for mattresses. Sorell tidied up the wool industry in VDL and improved its methods. Besides the Macarthur rams from NSW, he bought in English and Saxon Merinos. Of the first 300 rams brought from NSW, 119 died on the journey. The rest he distributed to deserving farmers and by 1830, over 1 million pounds of wool was being shipped from VDL. Wool had replaced sealing and whaling as the major export product and meat and grain markets were shrinking, as NSW became self-supporting. In 1826, the common opinion was that VDL was better suited to the wool industry than NSW, the pastures were better, disease less frequent and methods better. Pastures were improved and runs were fenced in VDL long before they were on the mainland. Other industries suitable to the VDL climate and landscape were being developed. Potatoes were exported to NSW in 1817, hops for beer in 1820 and the apple industry would begin in earnest in 1827. The Island was thought of as a fertile garden; only the markets were lacking. When the Commissariat stores in both VDL and NSW were full, there was no other outlet for produce. Agriculture declined whilst wool thrived.

This was the setting and background which the VDL Company agents reached in 1826. The company had great potential but a lot to prove. It would all depend on what initial steps were taken. The next five years are largely taken up with arguments between the company and the governments of VDL and Britain and this in itself became a recipe for failure.

Curr was not the last British manager of the VDL Company who did not succeed in that role. Following his dismissal by the Directors in 1842, a further succession of ill-equipped, untrained and ego-driven managers, appointed in London, tried to understand and conquer the colonial territory, but none came close, until 1850 when the colonial manager, James Gibson, recommended the company be liquidated. A special committee of one director and four stockholders was appointed to advise the directors on further steps but the committee's report was that the company's assets were less than its liabilities. Thus the directors were once again misled on the true value of the company's assets. For some reason, the committee fell for an accounting trick and accepted the capitalised expense of the company's properties in Tasmania as being the current book value of the property assets, even though current land and livestock sales and leases could not support the book values being used. The assets were overvalued in the books, probably as a way of convincing the directors that the capital had been spent wisely and to show the Government that the required development works (committed to under the original grant terms) had been carried out by the Company.

From 1850 there was a period of consolidation and liquidation, although again not in any rational way. What was showing itself to be the company's best, biggest and most valuable asset was being sold for a trifle. The forestry lands, which by the late 1850's were beginning to show some market interest and worth, were being offered for a fraction of their real value and on terms too generous to be of commercial intent.

The committee that handled the company's break-up must have realised it was a hopeless assignment, since they recommended delaying further action as they awaited a detailed assessment of the mineral worth of the company's lands. A mineralogist from the mainland examined all the properties, looking for gold and ores (tin etc) but found nothing within the company's boundaries. Running out of luck again, a new discovery of tin ore (like an earlier tin discovery) was made just outside the company's boundaries. The directors decided that, if they could not extract the minerals, they would handle their transfer from the remote mountain location to the company port of Emu Bay (Burnie) by a company-built railroad mainly over company lands. The thinking was sound—protect the company's main town and port, before the Government stepped in to open up a competitive port. Unfortunately the assessment was again uncommercial. Gibson, the manager who had blown the whistle on being able to keep the company alive in 1851, recommended the railway project. He suggested the rails should be built out of wood in order to keep the costs down and projected the cost to be £800 per mile. The actual cost came in close to £100,000, or £1,400 per mile, but the government, thinking it could do better, re-routed the line to its own port.

As with most VDL Company business enterprises, success was illusive. Activities undertaken, including such diverse programs as tenant farming (with the company offering lessee farmers a guaranteed buy-back of all produce), commercial livestock sales, timber sales, port operations, township land sales, wool production, railway operation and land development, almost always fell short of expectations. The tenant farming concept, of leasing land to immigrant farmers and then buying their produce at commercial prices, resulted in a company loss of over £30,000 when the produce could not be sold and was dumped in the Emu Bay Harbour. Not one of the business enterprises that commenced resulted in a direct company gain, even though the directors and stockholders were annually promised–'this next year is the one', 'success is just around the corner'.

It took until the 1900s for a rational plan from an Australian manager to emerge. However, the first 75 years had taken its toll on the company's finances and little was developed and ready to sell off, or even make productive. The 20th Century realised further consolidations and small progress, although concentration had returned to the Company's core focus, as set down in Bathurst's original instructions to Curr–growing (fine) wool, developing, and making the land productive, and improving the quality of the livestock.

Today, the first signs of success can be seen. Carrying over 40,000 sheep, 2,000 cattle and agisting a large dairy herd, the company's sole remaining property, 'Woolnorth', is profitable and productive. This 50,000-acre property is all that remains of the original 350,000 acre grant but, during its 175 years of operation, the stockholders made numerous capital contributions and received one large return of capital when property sales showed a windfall gain greater than the directors could spend.

It has taken 175 years, numerous controlling stockholders and many managers for the Van Diemen's Land Company to realise its original mission. Not many companies can experience such failure and remain in business. The shareholders carried the company, meeting many 'calls' on the capital obligations, waiving dividends, seeing profits ebb and flow and receiving little accurate information on which to base firm business decisions.

This then is the story of a company, historic in formation, whose history is largely the history of the north-west region of Tasmania. Its failure to realise its opportunities and potential is the failure of managers (mostly

British) to understand Colonial conditions whose personal shortcomings almost ended the company's existence.

Of course, this outline will need to be fleshed out with events, plans and results over the whole period of the company between its beginnings in 1824, until a suitable stopping point is found in 1900. It will include some of the less pretty episodes of its existence–dealing with the assigned servant problem, the aboriginal problem and the hiatus that existed for so many years between the company and the local VDL government. The policy conflict between Bathurst and Lt-Gov Arthur over the use of government land grants, convicts and scarce local funds in support of a corporate giant, based in London, weaves through the tale like a spat between spoilt boys that is never resolved. Being principally an economic history, the financial changes to the company are given special attention and treatment, but the overall story is simply one of missed opportunities and wasted advantages.

At this point, an assessment should be made about 'sources'. If not in profits, the company is rich in records, and the official records are replete with the correspondence between company representatives, the Secretary of State in London and the VDL Government in Hobart. Sources are scarcely under abundant and the challenge becomes mainly one of sorting through voluminous handwritten records in order to determine what is relevant and important and in what context.

Unlike much of our early history, there remains some original property to help put the challenges and opportunities of the VDL Company into perspective. The house built by Curr in 1826 still stands and reminds us of the lifestyle pursued by 'gentrified' folk. Most of the original maps, plans and diaries, as well as the original 1826 exploration records, also remain to offer a basis for assembling an economic analysis of the Van Diemen's Land Company between 1824 and 1900.

CHAPTER 2

SYNOPSIS OF SETTLEMENT AND COMPANY BEGINNINGS

- **The discovery of Van Diemen's Land**

It is not the intention of this chapter to identify all of the events, which led to the discovery, founding, and settlement of this island, south of the mainland of the Great South Land, first known as Van Diemen's Land. However, an outline of these events is necessary to provide the context of development.

When Abel Tasman began Tasman's diary of 1642 with the invocation 'May God Almighty be pleased to give his blessing to this voyage! Amen' he little knew that it would open a new chapter in exploration. Having sailed from Batavia in August 1642, his arrival on 1 December at Frederick Hendrik Bay was a pleasant respite from the angry seas which he had endured for four months. They then sailed into what is now Storm Bay, the entry to Hobart, where Tasman recorded 'This Bay (is now called Blackman's Bay'. He reported seeing saw people at the east corner of the bay, but found no fish, except mussels. There were many burnt trees, widely separated, such that they admitted an extensive view.

Tasman had naming rights, as the first European to touch soil in the region, but from 1772 a succession of ship's masters reached land on the Island, making the east coast a strategic port as well as a valuable location for rest and recreation. Captain Marion, who arrived from Mauritius in

1772, also anchored in Frederick Hendrik Bay, whilst Captain Furneaux arrived at the southwest cape, exactly one year after Marion had departed. Furneaux's decision that there was no strait between the east coast and the mainland led to Cook's decision that such a passage was not there to explore. Consensus between the various exploring parties (Tasman, Marion and Furneaux) appeared to be that the land was favourable for plant reproduction and grazing. In 1777 Cook landed at Adventure Bay while on his third voyage to the region. John Henry Cox in 1789 and the William Bligh in 1788 both touched Van Diemen's Land, Bligh leaving a mark on a tree and seven breadfruit trees as his evidence of touching land.

Governor John Hunter encouraged surgeon George Bass and his devoted military friend Matthew Flinders to test the Hunter theory that a strait existed between the Port Phillip and VDL, an observation based on Hunter's observations about the swell of the ocean.

Governor John Hunter was of the opinion that a strait existed, based on his observations about the ocean swell. He therefore encouraged surgeon George Bass and his devoted friend Matthew Flinders to test his theory as well as the discovery of Westernport Bay and its 600 miles of coast. Hunter's encouragement came in the object of an eight-foot open dinghy *Tom Thumb and he* requested that Flinders and Mr. Bass, a surgeon, sail in the *Norfolk,* through the strait, in just 12 weeks. In 1798, they came to a headland which they called Circular Head, from its resemblance to a Christmas cake. The extreme northwest, they named Cape Grim. A few years later these points both became landmarks in the VDL Company land selection.

- The first settlers
- **West,** in the *History of Tasmania* introduces his section on the first settlers by pointing out:
- '. . . *the establishment of a settlement in VDL, perhaps thus hastened by a jealousy of a rival power, was at first chiefly intended to relieve Port Jackson. Fifteen years had elapsed since its foundation, and from six to seven thousand prisoners had been transported to Botany Bay—dispersion became necessary to security—to repress alike, the vices of the convicts or places of*

> *punishment, and the indolent and intemperance of emancipist*
> *settlers, both of which endangered authority.'* (John West: *The*
> *History of Tasmania*–1852 Part 2 Section II)

Thus VDL was colonised–'a place of exile for the most felonious of felons–the Botany Bay of Botany Bay'. (West op cit Part 2 Section I p.30)

The first settlement was also encouraged by another motivation, the 400 rebels who led 'the Irish riots (uprising)' which, broke out at Castle Hill, seven miles from Parramatta in March 1804. The remoteness of VDL, its comparatively small size and insular form made it well fitted for the purposes of penal restraint–'a place where its most turbulent and rapacious could find no scope for their passions. Its ports could be closed against commerce, and thus afford few means of escape'. (Barnard: *A History of Australia*)

In '*A Statistical, Historical and Political Description of New South Wales* (London 1830–p.210*)*, Wentworth writes: 'In the great south land, labour and produce were redundant, wherein overwhelming harvests reduced the price of grain so low, that it was rejected by the merchants; goods could not be obtained in exchange; and the convicts at the disposal of government were a burden on its hands–almost in a condition to defy its authority.'

David Collins, the first Lt-Governor of VDL had long held the posting of judge advocate general in Sydney and was the recorder of the Botany Bay settlement in *Account of the English Colony in New South Wales* (London 1798)–the second volume of which was dedicated to Lord Hobart in 1802. Collins' first attempt at establishing a new settlement south of Botany Bay had been at Port Phillip but had been unable to construct the basics of an on-going settlement there. Collins, following a survey, preferred the west side of the Derwent (named after to a stream in Cumberland, England, immortalised in prose by the poet Wordsworth). He arrived at Sullivan's Cove with his party of marines and male prisoners on 30 January 1804. Collins named this new location Hobart Town but, by any standards, the settlement grew slowly and uneventfully.

In all, the administration of David Collins brought little progress. By 1810, the total population was still only 1,321 persons, even though the 410 persons had originally landed at Sullivan's Bay. There were no roads into the interior, no public buildings and Government House was a simple cottage. Only a few acres of land had been cultivated by convicts; cattle had arrived from Bengal and sheep from Port Jackson. Under his closed ports policy, even the most necessary articles had unavailable in the settlement. The earliest settlers purchased the clothing of prisoners, being preferable to the skins of animals in which they were often clad. This early failure was attended with disastrous results and in all; the administration of David Collins brought little progress. He died in Hobart in March 1810 at the age of 56 and was buried there.

The northern settlements were not brought under the governance of Hobart until 1812, for at the same time as Collins was naming Hobart Town, Colonel Patterson named the northern settlement (on the west bank of the Tamar) York Town, later renamed Port Dalrymple. Bass had noted this area as suitable for agriculture and pasture, whilst Flinders had simply noted the difficulty in obtaining local fresh water. The next important event in the settlement of VDL was the removal of the settlers from Norfolk Island (first settled in 1788). In 1803 Lord Hobart had issued the first direction to relocate all settlers but only four people had responded by 1805. The order was renewed in 1808 and enforced by Captain Bligh, with 254 arriving in October 1808 in Port Dalrymple. These new settlers were welcomed with unconditional grants of land (double their allocation on Norfolk Island) as well as support from the public store, loans of livestock and the establishment of a barter system whereby a keg of rum was worth more than a common farm.

Colonel Davey was appointed the second Lieutenant Governor in February 1812. He opened the ports for general commerce in June 1813, and local traders, Messrs Lord and Reibey supplied the colony with English goods, following their arrival in 1816. Encouraged by Davey, the resources of the Colony were developed and a military officer discovered a new species of pine, highly valued by artificers–the Huon pine. Birch, a local merchant, built a vessel to survey the western coast and discovered Macquarie Harbour in 1816. He was given a one-year monopoly over the fishing trade. The whale fishery was enlarged, corn was exported, the plough introduced, a mill erected, and the foundations of St. David's were church laid. A passenger Ferry connected both sides of the Derwent River and a civil court was established. The first local newspaper, the *Hobart Town Gazette* was published in June 1816.

Despite this marvellous progress, the welfare of VDL was retarded by the 'number, the daring, and the depredations of bushrangers' (Hobart *Gazette,* August 1816*)*. In response, Davey placed the whole Colony under martial law and encouraged flogging for those (free or bonded) that broke the evening curfew. Davey's term expired in 1817. The development of VDL was following the pattern of development in NSW but with a different accent. The land grant system was the same, so were the land sale regulations. English law ruled. Progress towards self-government was parallel, and the same economic depressions affected both colonies.

William Sorrell, the third Lt-Governor, landed in Hobart in April 1817. He set out to restore safety in the Colony and, armed with individual pledges, he offered large rewards which were sufficient to persuade the military, constables and private settlers to identify the culprits. This was successful and the greater portion of the bushrangers was captured within three months of his arrival. Whaling and sealing were bringing business and money to the town. Sorrell had commenced the practice of an annual muster of all settlers, and thus accounted for each family and their livestock and the name, residence and civil condition of every inhabitant became known. Sorell's progress in building population and livestock numbers was now well documented by the Governor's despatches of July 1821. Sorell's initiative in attracting free families with capital was applauded by Macquarie, who in his despatch during his visit to Hobart, writes, 'recent influx of several respectable free settlers with considerable property will not fail to hasten the period at which VDL will hold a high rank among the settlements of the British Empire'. (Governor's despatches July 1821)

This transfer of settlers from Britain was an important event: their efforts were experimental and their achievements prophetic. The arrival of so many emigrants led to the exploration of the inland of the island and the opening of many new opportunities–the VDL Company grew from such rich resources. To provide a settlement for strangers, Sorell explored the region lying between the Shannon and the Clyde Rivers to their junction with the Derwent: which area was free from timber and within 20 miles of navigable waters and this district welcomed several distinguished settlers. Expansion followed development and by 1820, £20,000 of wheat had been exported to Sydney. This prolific result came from the farming on the more fertile and open plains, already free of timber and scrub.

Vessels commenced arriving directly from Britain and in 1822 600 new settlers arrived bringing their capital—already a new tone was prevalent in the society. Much praise was being heaped on VDL in books published by explorers and colonists—'the fertility of the soil, and the beauty of the climate... 'These publications also generally contained a theory of pastoral increase—'geometrical progression towards wealth.' (Godwin) and include the books by W.C. Wentworth, Edward Curr, Commissioner Bigge, James Dixon, George Evans, Charles Jeffrey and Godwin's *Emigrant's Guide to VDL*. The results were impressive. Between 1810 and 1822, the population grew fifty-fold, whilst wool exports to Hamburg helped promote flock improvement.

However, the greatest landmark in the population growth of the early settlements was a decision by the British Government in 1831 that the principle of assisting the payment of emigrants' passages was accepted, and officials were appointed to supervise emigration. Australia was now seen, not merely as a solution to prison overcrowding, but as a relief for unemployment and poverty among law-abiding citizens. In the next 20 years 200,000 assisted emigrants entered Australia in addition to the almost 160,000 convicts transported to the country.

The position of VDL favoured its settlement and advantages offered to settlers included land grants, loans of livestock and seed: the price for wheat remained at an attractive 10s. Per bushel and meat at 6p per pound. By 1821, there were 7,400 residents, possessing 15,000 cultivated acres, 35,000 cattle, 170,000 sheep, 550 horses and 5000 swine. Scarcity in NSW led the Crown to buy £10,000 of meat in Hobart for transfer to Sydney. Land grants, between 1818 and 1821, rose from 25,000 acres to 250,000, whilst cultivated land tripled to 15,000 acres. Macquarie's final visit in 1821 was a great success, which was dutifully recorded in the *Sydney Gazette*: 'the architectural taste of the private buildings; the handsome church; the commodious military barracks; the strong gaol; the well constructed hospital' were all impressive and a welcome improvement over the Collins-style settlement. Macquarie also commented on the enterprise and industry of the people, the spacious harbour, the pier, the battery and the signal post.

It was the spectre of wealth creation and the prospect of large quantities of good wool that appealed to a group of wealthy merchants and gathered them into the VDL pastoral holding club, to which Curr and Sorell sowed the seed of new investment in cheap land and control of pastoral activities. It was surely a fitting salutation to a Colony, in which the wealthy merchant group in London (the VDL Company stockholders) was planning to invest. All they required of the Government, facilitated by Lord Bathurst, was a grant of 500,000 acres.

Towards the end of Sorell's administration, circumstances favoured commerce and development by English merchants in overseas colonies. The motivation was not only wealth; it was often the securing of regular supplies of commodities in an otherwise troubled Empire—the Napoleonic Wars had left Europe torn and withdrawn. All England's wool was imported from Germany and Spain, two countries interested in using strategic supplies to advance their own position against Britain. The commerce of the VDL Colony was assisted through the enterprise of some such merchants.

Following his visit to VDL in 1820, Captain Dixon, commander of the *Shelton* published a volume (*Narrative of a Voyage to NSW & VDL–1822*) on the capabilities of the colony. He suggested the formation of a pastoral company, having shares with a face value of £100, as a wealth creating opportunity. A speculative spirit was awakened amongst the merchants and investors in England, and they were willing to subscribe to such opportunities with enthusiasm, including the Van Diemen's Land Company. One object of this latest speculation would be to relieve Britain from dependence on foreign wool, and to improve the quality of the Australian flocks.

In 1823 a company was formed at Leith (Scotland), with a capital of £100,000, professing 'to promote the welfare of the colonies, by taking their produce in exchange for merchandise' (West p74). A succession of vessels was despatched, which transferred many families from Scotland. Their position and capital made them amongst the best in the land.

Sorell received his recall in 1823, and decided to return to London for a debriefing program. His successor, Colonel George Arthur, arrived as the fourth Lt Governor of VDL in May 1824.

• Narratives on VDL

As described above, there were numerous books published between 1800 and 1825 in support of VDL. Listed below are some that can still be tracked:

- W.C. Wentworth: *A Statistical, Historical and Political Account of the Colony of New South Wales and its dependent settlement of VDL* (1820)
- Edward Curr: *An Account of the Colony of Van Diemen's Land* (1824)
- John Thomas Bigge: Reports 1, II and III on various aspects–State, Judiciary and Trade and Agriculture–of the Colony of NSW (inc. VDL) (1821-1823)
- James Dixon: *Narrative of a Voyage to NSW and VDL* (1822)
- J.K. Tuckey: *An Account of a Voyage to Establish a Colony at Port Phillip* (1805)
- David Collins: *An Account of the English Colony in NSW* (1796)–Vol I
- David Collins Vol II of his account deals with his stay in VDL (1802)
- George Evans: *A Geographical, Historical and Topographical Description of VD'* (1822)
- Charles Jeffreys: *Van Diemen's Land Geographical and Descriptive Delineations of the Island* (1820)
- T. Godwin: *Emigrants Guide to VDL (1823)*

TABLE 1: EXPORTS OF WHEAT AND MEAT FROM VDL
1816-1820

	Wheat	Meat	Total Exports
1816	13,135 bu	10,000 lbs	£21,054
1819	24,768 bu		
1820	47,131 bu	36,000 lbs	£33,225

• The origins of the VDL Company

Edward Curr, a young Englishman attracted to and by the colonies, had returned to England from VDL following his father's death when he was invited to attend a gathering of the proposed VDL Company planning group in London. The publication of Curr's booklet on conditions and opportunities in VDL had drawn attention to the fact that he was in England. A group of wealthy woollen mill owners, wool merchants, bankers and investors had planned to invest in a pastoral operation in the new colonies shortly after learning of the apparent success of the Australian Agricultural Company (AAC) which, following its charter by the Westminster Parliament and being appropriately capitalised, had received a grant of one million acres in the Port Stephens region of the NSW mid coast.

Curr, having spent only a few years in the Colony, had returned from NSW and VDL, having received a small grant of land in VDL. Curr was a promoter and, while returning to England by sailing ship, he had written a booklet for publication with the intention of promoting the VDL Colony. *An Account of the Colony of Van Diemen's Land* was published in London in 1824 and, together with a collection of other similar publications of about the same time (refer list on previous page), became influential in awakening interest in the new Colonies of NSW and VDL, especially as havens for making money through absentee land ownership and emigration. In one of his more uncharitable moments, Jorge Jorgenson suggested Curr wrote his short story, during a moment of boredom, whilst becalmed near Mauritius on his way to England.

The 'syndicate' of influential merchants and mill owners applied to Lord Bathurst for 500,000 acres of land in the VDL Colony. Bathurst at first disapproved of the idea but he was willing to give it lengthy consideration and to receive frequent representations from syndicate leaders. He finally agreed to sponsor an Act through the British Parliament, under which a charter of incorporation would be issued and stamped with the Great Seal, through which the regulation, land selection and grant approval would be incorporated. In November 1825 the Act passed both Houses and, by this means, the company was required to issue One million pound in shares and employ their capital in cultivation and sheep farming; to lend money on mortgage and to persons engaged in fisheries; to undertake public works on security of tolls, but they were barred from engaging in banking and commerce. In return, the company would receive a grant (subject only to quit-rents) of 250,000 acres in VDL.

Bathurst had liaised with Sorell (who had returned to England following his recall), and Sorell offered support for the concept, but warned Bathurst that no large blocks of fertile land remained unallocated. Bathurst decided to limit the grant to 250,000 acres, to be taken on the northwest coast in one square block, bounded by Bass Strait to the north and the ocean to the west. Negotiations followed between Bathurst and Curr, who had originally been appointed secretary of the company, but was then appointed chief agent and manager of the company in the colony. Curr's conflict of interest commenced when he subscribed to a large block of shares, as well as being an employee of the company. The Managing Director, based in London, remained responsible to the Governor and Court of the company (also based in London) whilst the land granted was to be valued to the company at 2/6 per acre, and the whole 'quit-rent' charged was 'four hundred and sixty-eight pounds, sixteen shillings' per annum. This quit-rent was redeemable at twenty years in the lump sum of £9,575, although one-fourth could be offset for 'useless' land. The employment and full maintenance of convicts would entitle the company to a further remission of quit-rent, up to £16 per male per annum, and £20 per female. The terms of the Charter, and the Instructions from Bathurst signed off on by the Company are included in Chapter 4.

Curr sailed to VDL, arriving in Hobart in 1825, with handpicked officers of the company, Stephen Adey, livestock superintendent; Alexander

Goldie, agriculturalist; Henry Hellyer, architect and surveyor; Joseph Fossey and C.P. Lorymer, assistant surveyors. Curr was so anxious to select the land; he made little preparation to determine an outline of the parcel from which selection could be made. He was so confident of his success at selecting suitable land for grazing and raising sheep for wool that a boat, loaded with sheep collected from Spain, was only months behind their arrival in Hobart. In the Colony, not all was well for Curr' exploration plans. Because of constant bickering between Lt-Gov. Arthur, and Curr, the selection of land was not completed until 1830, and then only by Bathurst using a veiled threat to cancel the agreement unless speedy progress was made.

Our knowledge and understanding of those early years of the VDL Company come from a variety of sources. For instance, we learn of the bickering and disputes between Arthur and Curr; Bathurst and Inglis (VDL Coy Managing Director in London) from their voluminous exchange of correspondence, reported in Series III of the *Historic Records of Australia*. This offers us the thoughts, plans and desires of the governments and the Company but we need to look at the semi-official writings of the Company's directors to learn if rational planning took place in moving it forward.

That there was a frequent and almost alarming redirection of business strategic policy within the company is apparent from the annual reports of the company and the failure of consistency to pursue any one of these subsidiary business operations for any period of time. Today's corporations could not afford to be as shallow as to pursue turnarounds and turnabouts of planning and policies at the same rate as the VDL Coy did between 1830 and 1850. However, dealing with this superficial pursuit of profits without any apparent planning or strategic analysis is for another chapter. What we do need to point out here is that the company failed to plan and changed direction as often as was necessary to offer hope to the shareholders who year after year faced calls on the shares, and learned of no dividend again this year, and, in fact, in many years faced a technical insolvency, that today would have been an invitation to the liquidators and administrators to move in 'en masse' and close the operation down. However, for all the company records that are available in the National Library of Australia (NLA) and the Tasmanian Archives (TA), there are no minutes of meetings where a 'business plan' or strategic plan was unveiled and adopted. Instead we have these regular visits of the directors from London, who arrive in Hobart to visit the 'estate', (although sometimes not even leaving the domesticity of Hobart) and in return for the all expenses paid trip write a favourable report of how well everything is going, whilst the figures and statistics indicate the opposite is the case. Bischoff, the Managing Director after Inglis visited and wrote in 1832. Sir Edward Poole, representing the general directors of the Court during his visit in 1859, was the first to report in a practical fashion of what the company had by way of useful assets and what it could profitably do with them. This 'business plan' prepared very independently of the local manager James Gibson, who Poole declined to meet with during his visit was the first 'road map' of future operations and was followed for the next 40 year with success. Such a step some 30 years earlier could well have put the company on a sound financial footing. In the interim, the annual reports of the Agent-in-chief and Manager in Tasmania (as it became in 1826) was attached to the Company's Annual Reports as the means of keeping the demoralized stakeholders informed.

Before we return to the establishment of the VDL Company, it is timely to ask—Did the VDL Company fail in its objectives or mission, or just fail financially? The short answer must be 'no'. The two-fold main objectives were to produce a reliable source of wool for its merchant-owners in England, and upgrade the quality of local sheep flocks (hopefully through livestock sales). An amazing quantity of wool was exported from this small island over the years, and this story is told in Chapter Four, on gathering and interpreting the company's statistics. That this was a potentially reliable source of wool exports is not questioned either, nor is the upgrade to the company's sheep flocks which grew in numbers as well as quantities year after year, especially as the tenant farmers were encouraged to produce more and areas of fertile land held by the company was opened up to production.

However, the company did fail, not only financially, but also in a moral way, for nothing it started seemed to be given longer term support, and nothing the company started seemed to ever reach its optimum goal. For instance, the company in 1849, after having worked its lands for 20 years, was still only running 6,519 sheep on 325,000 acres (*Return of Livestock for the year ending 31ˢᵗ December 1849*). The company return for 1850 shows sheep on hand to be 6873, whilst only 1966 sheep were sold for an income of £708. Those figures suggest that the flock was not being managed for reproduction or growth, and so neither income nor gain was received.

In the same vein, unable to show major gains in the pastoral operations, the company turned to tenant farmer development (by leasing out farmland to immigrant farmers), and the development of a Port at Circular Head. Tenant farming peaked at 843 in 1850, at the same time company-employed workers were in decline. Company income from a third income area was only £1764 in livestock sales. The point here is that the company seemed to have no clear predetermined sense of direction, nor any particular goal. Even if cash flow had not been in annual crisis, the company could have optimised its flocks to cover the 350,000 acres granted; or optimised its tenant farming operation to a degree greater than having 800 odd farmers yielding poor results such as to put both them and the company at risk every year.

There is a need, at this point, to make a brief observation on the financial side of the VDL Company between 1826 and 1850. It would be thought that a company of VDL stature and capitalisation would have an attractive set of financial statements–should they be optimistic in order to attract new capital and stockholders? Should they be less than honest in order to justify further capital calls on existing stockholders or should they be minimalist but honest in order to show that the managers are performing, even if at less that desired levels? Well, the 1850 Balance Sheet, which is unlike any we could observe today, shows 'investment in livestock at £28,186.17.9 (even for a pastoral company of VDL Company's standing, this was remarkably low–sheep averaged about £4 per head); debts of £7241 for unpaid wages, commissions, obligations and promissory notes; and accepting that the 360,000 acres of land granted to the company came at nil cost, the balance sheet states 'investment in land' at £108,054. Of this sum, £35,471 was the value of the Circular Head 'head office', which merely reflects that the company had invested in office buildings, houses, ports, wharves etc rather than the pastoral arm of the company. Losses for the year of 1850 reached £23097, although the cumulative losses are not recorded in the Balance Sheet at this time. Cash on hand was less than £1,000, but bills receivable were listed at £6977.

Later chapters will pursue this analysis of the company operations, but it is sufficient at this point to say that the company failed in every way except for the self-serving production of quality wool for its merchant stockholders, which occurred in ever decreasing quantity.

Although Curr's writings on the condition of the country in VDL were clear and precise, the first selection of land around Circular head was not encouraging. Nor was the opinion of Adey and Hellyer on the worth of the land between Circular Head and Cape Grim. Opinions on the initial selection possibilities were poor as was the land itself. Curr would not accept any responsibility for such selection criteria, required of him, but wanted to keep an argument running with Arthur over what Bathurst intended in his written instructions to the company–where was the north-west region, why couldn't the grant be in separate parcels; was the 250,000 acres granted to be of 'quality or fertile, arable lands' and exclusive of waste-lands?

In the end Curr achieved better than he deserved by mere bent of the other side being exhausted through this continual stream of questions, complaints and misinterpretations. In 1830 Curr accepted the grant of six parcels in the northwest region, amounting to over 350,000 acres, indicating that at the equation of less than 70% arable land in each parcel, the productive land would net to the originally intended 250,000 acres. One side benefit of these numbers was that the average value per acre reduced from 2/6 to about 1/6.

The land grants were as follows:

- 'Woolnorth' 150,000 acres
- Circular Head 20,000 acres
- Hampshire Hills 10,000 acres
- Middlesex Plains 10,000 acres
- Surrey Hills 150,000 acres
- Coastal Islands 10,000 acres

Total Acreage 350,000 acres

An indication that Curr was perhaps under growing pressure to take up the offered land was that the high lands towards the westward of the region were found to be barren and cold, and unsuitable for the imported breed of sheep. As a result, in the years 1831-1833 the company lost its entire flock to climate and disease problems, and psychologically, probably never recovered from this near-fatal blow. The essence of the conflict between Curr and Arthur was that because of the barren land and unfavourable climate, Curr wanted to move his region as far north towards the sun, but Arthur held him to the literal agreement. So in the end, Curr was granted 350,000 acres of land but much of it was in unacceptable locations (unacceptable only to Curr, for it suited the VDL governor to open up new regions of lesser quality land). The whole scheme of granting the VDL Company such a huge parcel of land was distasteful to Arthur—he was aware of the potential risk to and challenge of his authority from a large company, headquartered in London and unable to be reined in without political brinkmanship. An oversight by Bathurst had failed to place the raising of capital in the covenant between Government and the company. Bathurst could only delay the issuing of the charter until satisfactory assurance was received of the subscription to the capital. The public works undertaken by the company were far from what Lt-Gov Arthur had envisaged, even with the assignment of convicts specific to building roads and connecting tracks between each of the properties. The instructions by Bathurst to the Company were largely ignored, even though they appear to be clear, to be commercially viable and in the end result, performable to the benefit of the company, its employees and its subsidiary operations.

West offers us a fairly 'grim' look at the company operations before 1850 (p. 91).

"The operations of the company were conducted on a liberal scale: artisans were sent out. The proprietors had been promised a remission of £16 for men, against the quit-rent. This was the first encouragement of free immigration, except for employers, to this quarter of the world. A road was opened to Launceston, chiefly useful to absconders.

The importation of sheep and horses was of great value to the country. The value of the grazing flock to the company was £30,000 when the value of wool exports from those sheep was only £2,000. The servants of the company left them on the expiration of their engagements: many before. The company supporters, claimed no police, no prisons, and none required. Those statements vary from the facts. The company provided no religious teaching for its people, although it had built a church, at some expense in Circular Head as a token gesture. The losses incurred by the company were great: the cold and disease had destroyed the livestock; and their crops often perished from moisture, in many forms. Sometimes the season never afforded the chance to use the sickle: in the morning the crop was laden with frost; at noon it was drenched with thaw and in the evening it was covered by dews; and thus rotted on the ground." (West: *A History of Tasmania*)

Although Curr had numerous staff at his disposal, his attitude and demeanour drove him to fulfil his nickname of 'potentate of the north'. His demagogic style left his subordinates—an agriculturalist, an architect and surveyors usually without firm or useful guidance. Servants, engaged in England at low wages, often escaped upon their arrival and after a short survey of life in the region. In 1834, the population on the company estates was about 400, half of whom were prisoners of the crown. However the company remained unprofitable for many years.

• The VDL Company-formation, land grant and convict disputes

The VDL Company could not have begun on a worst footing that it did. Challenges to the Secretary of State for the Colonies (Lord Bathurst), and to the Lieutenant–Governor of the Colony, were frequent and acrimonious. Nothing positive could be achieved out of such friction and nothing was. The beginning of the end had been realised before the beginning could be fully fleshed out.

Whether for self-preservation purposes, or self-protection, company sponsored recordings and reports of the foundation and progress of the VDL company are the most numerous and reliable. Curr's own diary and then the writings of Bischoff, Poole, Hellyer, Jorgenson and Adler provide an interesting insight into company operations, especially since planning was not recorded, if it took place at all. An early researcher into the origins of the company, Meston, did not paint a very encouraging or positive picture of the actions taken by management or of the prospects for company success. The exchange of correspondence is reliability reported within series III of the HRA, and is unexpurgated and uncensored in this form.

The formation of the company had taken place in 1824. In the initial stages some opposition was received from the Australian Agricultural Company. The AAC was authorised by 5 Geo.IV, cap. Lxxxvi, and was incorporated by letters patent, dated 1st November 1825.

Although the operations of the two companies were restricted to NSW (the AAC) and Tasmania (the VDL Company), the directors of the AAC thought their interests might be adversely affected by competition between the two colonies and by a rise in the value of sheep in Europe. Macarthur expressed the opinion that the introduction of a large amount of capital into each colony would have an evil influence on that colony. After negotiations, the AAC proposed (1) that the VDL Company not purchase any sheep in NSW, or any sheep imported from NSW within VDL for a period of twelve years, and (2) that VDL should not purchase sheep in Europe for a three-year period. At a meeting in February 1825, point (1) was accepted but (2) was declined. Bathurst wrote with this resolution to Curr, in Hobart dated April 1825. The statute 6 Geo IV, cap xxxix, was passed in June 1825 authorising the granting of the charter to the VDL Company and the charter received the great seal in November 1825. Bathurst had restricted the sale or issue of shares to the public until the charter was granted. In consequence, no prospectus was ever issued.

Bathurst advised Arthur of the formation of the VDL Company on 2nd June 1825. He wrote "The establishment of a company for the cultivation and improvement of waste lands in VDL is deserving of the support of H.M. Government. A company has been formed under the title of 'The Van Diemen's Land Company' and offers the immediate advantage of introducing a large amount of capital for investment in agricultural operations, but more especially to the rearing of flocks of sheep of the purest and finest breed. You will also note, (writes Bathurst to Arthur), from the Bill that the Company has certain limitations. You should also note that the land grant will be contained by the Basse's Strait to the north, by the ocean to the west and on the east and south by lines drawn from either shore, and these lands should be reserved until the Company selection has been finally made.

He also asked Arthur to 'afford every facility to the Company officials, who will be carrying out survey and valuation of the lands to be conceded to the Company'. A month earlier (April 1825) Bathurst had written to Edward Curr, the then Secretary of the company, setting out the terms for the formation of the Company.

Its main paragraphs contained information as follows:

a. The formation is to be encouraged because of the advantages of new capital being transferred to the colony of VDL. 'It is our conviction that the judicious introduction of capital into the colony cannot fail to produce the most beneficial results'.

b. 'The essential basis of any agreement for the formation of the company must be the subscription of the nominal capital and putting the avowed designs of the company into effect'. (Bathurst had accepted the plans of the company to improve the sheep flock in the colony and export wool from the colony to the woollen mills in England).

c. 'Before I can introduce any bill into the Parliament I need to see 4/5ths the nominal capital subscribed, and I need to be assured that the subscribers are men of substance and honour in relation to payment for their shares'.

d. 'Before the charter is issued, the subscribers must actually pay 5% of their initial subscription in cash to the company. I would like to also render the shares inalienable for a few years, or else I will accept that the nominal value of each share shall be £50, as set down on the share certificate. The Government may from time to time authorise the issue of additional capital. These shares shall be preferred to existing shareholders as a second set up to the number of first shares taken up'.

e. 'Conditions of a resolution of a general meeting will precede the government approval of additional capital, as will evidence that the original capital was put to good use (especially as to Public Works and Improvement of the Lands)

f. 'The original subscription of capital will be for £500,000 in £50 parcels. Each director and auditor will be required to have 50 qualification shares'.

g. 'Any variation to the employment of this capital other than as specified will be deemed a violation of the charter'.

h. 'Upon the issuance of the charter I shall direct His Majesty to approve a grant of 250,000 acres of land in the Island of Van Diemen's Land. One of the primary objects of the use of company capital shall be the clearing, improvement and cultivation of this tract of land. Improvement will include the construction of roads, drains, bridges, erection of houses, mills and other works and machinery necessary for the occupation, or cultivation of the soil and or the depasturing of sheep or cattle.

i. 'Another primary use of original capital will be the sponsorship of emigration of persons intending to settle upon any part of the company's estates. Full assistance will be provided to these people.

j. 'A third primary purpose of capital will be the encouragement of mining. The crown will reserve mining rights to itself; however, permission will be given to the company for leasing rights for mining. Mining can only take place on land the subject of these grants.

k. 'Capital may be used to make loans to settlers, provided they are publicly recorded with a limit of £50,000 to any one settler. The company will not be permitted to lend money on mortgage other than to settlers on company owned estates. I do not intend to limit in any way the amount advanced to settlers using company owned lands for production.'

l. 'The company may not enter into any banking operations, nor lend money on interest'.

m. 'Regarding public works, there will be a limitation of £50,000 in any one undertaking. This restriction will cease ten years after the date of the charter'.

n. 'The company may loan up to £100,000 to the governor or treasury at any one time. This limitation will expire after ten years'.

o. 'Whaling and fishing investments, because of the risk and management time demands must be limited to £20,000'.

p. 'The company is not to engage in any species of general trade, which shall include barter or sale of the product of the company's lands'.

q. 'Further land purchases will not be permitted without the authorisation of the Governor. However some capital may be invested in the purchase or erection of housing, wharves in company townships. The limit of such investment will be £20,000'.

r. 'The following rules will apply to the selection. The company will receive its grant in the northwest district of the island, bounded by Bass Strait, the Ocean and on the east and south by lines drawn from either shore. The company will have discretion in selecting land within that specified region, but all lands must be contiguous and approximating a square'.

s. 'The whole quantity of useful land, that is land capable of tillage, is to be 250,000 acres. Whatever useless or unprofitable land may be accepted will be granted to the company gratuitously, as an addition to the 250,000 tillable acres'.

1. 'The survey and valuation of the selected land will be carried out to the mutual satisfaction of the company and the Governor, and the parties shall share its cost equally'.

2. 'The report of the surveyors and valuers (to the Lt-Gov) shall be binding and unanimous, and will be the formal accounting of the limits of the grants and operational area of the company'.

3. 'Quit rent shall be charged at the rate of 30s for every £100 of land value, and will become payable at the expiration of five years from the date of the grant. The company will be able to offset the quit rent by fully maintaining convict labour for 15 years, provided it can be verified that the company has saved the governor an expenditure of at least £25,000, using the rate of £16 per convict for a whole year'.

Bathurst confirmed to Arthur on the 12th September 1825 that the Charter had received the great Seal. Bathurst again urged the cooperation of the governor towards the VDL Company, by assigning convicts, offering a military guard to surveyors whilst carrying out their surveying duties, and meeting equally the costs of the survey and the valuation process. He suggested, where practical, the utilisation of natural boundaries, and the early issuance of any licence of occupation of lands to assist the company. Bathurst extended flexibility for the governor to negotiate the location of the grants with the company's agent reserving to the government any stands of valuable timber suitable for naval purposes, and also any lands near harbours suitable for naval or military purposes. He was further authorised to waive quit rents under certain conditions. Bathurst ordered any mining on Company lands to be approved.

On 26th January 1826, Arthur replied to Bathurst's communications and assured Bathurst of his loyal support for the company, with the reservation that Macquarie harbour penal settlement may be impacted by the selection of Company grants. He was most concerned that company lands may be used to hide or harbour escaped convicts. "Every countenance and support, wrote Arthur, which your Lordship has desired to afford to the company in England, would be zealously and cheerfully continued by this local government."

Arthur added that there was a scarcity of convict labour and the company's request for convicts could not be met–'the applications by settlers for convict labour already exceeds the present capacity of the government to supply.'

I expect you will increase the number of transportees to meet the new needs and the demands of all. Public works has slowed due to the shortage of mechanics, and I urge your consideration of free settlers to provide additional labour.

Arthur advised Bathurst that military protection for company officials was unnecessary. "If a good system is introduced and order and regularity follow, the prisoners will generally behave well; if the arrangements of the company are defective, a whole Regiment will not insure harmony". I have promised Mr. Curr and Mr. Adey that a few soldiers would be available to accompany them on their travels.

Arthur had already seen evidence of Curr being difficulty to deal with and he advised Bathurst "Your instructions will be carefully observed, although a question has arisen concerning ambiguity in the instructions. Arthur was merely covering himself in the event Curr challenged the instructions. Arthur stated 'I fear a difficulty will arise in determining what land is considered available to the company and what may be rejected'. Again Arthur was putting Bathurst on notice of future complications, which may arise and be the responsibility of Bathurst and not Arthur.

Arthur reiterated again that Macquarie Harbour penal settlement might have to be abandoned if the company selected land adjacent to Cape Grim.

On November 14 1826, Arthur once again appealed to Bathurst to withdraw his offer of convict labour for the company. 'I venture to state, writes Arthur, that between Mr. Curr's arrival in the colony and this very hour, I have received requests for over 800 prisoners by free settlers, who are most anxious and pressing to obtain their services, and without seeking the slightest gratuity would esteem the assignment of a prisoner as a great favour. It would seem most contradictory to draft the prisoners off to VDL Company with the concession of 16 pound per head per annum.'

Arthur points out that Curr's position is simple–the Home Government made a bargain and must be made to meet it, otherwise compensation will be sought from the government. In response 'My decision has been to grant the company the convicts they desire, as I would on no account be the means of their suspending operations, or give them occasion to ascribe their failure to measures taken by this local government, but to notify their Agent that I have taken action purely from the desire to relieve government from any liability or damages'.

Arthur is demonstrating to Bathurst that it is really Bathurst's inept action that is causing these problems; that he (Arthur) does not really agree with the commitment by the British government to the Company but he wants to remove any disloyalty or claim or charge of inaction from against himself.

This was *mea culpa* by any other name. Arthur finishes his letter with a gentle rebuke to Bathurst 'I read from Mr Undersecretary Hay's letter to Curr, that Your Lordship has promised the Company further support and assistance in the prosecution of their *ulterior views so far as they may not be injurious to the general interests of the settlers, or as may not on other accounts be objectionable'*

Arthur is once again appealing to Bathurst to cease making commitments against the colony of VDL without reaching some consensus with the governor (who has to implements these policies made on the run) first.

Arthur, in stating he was responding to an application from Curr, was acceding to Curr's request of 5th October 1826 when he wrote to Arthur's office 'I have to request that 25 men be assigned to the VDL Company. I need laborers, tree fellers, gardeners and timber splitters'

Arthur responded to Curr's letter advising that 25 men would reluctantly be made available but that Lord Bathurst, when making the arrangement for convict labor with the company 'labored under a misapprehension as to the State of the colony, and that instead of a pecuniary allowance being made to the company, a charge should have been made for using convict labor'.

Arthur reminded Curr "There would be an apparent injustice if the Company were to obtain servants on more advantageous terms than other settlers."

Arthur further informed Curr that any future convicts could only be assigned conditionally, and that is because convict labor can only be used to complete public works required of the company.

Arthur then referred these 'delicate' points to Bathurst for adjudication, and raised the question of another settler having been granted 2,000 acres of land within the reserved area for the VDL Company. From the tone of the Arthur letter and the Bathurst reply, it is apparent that both parties were getting very tired of Mr. Curr's inability to work with the system, instead of against it. Arthur again points out that most of these disputes arise because of the difficulty of understanding the original Bathurst instructions on the location of the land grant, as well as the impracticality of offering a grant of so large an area on this Island. "Your Lordship should have raised a doubt as to whether so large a tract as the company required could be found available in this colony, and the company expectation of getting 3 to 5 hundred thousand acres (Curr suggests it may take one-quarter of the whole island) should not have been accepted by Your Lordship without the benefit of discussion, survey, long consideration, and checking with the VDL administration". Curr writing to the Colonial Secretary on 27th July 1826 finally reveals his plan: "The current discussions are founded upon an erroneous view of the subject. Lord Bathurst never indicated any intention of excluding certain areas (e.g. Port Sorell) from our consideration. Although Lord Bathurst did not clearly define what he intended by the Northwest district, yet his words, taken by themselves admit only the construction placed on them by myself".

In response Arthur accepts Curr's interpretation and gives permission for selection of the grant to include port Sorell. Furthermore Arthur apologizes for having made a mistake with the 2,000-acre grant, which is the subject of much correspondence. Arthur does not apologize lightly nor allow his judgment to be easily swayed. The sting is to come. Arthur advises Curr that: Lord Bathurst originally gave instructions that "the Company will receive their grant in the northwest district of the Island, that district for present purposes being the square thus drawn from seashore to seashore which shall be the only area considered for the grant. I consider Colonel Sorell's letter to Lord Bathurst as not being in disagreement with the above. Therefore, I have determined:

- *Some* latitude of selection should be allowed to the company, and
- It is equally evident that no selection can take place unless the district is larger than the land to be selected, therefore
- Lord Bathurst's intention was that 'within the district I have directed their lands should be received, they may select any un-granted lands at their own discretion'.

I urge you to act, without loss of time, on completing the survey and measurement according to Lord Bathurst's directions."

This ultimatum would not be pleasurable to Curr and he would have to decide if he had taken his fight to the full.

Curr decided to continue his fight, and turned back to Bathurst with an argument for concessions on quit-rents. One can only conclude that Curr had a lot of excess time and little inclination to finalize his land selection and move the property into production. More and more letters and more and more arguments were produced in this voluminous exchange of correspondence. On 30th October 1826, Curr claimed to Colonial Secretary Hamilton that unless the Government gave in to his demands, there would be 'possible injury to the company's interests and he would be making a tentative claim for compensation from the Government on behalf of the company'. By 15th November 1826, Arthur was telling Bathurst "I have not permitted any interruption to take place in the good understanding that has hitherto existed between Mr. Curr and me. My arguments with Mr. Curr have been founded entirely upon the reasonableness of the objections; and although he is very anxious to remove them to the interest of the company, he is, I believe, sensible that they are brought forward and naturally arise out of circumstances not fully anticipated at home'.

Arthur again was covering his rear. He was not fully privy to correspondence between the company and Bathurst, and if there was any such correspondence, Arthur was sure that it would be critical of Arthur's threat to cancel the agreement, so Arthur was getting in first with Bathurst. 'My discussions with Curr, implies Arthur, have been cordial and I could only commit to carrying out your intentions, and not making a revised deal'.

Lord Bathurst was being pressured by Arthur on one hand, who was opposed to the great concessions being made to the Company, and by Curr and Inglis (the London-based Managing Director), on the other hand. Curr and Inglis had different strategies, however Bathurst shot at both of them.

"If Curr went to VDL suffering a misapprehension (as implied by Inglis) he has taken three years to produce his arguments and maps. This should have been divulged earlier. Bathurst then argued that there was a dichotomy between the company's wish to use their map to base the area for selection, and the company's intention to obtain the best grazing land. Bathurst says that the Crown Surveyor opines the map coverage is not good grazing areas. However, Bathurst concedes, 'go ahead and select from within the lines on your map. I will instruct the Governor of this change." Two days later, Inglis responds to Bathurst and argues about the quit rent concessions, admits his map has been misunderstood and withdraws any threat against the government for compensation. This may now be the turning point for offering concessions to Bathurst so as not to lose out altogether.

Another red herring arrived from Curr. He wants the governor to give him grazing rights over 10,000 acres whilst the land grants are being finalized. He does not wish to pay for them. Bathurst decides he can have the grazing rights but only at the same cost as would be the case in NSW, which is a rent of one pound for every hundred acres. This charge may well decide the company's future, as Curr has already made his report to the Court of VDL Company in London that if 250,000 acres is accepted on the northwest point, it will cost £13 to improve each acre of land in order to make it finally worth only 2 pound per acre. The Court offers a concession by claiming that one continuous parcel of land is not possible, but a number of parcels would be acceptable. "The court, writes Inglis, have no wish to avail themselves of a literal interpretation of the agreement, to press for an area of territory which could be of no advantage to their undertaking, and are therefore content to take detached portions of useful land, in any part of the Northwest Territory.

These concessions were to enable the disagreement to reach settlement although a further two years would elapse before the surveys were completed and the company made plans for various settlements on their land. Of course, we have only observed the relationship between the company and the government from the written word and without the benefit of a company representative offering an interpretation for their confused and beleaguered approach.

A variation on the correspondence can be found from the writings of Bischoff and Curr (to be found in the Appendix to this volume).

The Annual Reports

We learn from the writing of the annual reports that Curr's reports were not always included, and that Bischoff misstated the quality of the land grant in order to ensure 'calls' were paid, and in order to allow the stock to trade at a reasonable value on the London Stock Exchange. What we don't read very much about is how the company performed financially.

So we can work within certain parameters in order to better understand the company's performance.

The company's fiscal year was the calendar year–January to December. Two separate sets of books were kept (one in London to cover 'Head Office' expenses, and one in Circular Head to reflect VDL expenditures) but they were not fully reconciled, and even though they were officially audited, the 'advances to' Circular Head in the London accounts, never quite balanced to 'advances received from Head Office' in the Circular head books. There is an explanation for this but not one that was ever brought to stockholder's notice in the audited accounts, nor was the audit report ever included (before 1901) with the Annual Report, as is the case today.

So the observations that can be made from the published accounts are done so without the benefit of seeing the comments made to the Directors by the Auditor.

a. The first observation we can make is as to the Organization structure. The Company had a fully supported office in London (it started at 31 Finsbury Circus), before moving to 6 Great Winchester Street, and then moving again to the final registered offices at Blomfield House on London Wall.
b. We learn that nepotism abounded. In 1857 the chairman was John Cattley, whilst the Company secretary was Henry Cattley. Two Pearse family members (Brice and Charles) sat on the Board at the same time.
c. In 1856, the shareholders were advised in the annual Report 'The funds in London are not sufficient to admit of an immediate distribution of (i.e. a return of capital) ten shillings per share (par

was £100)", however, the report concludes with the statement "The directors consider there is nothing in the present circumstances of the company to lessen the confidence of those who have hitherto been disposed to think favorably of its future prospects". This statement in spite of the 'Liquidation Committee' reporting only two years earlier.

d. The 1873 report states, "There are 9,000 effective shares, limited to £30 each, and of which £28.10.0 has been paid".

e. New auditors appointed in 1871 again revalued the company's assets, and recapitalized the land grant properties with accrued expenditures for improvements at £255,796, an increase of £138,156. The cash position was worsening with only £23 pound in cash in the colony and receivables of £4,225. Cash in London was little better with only £1171 on hand, which include petty cash of 5/7 (five shillings and seven pence). Receivables in London were 100 pound. Revenues in the colony for 1871 were well down on previous years at £2,528, including land sale installments of only 45 pound. The company had been floundering now for over 20 years, and obviously a new approach was overdue.

f. What is surprising is that even with revenues down; expenses were down even further and in line with plans to re-build the cash reserves. So the year 1872 ended with an increase in reserves of £755. The support, on the board, for increases in Head Office expenses was apparently nil. They lived off accumulated reserves and received no fee income from the colony, or from the efforts made by Directors towards operating the company. Cash on hand in London had declined by about £1,200 to the unhealthy £1,171. Deferring the dividend was obviously not the answer. For its whole life, dividends had been paid out of capital and not out of profits. Any profits declared were merely book profits and derived from revaluations of land and livestock assets in the colony. Auditor emoluments for 1871 were set at £6.6.0, which was the same amount actually paid (according to the annual report) for a 'small iron safe and stand'. g. From the 1856 accounts we learn of two new operating areas. The mining and extraction of slate, which ran out at a depth of 12 feet, but in addition was of poor quality, and not suitable for roofing as had been planned. The accounts for the year showed a healthy increase in port activities through the Company Port at Emu Bay (Burnie). Between 1853 and 1856 tonnage processed had increased from 433 to 892, whilst value of processing rose from £3487 to £14353.

h. An observation of interest but without adequate explanation is that the auditors appointed were individuals rather than a firm (which would have provided continuity) and those individuals usually lasted not longer than two years. We know not the reason for this continuous change but could conjecture that:

- The emoluments at 6 guineas were not attractive (especially for the work required to be performed); or
- The accounts were in such a bad condition that no auditor could risk his reputation by being associated with the company; or
- The auditors demanded accounting changes, which were not acceptable to the directors and new auditors, were then selected (when questions began to be asked).

i. From statistics included with the annual report of 1849, we know the extent of livestock in the colony, owned by the Company. Sheep numbers ('in the company's possession') were 6,519, but were recorded in the Balance Sheet at only £7979. Cattle numbers were 2282 but were not separately valued in the accounts. 185 horses were valued at £4948, whilst deer numbered 76 with a value of £133. Valuations from year to year showed no rationale. Sheep killed for food in 1849, numbered 316 but there is no write off in the accounts for this 'personnel' expense. Similarly, the various properties were all 'valued' but there is no relationship to a value per acre. There was no 'unimproved value' with improvements being identified and capitalized. The accounts for 1851, although audited are not in balance, and no explanation is offered for this situation. The total assets are made up of Land, livestock, machinery and stores and sundries (including cash of £164) and amount to £223,330, but liabilities total £255,900. The difference is not accounted for against 'shareholders' equity'.

CHAPTER 3

COMPANY SPONSORED EXPLORATION

• Exploration

When Curr arrived in the Colony in early 1826, his first step was to send his assistants on an exploration program, in order to discover the reality of the northwest region.

Lorymer and Hellyer explored passionately and wrote lengthy reports of their travels and findings.

Meston also offers a summary of these travels based on diaries and notes, other than the official reports to Curr.

Meston points out that "Bass and Flinders on the voyage of 1798 named several of the prominent landmarks and features of the north-west coast–Round Hill, Table Cape, Rocky Cape, Circular Head, Hunter's Island, Cape Grim and Trefoil Island". HMS Buffalo added Robbins Island to the map following an 1804 visit to the location. This whole coastline was a favourite resort of whalers, and the Tamar River plus Rivers 1, 2 and 3 west of the Tamar were probably well known to early visitors. These three rivers had not yet been officially named and were commonly known in the district as Rivers 1, 2 & 3.

'Gov. Sorell had encouraged exploration of this region during his administration, whereby he would locate extensive tracts of grazing country, but the reports he received were not favourable and a practical stock-route to the area could not be found'. This statement by Meston is questionable in view of the information; report and recommendations Sorell later gave to the promoters of the VDL Company. The Sorell assessment (as offered to Lord Bathurst) is that the Cape Grim area was "useless for agriculture, except in small patches"; Port Sorell area was 'delightful', whilst Rocky Cape to the Tamar was 'unfit for human habitation'; of Circular head he gave a glowing report. In spite of Sorell's opinion, or perhaps because of it, Bathurst insisted that the VDL Company select land only from the Cape Grim corner (the north-west corner) of the Island. How easily tribulation can be imparted to antagonists, by offering them a land grant in an area 'useless for agriculture'.

In his first presentation to the VDL Company Court on 18th December 1824, Sorell advised, "All the good land has been granted away and two-thirds of the Island is barren rock, although (Sorell said) I have no knowledge of the north-west district". Sorell, in his second presentation, following the release of the Curr booklet on VDL, spoke very highly of its author and supported Curr in 'his enthusiasm of the opportunities awaiting a judicious use of capital". John Pearce, the 1824 President of VDL Company asked Sorell for a memorandum 'upon the detached and unallocated parts of VDL and the openings for an extensive grant'. In his response, Sorell advised, "From Port Sorell to Circular head would be the most suitable tract for any extensive alienation of land. To whatever extent the quality of the country might admit of a large grant being carried back from the sea, even were the interior to be found so unpromising as to narrow the location materially, the space from Port Sorell to Circular head would afford all that would be required". He warned also that 'there were good prospects of producing fine wool and the Island offered a splendid opportunity for the use of capital in pursuing the black whale fishery, in opening up iron deposits at Port Dalrymple, in exploiting the abundant beds of limestone and in carrying out distilling, brewing and tanning'. It was unfortunate that Sorell recommended two potential industries specifically negatived in the Bathurst instructions–Whaling and Mining.

Curr's exploration objection was to find open, lightly timbered plains similar to that on the eastern side of the island, so eminently suited for sheep, and spared no pains in this effort. While the charter allowed Curr to spend company capital in cultivating and improving lands, the acquisition of forestlands and the clearing of them did not appear cost effective to Curr or the best use of the company capital expenditure. On 22nd April 1825 Curr, along with Hellyer, Fossey, Lorymer, and five men with two laden carts, set out from Launceston to cross the River #1 (later named the Quamby River) and entered the area reserved by Bathurst and Arthur for the VDL Company selection. By May 20, they had found no suitable land and had reached river 2 (west of the Tamar) and named it the 'Mersey'.

Going further west to commence their exploration, Goldie and Adey commenced working down the rivers, but soon concluded 'the whole district from Port Sorell to Circular head was worthless'. Fossey and Goldie, in July investigated the Circular head to Cape grim area and decided only about 4,000 acres was open and suitable, although more could be attained at reasonable expense. As a result of these journeys, Curr decided to headquarter at Circular Head and sent his brig with livestock aboard to that port for unloading.

From that time, individual efforts were made by the assistants, Lorymer and Hellyer into the afforested areas, and the notes maintained by these men and their final reports to Curr are now included, below, in this text–the first time revealed. Jorgenson led a third team, but this team experienced problems with severe weather and flooding and eventually abandoned their efforts within a couple of weeks.

• Exploration Report of C P Lorymer–Circular Head 29.1.1827

"This day I proceeded hence in the whaleboat across the bay to Crawfish River at which point I landed. The following morning I took the boat to Rocky Cape entered the plains and proceeded to the south point. Here I commenced my route for the purpose of exploring the country in the direction of the large tier of mountains bearing SSE from Circular Head and distant about 30 miles.

This range extends in a north and south line from the sea. I ascended the hills, which presented themselves from the plains–upon reaching the summit I clearly discerned Circular Head to the north–northwest–and Rocky Cape to the north east by north. From these heights the country appears to be one entire forest–to the east and along my intended route a clear open but a healthy and hilly country. The valley to the east of the plains below (over which I had passed) is very scrubby and heavily timbered. Through the vale a river takes its course and empties itself into the sea at Rocky Cape–from the heights I began examining the country to the south, found it impossible to make much progress in consequence of the wire scrub and the ground being intersected by deep and perpendicular ravines–to penetrate which could not be effected without encountering many difficulties–not only in labour and fatigue but expending much time without gaining anything. Perceiving the obstacles I had to encounter on this line of route compelled me to return to the heights and continue my course southeast along the range. After traversing about a mile and reaching the side of a very deep gully (about a mile in width) thickly intertwined with the wire scrub, I crossed it, which occupied five hours. Before I reached the foot of this ravine I had to descend a precipice of nearly two hundred feet and it was with much difficulty I affected my descent in safety.

Having crossed the river at the bottom, which from its course must be the same as described as passing "through the valley" I entered a flat piece of ground about two hundred metres wide consisting of light soil growing a quantity of fine timber consisting chiefly of Blackwood, Pine, Stringy Bark, and Sassafras. Also, we came across a tree of large dimensions, the wood of which is white in its nature; close in its texture, fit for every kind of building purposes and inside lining for furniture etc. I am of opinion that an easy road can be made from this part of the river to Rocky Cape plains through which it runs when the timber could be shipped on board of small craft and conveyed to Circular Head.

The next morning I ascended the opposite rise, which was thickly wooded. After encountering much scrub I again entered upon the hills, which consist chiefly of sand growing quantities of heath coarse grass as well as the grass tree. Continuing a southeast course for a few miles I once more changed my route to the southward and westward. Upon leaving the hills I entered a thick forest in which I found small trees of the sally pine, also the narrow leaved gum of large dimensions. In this forest I continued travelling four days when my efforts were again frustrated by deep ravines or gullies surrounding one on every side excepting the link I had traversed.

The range, which I was desirous of attaining, bore south by east. The country between me and the hills, and also to the southwest appeared to be one entire forest intertwined with scrub and impassable.

Perceiving I should have a difficult task in advancing forward I came to the resolution of returning to the edge of a valley over which I had passed and endeavour if possible to make my course to the southeast. Here I met with a strong opposition from the wire scrub, which was fifteen feet high. In making the attempt I was two hours in accomplishing a distance of two hundred yards. This compelled me to trace my steps to the hills I had left. Upon regaining them I proceeded in a south east direction, ascended a rise of ground which commanded a view of the surrounding country–Circular Head bore 320 degrees–Table Cape 60 degrees–very distant hills to the east 100 degrees–Seal Hills 105 degrees and the range south east by south.

In descending this hill I kept the latter course before attaining the foot. I entered another scrub and continued two days traversing through it when a tremendous ravine or gully presented itself of so terrific a creature I could not with proprietary make the attempt to go down it without running a great risk it being nearly perpendicular and its depth about 300 feet.

Had I been successful in crossing the gully I should have ascended the mountain range and have accomplished the object of my route? It was with great reluctance I abandoned the attempt.

I commenced my return to Circular Head at which place I arrived on 14 February 1827, the whole of my provisions being consumed.

The range of the hills appears to run about six miles in extent–soil sandy, vegetation heath, horse grass, and the grass tree. The intervening falls from the hills woody. The summit of the range stony and in places thickly wooded. The south end of the tier appears to terminate with a gentle declivity into a valley through which there appears to be an opening on the other side to the south.

(Signed) C P Lorymer.

Extract letter of Edward Curr to the directors.

During my stay at the (VDL Company) establishment, Mr Lorymer returned from a journey, which he made in a southeast direction from Circular Head. He stated himself, to have found at the distance of about fifteen miles, two tracts containing 20,000 acres of good pastureland; on this I am obliged to say that I place no reliance. He however bought with him some samples of very valuable timber which he found within five or six miles of water carriage, which if it should prove to grow there in abundance may be both very useful to the company's work and very valuable in the colony. One of them was pine and the other an inferior quality of cedar.

The bluff is a block of granite not very hard to work but which becomes harder by exposure to the air.

• Exploration Report of Henry Hellyer–The Discovery of Hampshire and Surry Hills

(Submitted at Circular Head 13 March 1827)

I have the honour to forward, together with a panoramic view from the peak, a map of all the country I have yet seen or examined, laid down to the scale of a chart which I thought would afford more information than merely a written description and show the extent of good country which I have now seen. Agreeably to the arrangements made by you when here during the latter end of January I started on the first of February to explore the country in a southerly direction from Rocky Cape, taking with me four men, three packhorses and a month's provisions. Having sent the horses round by the shore I crossed the bay and landed about three miles up the Detention River and on the 5th I arrived at the west side of the base of the south end or dip of a lofty tier of heathy mountains, the summit of which I expected would afford a good insight into the country beyond, and determine my future proceedings.

On the 6th, I ascended the Dip and saw from it a plain about fifteen miles south of Table Cape and a large tract of open grassy country, south east by east, lying beyond the north side of the peak which I considered was the most desirable route for me to take and to endeavour to ascend the peak. The country to the south being all high forest, tier above tier, and to the west one mass of low forest so flat that I could see Mount Cameron and Cape Grim forty miles off, neither of which are very lofty.

After taking minute observations of every feature of the surrounding country I descended and took the horses down through a steep forest into an extensive green flat which I called "Dipwood Marsh" and knowing it was all forest beyond for many miles in every direction and finding here an abundance of fresh young grass and herbage (although very coarse) with grass trees and fern, I left the horses and the two prisoners who were already knocked up and started for the open country, beyond the peak, each of us carrying a gun and a knapsack containing a large blanket and a fortnight's provisions–my strength I feared was scarcely equal to it but I was determined to go as far as possible.

The country, from Circular Head as far as Dipwood Marsh is everywhere sandy and of no utility whatever for the purpose of the Company–it consists of barren rocky and heathy hills with useless stunted trees, heathy swampy plains and rocky forests. I have observed there is a sharp white sand freestone, to be had from about the Dip but its carriage would render it almost unavailable–it would I think make excellent grindstones, rubbers for scythes, etc. Dipwood Marsh extends from about four to five miles in length and is about half a mile in width–the soil grey sand mixed with lumps of milky quartz appears to be a place much frequented by the natives and has been burnt a few months back. We found several kangaroos upon it when we came down.

I left Dipwood Marsh and had a most fatiguing march for several days, through a thick dark forest–a succession of woody mountains and although the men climbed trees upon every top where it was likely to obtain an observation, we found such a mass of foliage everywhere that no distant object could be seen until the evening of the 11th when we were fortunate to see the Peak which appeared to be a good three days march from us. I began now to consider we had travelled five days out of our fourteen and as I could not go near the Peak if I went on for the open plains, I determined to ensure at all events my ascending the Peak.

On the morning of the 12th, having altered my course from south east by east to south east by south I found the travelling the same all that day, but on the 13th we saw an Emu track down the side of a hill, which assured us we were getting into a better country, and about noon we suddenly came upon grassy hills, the extent of which we had then no idea of—the change was quite dramatic and we saw the Peak was some miles before us yet so we went over these hills and passed through a considerable tract of myrtle forest similar to our last six days travelling, and came to the widest and deepest river we had seen since leaving Circular Head and we crossed on a fallen tree bridge about twenty feet above the water. Its course here is from the southwest and going east northeast. I have since named it "Emu River". I expected this river skirted the Peak and we afterwards found seven distinct tiers of hilly forest before we arrived at the base of the principal eminence.

On the night of the 13th we rested on the fourth hill of ascent and on the 14th being very unfavourable, wet and gloomy, we could not wait for the weather and about 2 o'clock we had reached the top of the north pyramid of rock

The highest part being yet far above us and in the clouds and seeing the weather thicken to windward and fearing the scene around me would soon be eclipsed I hastened to take a sketch of it but the clouds descended and it poured with rain. We could not see each other for there was such a thick mist and it rushed past us so furiously we were obliged to take shelter in a nook of the rocks and wrap up ourselves in blankets. The cold was perishing. I wanted to see if it would blow over and waited till 5 o'clock and finding there was no chance of it clearing we descended and determined on going up again the next day.

I had just sufficient time to look around and see that there was a fine open country to the northeast and southwest. We found it very difficult to get down being obliged to hold on pulling perpendicular rocks and the small twigs which grew between them and finding water just before dark we made a stand before a large fire against some trees. (The rain continued a great part of the night.) The country from Dipwood Marsh to the Peak is not by any means barren. After the first three miles from the Marsh, it changes from a hungry sandy soil to a deep rich loam and there is not a stone to be seen except at the bottom of brooks which are mostly in deep ravines and gullies which intercept and drain the forest in all directions—the surface soil is actually rank with constantly decaying vegetable matter. It seems being quite disagreeable and the air in these dense forests is putrid and oppressive swarming with mosquitoes and large stinging flies the size of English bees—daylight is completely shut out by masses of foliage impervious to the rays of the sun.

Myrtle is the principal timber throughout this district, its appearance as to a rough bark and thick foliage very much resembles the Elm but there are no Elm equal to those gigantic trees being in general 150 to 200 feet in height and 30 to 40 feet in circumference—the wood is very like cedar. Sassafras is found here in great abundance and of fine growth and on many of the higher tiers is celery-topped pine of considerable size. Fern trees twenty feet in height, laurel ferns and feather fern are everywhere to be found except in the thickest scrub—the rivers and brooks are so numerous we were scarcely half an hour during any day without passing one or the other.

Dead logs and branches impeded us at every step and we were continually meeting with large tracts of dense thicket, from 30 to 40 feet high, so closely interwoven and matted together as to be impenetrable below and we were often obliged to be walking upon these never dry slippery branches covered with snow as much as twenty feet above the ground which being in many places rotten occasioned us in many awkward falls and tore our clothes to rags. We were not able to force our way on 500 yards in an hour in some of these horrid scrubs. I was glad I did not attempt to bring the horses on any further.

The grassy tract of country which we had crossed north of the Emu River appears to extend many miles to the south west and unites with the large open country to the North–it is covered with luxuriant grass and there are a few large stringy bark trees on the top of the ridge which runs down the centre of it. The hilly forest from the Emu River to the base of the Peak is of the same description as all the other myrtle forests we have traversed, except that the soil here is rather rocky and there are some stringy barks on these hills.

The Peak is composed of pudding stone, (like several other of the principal mountains which I have examined) and is in shape when viewed from the East or West side, like a three masted ship in full sail, and when observed from north or south it is as sharp as any peak can well be imagined, the sides being nearly perpendicular, its base extends six miles in length and about three miles in width. There is a companion hill on the northwest side, which is of considerable size and very lofty but woody to the top.

The morning of the 15th was fortunately very clear and serene. There was not a cloud to be seen and we again toiled up the mountain with our loads not knowing which way it would be most desirable to go on after getting to the top. We were several hours struggling through thick scrub and wire weed and climbing over immense masses of rock, the scrub was dripping wet from the heavy rain, which had fallen in the night. We had arrived upon the very highest point three thousand feet above sea level. The view from the spot or apex I have endeavoured to give an idea of by a panoramic sketch laid down to the true bearing of each object, having made it a sketch of the country all round.

I found the stump of a withered box tree and cut upon it "Saint Valentine's Peak" together with the date of my ascent, which I drove into the clefts of the rocks at the top with its root in the air. The men rolled off some huge blocks of rock which in their fall appeared to make from the splinters which flew off as they struck and rebounded from one massive projection to another. I had now to consider which way I should proceed on my return to see as much as possible of the good country which I had discovered from Valentine's Peak, and as that portion lying to the north east might be more easily examined from the coast, I descended at the south end after collecting specimens of the rock by breaking off several lumps sparkling with crystals and brought them away although I had a long distance to carry them in my knapsack.

We alighted in the evening upon an open spot, which had caught my observation from the top. I found it consisted of grassy hills and knolls and resembled a neglected "old park", one thousand to fifteen hundred acres in a patch without a tree (except for a few clumps of Blackwood), dead trees lying to rot where they had fallen, grass run to seed, the tops of which appearing at this season nearly white made it very conspicuous when viewed from a distance. Here we saw kangaroo in abundance and tracks of them in all directions. A brook runs across this district from the Peak in a southeast direction (which I think is very likely to be the source of the Seven River). The banks of the brook are green with trefoil—we found here as good mushrooms as any I have tasted in England.

As I only had time to make one straight line to find my way over the mountains of forest which divided me from the horses, I determined from what I had observed above to go from this west south west and see a fine large open tract about ten miles off. We went on in excellent country consisting of gently rising dry grassy hills divided from each other by brooks, the sides of which are adorned with Blackwood and other elegant trees and shrubs and on the hills are a few tall peppermints and stringy barks.

About sunset having routed some emus we fired at them but without impeding their progress, and having shot two kangaroos we halted for the night. As soon as we had made a fire, the flames caught the grass and it spread to a great extent quite illuminating the atmosphere till rain came on and by degrees extinguished it.

On the 16th we proceeded west south-west and after walking about half a mile crossed the Emu River where we saw several wattle birds then went over many considerable hills burnt by the natives, found a lot of native huts and saw several trees from which bark had been taken to cover them, soon after which we came down to a noble river with a strong current gliding smoothly along from south to north which I called the Don (later renamed the 'Hellyer') by way of distinction.

It is fifty yards wide and took us to the middle at the shallowest place we could find. On its banks are complete-stopping shrubberies. This river appears to rise about eight to ten feet in time of flood. At some short distance from the Don we ascended the most magnificent grass hill I have seen in the country consisting of several level terraces as if laid out by art and crowned with a straight row of stately peppermint trees beyond which there is not a tree for four miles along the grassy hills. I had now arrived at the ground opening seen from the Peak beyond a brown forest (here the natives had been burning large tracts of grass). The morning being cloudy and wet I was just able to discern the peak through the mist; its top was in the clouds. I congratulated myself upon having a fine day yesterday or I should have had a very imperfect idea of the good country here.

The plains, or rather hills from the south foot of the Peak I call from their great extent and importance "The Surry Hills" (which name I here cut up on a large conspicuous tree). This country being about the same distance inland as that county in England. They resemble English enclosures in many respects being bound by brooks between each, with belts of beautiful shrubs in every vale including blue leaf, tea tree, box, sassafras, Blackwood, wood spear, birch, shoe loaf, musk, holly, celery top pine and myrtle—the whole country is grassy. The grass is principally in the line of our walk, Timothy, Foxtail and single kangaroo.

The surface soil is dark vegetable mould upon a rich brown open loam of various depths and lighter in colour according to its depth, but on the tops of the hills there are rocks above the surface in several instances and from that I could observe where trees had fallen by the roots, the sub stratum is everywhere gravely which appears to render these hills perfectly dry and all the brooks have hard pebbly bottoms free from mud and the water clear as crystal.

The timber found in these hills is in general of fine growth, very tall and straight. Some of it would measure 100 feet to the lowest branch. The trees are in many places 100 yards apart—they are principally peppermint and stringy bark which having lately made their summer shoots, the whole country appears to be a lively brownish line which I have marked "brown forest" on the map and from what I have seen of the brown forest thus far, I do not think it at all too thickly timbered to afford a little shade from the summer heat—it will not in general average ten trees to an acre and there are many open plains of several square miles without a single tree.

The kangaroo stood gazing at us like fawns and in some instances came bounding towards us like a flock of sheep. We never before saw so many together.

The plains or hills to the north of the Peak being nearer the coast I called "The Hampshire Hills". They appear even more park like than the Surrey Hills and are handsomely clumped with trees. We continued travelling in the Brown Forest until the morning of the 18th. We found it still the same grassy kind of country which I have before described all the way from the Peak—our course in the Brown Forest has been nearly twenty miles and as far as we were enabled to view it on both sides as we came along, there were grassy hills out of number which it was delightful to look round upon from one higher than the rest that commanded such a prospect which continually occurred in the course of our walk.

We now approach the high forest tier of woody mountains near which we came upon a marshy country and saw several snipe. We found here two native huts and marks of many fireplaces in the neighbourhood as if place had been lately occupied by a large body of natives. In one of the huts I saw a drawing of the moon done with charcoal upon the inside of one of the slabs which formed the hut, and regarding it as being evidence of there being artists among them, I cut out the piece and placed it carefully between two other pieces of bark in my knapsack. I sketched two figures of the moon with charcoal on the back of the hut and put the date of my visit.

I was now travelling North West by north towards the Dip Mountains until I might be able to get an observation to correct my course, and having ascended the high forest tier we hope to obtain a bearing that would guide us in finding the nearest way to the horses, but there was no chance of it. Nothing could be seen but tops of trees upon the next high tier. We descended, and on the 19th came down through a very thick forest to the head of a large deep and rapid river, longer than the Don and at this place more than ten feet deep close to the bank. It was here coming from south-southeast and going west by south. We did not therefore suppose that we should see any more of it and pursued our way along a considerable tract of low flat forest which had every appearance of being inundated in the rainy season beyond which we again found this large river running north east.

We were obliged now to wade through it at the best fording place we could find, and it was in some places so deep and dangerous we could scarcely withstand the current, but by holding onto poles we all got safely through it and having wrung our clothes we went on over several steep hills of forest and scrub and about sunset had arrived on the top of a very high forest tier.

The men climbed the trees as usual and could see nothing but tops of trees upon the next tier which was a great disappointment to me. On the **20**[th] we came down from high mountains of dark forest and went over many steep hills without varying the dismal scene, but suddenly it changed. For a few minutes we came down upon an excellent level spot of high fern and stringy bark–a capital soil for the plough and easily cleared, its extent might be a hundred acres. It appeared to be a long flat terrace off the side of the mountain. Here we again heard the great river just below and found it running west–we had no alternative but to find our way over and it appeared so much larger that we all thought it had united with the Don since our first crossing it.

We were however lucky in finding here a much better ford with an island of gravel to rest upon, and the current being wider was not as powerful as at the former crossing place. This spot would suit for a ford and depot if ever such a step should be made in that direction, which I think is most improbable because of the lofty mountains surrounding the location. I have taken the liberty of styling this large river "The Arthur" in compliment to his Excellency the Lieutenant Governor of VDL–it being one of the principal rivers in the island.

After travelling north north west over several high mountains of forest we at last obtained a view of the east end of Blue Peak range from which we know we were many days journey from the horses and too much to the west. We now changed our course to north-northeast. We had no provisions left except flour which mixed with water only is poor living to take such violent bodily exercise upon. On the 21st we came down upon the Arthur again, running east but seeing it turned to the north we went round the bend and from it ascended its very high and steep bank in a north-northeast direction and came up to the foot of a long line of perpendicular cliffs of slate from two to three hundred feet high.

Upon examination they proved to be slate of the best quality–splitting in parallel thicknesses to the size of ladies countesses and duchesses and lying in regular horizontal strata from end to end. I brought away specimens and engraved a large slab standing under the cliff "Whoever is found stealing slate from this quarry will be dealt with according to law" with the date below it. If the Arthur should be found navigable from barges from hence to the coast, this discovery so near the river might be valuable. These cliffs appear to extend for miles and would supply the entire world in slate.

We continued travelling in the dreary forest over high mountains of slate with an abundance of capital white stone in every deep ravine. A great part of the 22nd we were obliged to make our way for many miles along the top of a very dangerous, serpentine, stony and rocky ridge, so narrow at the top that a single tree would often occupy the whole width of it and we were obliged to creep along its almost perpendicular sides to get past such a tree. It resembled the top of a wall of a large castle and on either side below us was a rocky ravine many hundred yards deep, and after getting over several high hills of forest we came down to a large river which we knew could be no other than the Don and now discovered that it had not joined the Arthur as we before had reason to suppose.

It here ran west in a deep valley of rugged rocks among mountains of rocky forest. Having, with difficulty, waded through it about three hundred yards above a noble cascade where the whole body of water fell twenty feet perpendicular with an astonishing noise, we went up one of the loftiest forest tiers yet encountered and found it to be perfectly level on the top and thickly covered with an almost impenetrable espalier growth scrub that a dog could not get through. We persevered in getting over it till dark. It had poured with rain nearly the whole day. The water streamed from our finger ends yet we were obliged to go on or starve. This compulsory moving on past our strength, and the anxiety we all felt as to our ever being able to get back to tell of what we had seen, rendered our situation at this moment by no means enviable and the men began to consider it hopeless and said they should never be heard of any more, just like the seven soldiers that went from Macquarie Harbour after bushrangers.

But if we have strength left to crawl on at all, I told them we should get out; we could not be far wrong in our course and at all events could make the sea coast, even if we should be so buried in Dark forest as not to be able to get an observation. On 23ʳᵈ we toiled over several tremendous mountains of forest and had some thoughts of throwing away everything we carried, being all nearly exhausted with fatigue and want of food.

On 24ᵗʰ we came to the brink of a frightful precipice and saw a river below running north east and knew it must be the same which we had crossed going to the Peak which runs into the sea at Table Cape and from a tree on a high hill, further on, we saw the sea near Table Cape. We immediately altered our course to northwest and on the 25ᵗʰ after surmounting several steep and lofty ridges of forest we caught sight of the Dip only five miles from us, bearing west-southwest. We became a new set of men in a moment, and struggled hard to get out of the forest as quickly as possible, knowing now exactly the ground we had to go upon. We soon arrived upon the heathy hills surrounding Dipwood Marsh and when, within a mile of the spot where we left the men and horses, we fired a signal and as we walked briskly on, we had the satisfaction to hear a report in answer to it, which I was rejoiced at as we could not tell whether the men had not been murdered by natives during our nineteen days absence.

As we descended the last hill we were grieved to see two of the horses lying dead. The men came to meet us, glad at our return, having given up all hopes of it and were going to leave the place the next day and endeavour to find their way back to Circular Head. They said the horses had fallen off every day since they were brought here and one of them died six days after I left and the other one died the day before I returned—the third horse was nearly dead. I found the poor animal very weak and scarcely able to eat a piece of bread.

I had now an opportunity of putting on clean linen, which I had not been able to do for three weeks. On the 27ᵗʰ we quitted Dipwood Marsh for Circular Head. The country through which we had been travelling the last seven days from Surry Hills to Dipwood Marsh was much more difficult to get through than that by which we went to the Peak—the mountains being considerably higher and the ravines much steeper with bold, rocky sides and giddy precipices requiring the utmost caution not to descend too far to be enabled to reascend which we were often obliged to do and toil back again to find a more practical declivity along the mountain side often getting a considerable distance down which was very harassing and seemed often to render our return hopeless, having no provisions left during the four last days except a little flour of which we could only allow ourselves a pint a day stirred into hot water and we had only enough left for one more meal when we returned to the horses.

The timber I found chiefly to be myrtle, sassafras and stinkwood and on the mountains west of the Arthur I saw several pepper trees, large tracts are covered with closely matted scrub and cutting grass, fern trees and fern occupy the more open spaces under the dark spreading branches of the large forest trees. A great number of fine stringy barks are to be met with where the soil is dry but the principal part of this extensive country is as completely overshadowed with enormous myrtles as that through which I went to the Peak. A great proportion of the soil here is mixed with slate and rock but there are many cultivable tracts of great extent with a rich loam of considerable depth. Creeks and cascades are to be found in every gully up to the very summit of the mountains.

March 3rd seeing no boat coming we proceeded around the shore and in going along my attention was attracted by some curious appearances of metal among the rocks, where I broke off some grains resembling copper under a kind of old metal sheathing which covered great part of the rocks, and, in stagnant water near, I picked up shells dyed bluish and observed a greasy scrum upon the surface of the water. I am of opinion that there must be a large proportion of copper in it, and saved the best specimens I could procure. These rocks extend about two miles along the shore and considerably inland near Crawfish River.

March 4th reached Circular Head.

We saw no natives but several huts and marks of them; we picked up green boughs by the embers of their fires that had not been gathered two days.

We supposed they were not far off and might have used the boughs for mosquito fans.

Twenty miles from the sea we picked up the claws and shells of very large lobsters and crawfish, which they had roasted.

The only creatures inhabiting these large forest appeared to be opossums and bandicoots and I suppose Tigers or native dogs as they are called as we often heard the crackling of some heavy creature after dark (as we lay like mummies rolled up in blankets to keep off the mosquitoes by our fireside upon our bed of fern leaves, this the owls doleful cry of "more pork" and the screaming of opossums were the only disturbances we experienced during the night. Parrots &c

We also occasionally heard the trumpeter or black magpie and black cockatoos in large mobs, but they kept so much aloft we were only able to shoot one of them and one parrot during the whole journey.

(Sgd) Henry Hellyer.

P.S. "A store could not have been built at the farm ("Highfield") because of its inaccessibility until a road was made, which I daresay is not completed by this time, and the reason for not building it at the jetty was from the fear of its being plundered by privateers or runaway boats. When proper buildings are erected at the farm the present store will probably be converted to other purposes."

"Extract letter of Stephen Adey Esq"

"From a high cliff on the east side of Circular Head (consisting of a stupendous rock of granite whose area is upwards of 40 acres with good soil on the top) a somewhat level extent of country appeared to the eye to extend between the ranges of hills on each side about 20 or 30 miles south of the Bluff and on the S.W. I saw plainly with the glass some considerable tracts of clear ground 8 or 10 miles distant and just behind them a range of hills from which I thought it possible that a communication might be made with some heathy hills (but of a better description than those of Rocky Cape) which Frederick stated he had been on, and to lie from

15 to 20 miles in a South Easterly direction from Cape Grim. I therefore requested Mr Goldie to go with Frederick and Weaver to examine them. They started on the 1st July and returned on the 4th having found the clear ground to be a complete Marsh and up to their knees in water and without having succeeded in reaching the hill I pointed out.

A very interesting extract from a letter of Mr Alexander Goldie to E Curr Esq which exhibits the mode in which the Anglo Saxon civilization was imparted to the savages of Tasmania, who benighted in ignorance refused to participate in its blessings.

Emu Bay, 16th Sept '29.

"The day the "Fanny" last sailed from this (21st August) I was putting up a shed for the rams towards the barn, and when looking at the feed, I came upon a mob of natives. Seeing them on a point I returned to the men and determined to endeavour to take some of them. For this purpose I took my horse and the men, one gun and a couple of axes. On getting within 200 yards of them we were observed and they began to make off. I order the men to keep outside while I took the scrub. This had the effect and the Natives kept along the sands. Russel fired at one just as she was taking the scrub and shot her. She was very badly hit about the bottom and belly (!) and she must soon have died. I rode down another woman in the scrub and before I returned with her the men had killed the other. The woman that was shot had a child about 6 years old (a girl), which we also got. I saw other three, but whether there were any more, or any men among them I cannot say. The child is very thriving. They were both very much scabbed but I have nearly got them clean. The woman is in irons (!). I make her wash potatoes for the horses and intend taking her to the hills and making her work.

They eat nothing but potatoes, bread and shellfish. If I had that piece of lead ore perhaps we could discover where it is to be found but I daresay Mr Fossey can give the necessary information as Mrs Crabtree and Barras got some very fine on the Emu Plains or a little further to the southward.

The child is very lively and perfectly happy with a sharp intelligent eye. She begins to pick up a few English words, but the Woman will not speak and is often very sulky. She broke her irons once and was nearly getting away. I think she is about 20 or 22 years old.

I have no doubt she will work. Barras can make her do anything. She now bakes her own bread and with good <u>treatment (!!)</u> I think could be made to do anything."

(Sgd) Alex Goldie.

Curr, having read this letter, then reacted in an indignant and high-handed matter, as much it is thought in an endeavour to be rid of Goldie, as to be offended by such an outrage against the natives.

Alexander Goldie, Esq.

Highfield, Circular Head

30 Sep 1829.

It has never occurred to me since I have been in the service of the Van Diemen's Land Company to read a more revolting detail than that contained in your letter of 16 Sep; respecting the destruction of the Native Woman at Emu Bay on the 21st August and the manner in which the barbarous transaction is related without one word of disapprobation being expressed against your associates in the deed or one word of regret is scarcely less offensive to every feeling of humanity than the deed itself.

That the killing of the woman amounts to murder in a moral sense I have no doubt whatever, nor that you are a guilty accessory to the crime. What may be thought of it in a legal sense I do not know but it is my bounden duty to communicate to the Governor &c.

These sentiments arise solely from your own statement of the case.

(Sgd) Edward Curr

1st June 1828 A Goldie to E Curr

Burleigh (so named by Mr Fossey) is a part of the Surrey Hills lying about 2 miles south by east of the hummocks on a branch river running into the Seven, which we have called the Medway being midway between that river and the Blythe. The country is very open and it consists of dry rising hills clear of all under scrub (S.E. from Peak).

May-day-plains run along the bottom of May-day-mount. They are very extensive and excessively cold and wet. They extend to the S.W. range of the Black Bluff.

Vale of Belvoir in my opinion is both cold and bleak with coarse feed.

23rd June 1828 E. Curr to Directors

Burleigh is more lightly timbered than other parts of the Surrey Hills. The soil is light, rich, warm and dry and though from the irregularity of its surface it could not be considered an arable district, yet wherever the plough could be worked, it would produce abundant crops of any kind, which suited the climate. It is certainly a very beautiful district; nothing can be more pleasing than the banks of the rivers, which in one place spread into lightly wooded and almost level expanses of plain, and in another rise in bold hills not exceeding 200 feet in height and which in many parts are only accessible to sheep. The silver wattle grows in some parts of it.

17th October 1828 Henry Hellyer to E Curr

At Moory, Mount 3 miles E. of Mount Pearse

Which latter is the west end of a high ridge running nearly east to west and the dividing ridge of the race course is a continuation of the same line of country only much lower than that remarkable eminence. The Hellyer River rises from the north side of the ridge, the Medway from its east and I expect to find the Seven River receives much of its water from its south side. The soil of the racecourse plains is a rich loam upon a gravely or stony sub stratum. On the 16th, Mr Fossey and I came upon a native hut full of paintings, done by the natives representing men, emus, kangaroos etc. We came out on extensive plains, which I called "Painters Plains". Wattlebirds are plentiful on the racecourse plains and it is singular to remark that we saw a cormorant flying over them.

On the 1st November 1828, Hellyer reported to Curr as follows:

Painters Plains is a grassy tussocky flat with light soil and stony. Medway River runs northeast along the northwest end of the plains.

On October 20 we came to a curiously constructed native hut formed by placing bark against the two lower branches of a small tree—the centre aperture being its chimney.

We saw a deep ravine down which a vast accumulation of water, from the south side of that ridge of which Mount Pearse forms the western extremity, was pouring at a tremendous rate and loud roar. Descending from the open forest and the open plains and found them extending on both sides of this great southwest river (the grass is not thick).

We ascended to the level top of the first set of plains, which by way of distinction we called "Hatfield", after a race royal domain in Hertfordshire, now the seat of the Marquis of Salisbury. In a deep ravine ran a branch of the southwest river from Mount Pearce—Hatfield is between these two ravines.

"Netherly" is named after Sir James Graham's seat in Cumberland.

On 29th November 1828 at Emu Bay, Hellyer announced the discovery of the Macintosh River and the Eldon Range.

I have the honour to announce the return of the exploring party from their third journey—the particulars of which I take the earliest opportunity of reporting.

Having made arrangements before leaving Burleigh to enable the party to take a fourteen day's journey, I had determined to take a south-southwest course from that place leaving the mountains on our left and to go as far southward as the line of demarcation agreed to by Lord Bathurst and the governors of the company, after which it was my intention to have returned through the country to the south west of Mt Pearce, but that design was frustrated by a change of the weather after we had crossed the large rivers which obliged us to go to the east until we could re-cross these rivers, and we had to endure the most dreadful weather as well as the most laborious and dangerous travelling, and with great difficulty reached Burghley on the 17th day.

Seeing we could only keep the field eight or ten days unless heavier loads were carried we felt obliged in accomplishing this task to set the men the example by ourselves carrying enough for 14 days and ordered them to do the same, and having had one week's bread baked we left Burghley on Friday November 7th, each person's knapsack weighing about 55 lbs, which required no trifling exertion to endure.

We proceeded down the Burleigh Road about three miles and after getting beyond Firstock Hill, took a south-southwest course and travelled along an elevated ridge of open forest forming the west bank of the Seven River, which decidedly takes its rise from Mount Cripps. We walked several miles upon an excellent dry and healthy soil, producing the same kind of grass as the other part of the Surrey Hills and much intermixed with low gum bushes, we did not cross a rill exceeding 12 inches in breadth along the whole ridge since leaving Firstock Hill and there were springs: we at length gradually descended and crossed two strong creeks running Westward. We went on through open forest and soon after crossed a waterlogged marsh and observed in our left a Grass Tree Hill. We went on ahead to a rising open forest and the dogs having caught us two kangaroo, as we were all very tired and drenched with pouring rain, I had the tents pitched and large fires made to restore animation.

Saturday Nov 8th: We have had a shocking night of it and the ground is still covered with snow—wind south westerly—there was no cessation of the storm until about noon, and by that time the snow on the neighbouring ground had vanished. I walked with Mr Fossey to the top of the Grass Tree Hills to look round, from which we saw several distant ranges covered with snow and found that this Grass Tree Country forms the boundary of the grassy country in this direction. We saw some open plains to the northward (N.W.) about a mile from our camp, which we went to and examined. These plains rise from a low marsh on their south side and run about half a mile due north. They are much exposed to the south-westerly gales, the grass is tussocky the soil not bad. We had now such a heavy fall of hail and sleet that we could see nothing of the country. I therefore remained where we were.

<u>Sunday, Nov 9th:</u> This morning promises better weather, the sun is shining, and the clouds are of a light fleecy nature, the wind is south-westerly, generally the clearing quarter. Proceeded on our journey crossed the tract of open forest and entered a small open plain lately burnt by the natives, crossing which we went out upon an extensive tract of grass-tree country appearing to extend as far as May-day-mount. We crossed a creek running to the westward and from a south-southwest forming part of Cripps range and I hoped that a prospect from that Hill would afford us much information.

We descended and went down a grass tree plain nearly half a mile beyond which we entered a belt of Myrtle Forest and descended to a considerable River coming from the south east, shallow, but 30 yards wide (which for the sake of distinction I call the Allowell). We ascended a rough grassy and bushy hill and soon after finding the Allowell running to the south, we crossed it and went up a rough grassy hill same as last and down over a creek running to the Allowell.

Went over more Grass Tree Country, and descended to a fierce and deep creek also running to that river. We now came upon a better country, being grassy plains, extending from Allowell a good distance to the west, beyond which we crossed a track of open forest gradually becoming bushier with pepper tree and other shrubs. We then came out upon a grass tree valley in which ran a creek North West so beset with leeches that I named it Leech Creek, forded it on knots of spongy moss and rank silver sword grass and went up a grass tree rise.

We then entered a green forest with all its attributes and continued ascending for some hours much impeded by a dense <u>horizontal thicket</u> covering every creek and gully, several of which we crossed, and at length seeing no hope of getting out before dark, I halted for the night, determined to make the best shift we could as to firewood to dry our clothes, for although this has been a very fine day throughout, overhead yet the forest was very wet.

Monday, Nov. 10th: (Charter Day). The night has been dry and the morning seems fair. Soon after starting on in our course we arrived at the tip of a lofty forest ridge from which we saw grass tree and heathy plains below bearing south east by south. I considered it would be better to make for them, as they were not a mile off than continue in the dense green forest and began to descend for that purpose. We found it very difficult to get down from the steep ridge with safety; it was so slippery and dangerous. At last we alighted on the plains and found that they formed part of the range we were upon, which we now saw was partly open and heathy and partly covered with green forest, and seeing we had now the lofty eminence on our right which we had before us yesterday, I left two men to take care of the knapsacks, and with Mr Fossey, proceeded up the steep heathy mountains side, and after about an hour's difficult climbing we reached the summit from which I was happy to observe the snow had disappeared, except a few patches on the highest mountain tops.

We saw extensive open plains south by west between two ranges of secondary mountains, and beyond them a mountain which from its size and situation can be no other than the Mt Heemskirk upon the chart–seeing nothing equal to it in point of height or magnitude to the west of it, and I concluded that it is placed on the chart several miles too near the west coast as we could see two distinct lower ranges westward of it. We could see nothing of the northwest for the forests, which cover that portion of this mountain we were upon.

We returned to the knapsacks, and as the day was far-gone went on along the heathy country until we found a place to stop at, which we could get some firewood.

This has been a delightful day: the large flies and mosquitoes were very numerous in the evening. I have named this place "Charter Mount" in commemoration of the day.

Tuesday Nov 9th: A fine morning at Charter Mount, dense fog in the valley below, but it soon cleared up.

Went along the heathy and grass tree range having on our left a wide gully clothed with green forest and crowned by woody and heathy ranges on each side, in which we heard a roaring river. Our course was now south south-west, intending toward going off the range into the gully until we were obliged, which soon occurred, for we came to a gully side opening from the north and descended it south south-west through a very steep green forest, and at length came to a wide creek running to the left, pursued our way over a green forest ridge, descended and crossed another similar creek after which ascended a very steep mountainside in the hope of regaining the open and heathy top of the range which occupied us several hours.

At length we came out upon some lookout rocks surrounded by honeysuckles, mountain tree and various shrubs and soon reached the top, which I call "Mount Block" from the enormous rock which crowns the summit. The rock is of a coarse reddish kind veined with quartz. Mt Block afforded us an extensive prospect commanding all the great features of the surrounding country, particularly the gullies and rivers and it seemed very doubtful then whether we should be able to explore much further to the south unless the rivers were down. The next difficulty was to get down from the nearby perpendicular eminence for there was no more heathy top. Mr Fossey had a bad fall and broke his bottle of brandy in slipping down the rocks. We at length found a spur jutting out a little from the cliff down which we carefully lowered ourselves for some distance. One of the men then climbed a tree and called out–"The Big River is right under: the plains look like good grass. We may get to the river tonight. The peppermint and tea-tree run a long way down".

We continued descending with the utmost caution, sliding down rock and steep places very bare of vegetation of any kind to hold on by as the trees or shrubs grew only in fissures of the rock at wide intervals. We all eventually arrived safe at the north bank of a noble river larger than the Mersey at Gads Hill and very deep and subject to rise 20 feet above its present surface as we were informed by the driftwood lodged on its banks. The dogs caught a porcupine close by the river, which we killed and found to be as tender as a young pig.

McKay tried to catch a fish but the current was too strong–the river's course here was from northeast to southwest. To distinguish this from other rivers, I call it the "Mackintosh" after the eminent statesman of that name.

<u>Wednesday, Nov. 12th:</u> A dry warm night and hopes of a fine day. I determined to follow the Mackintosh to the south, which we found very difficult to accomplish from its ravine being composed of a succession of gullies and rivulets of various sizes and a dense gum forest to labour through. The ground everywhere sloping hideously.

We were obliged to rest many times with our loads, and by degrees we left the river further on our left by which we headed many of the gullies, which would have come in our way. Our course here was nearly south southwest. We hoped we had got over many difficulties by keeping so high, but all at once we came to such a dreadful chasm that we wished we had kept lower down. We were obliged to descend from tree to tree nearly perpendicularly for at least one thousand feet and at last got safe down when we crossed a rapid roaring creek which I doubt not had in the course of time torn out the whole of this chasm or chine from the level of its issuing from the mountains.

As I crossed it I looked up at the opposite side, which we had to ascend and seeing the trees growing out of its side affixed to a wall, I thought some of us might revisit the creek before we wished to do so–it was awful. The poor dogs had no chance of getting up. They fell backwards as fast as they attempted it. Our only chance was by helping or rather fishing each other firm one root to another. The dogs at last scrambled up. We found it less steep after we had surmounted the first hundred yards.

We were now after incredible fatigue only two miles from our last night's halting place–we rested a while on the top and proceeded south-southwest. Went through a continuation of green forest–with here and there a Stringybark tree and a wattle. We had observed that the river had turned away to the south on ascending a hill covered with wire weed ten feet high which exhausted the men quickly; after which we entered a forest of Stringybark and dry fern, intermixed with scrub and saw on our right an open heathy country below and in half an hour came out upon open plains of heath and grass tree.

We saw a curiously shaped hill somewhat like a venerable old castle (the north end of Eldon Range) bearing south by west and plains between us and it. We went on towards those plains and soon saw more extensive plains to the left, which had been burnt—this I concluded was the beginning of the open country seen from Charter Mount. We went on wading through the heath and grass-tree until our progress was suddenly stopped by the Mackintosh which here bent its course from east south-east to south-west. We descended to the water's edge and looked up and down. A cormorant flew up the river and as it passed along it seemed alarmed at seeing us there. This bird had no doubt flown up from the sea coast—and accounts for our having seen one before at the Race Course, which had probably flown up the other branch, which I call the "Huskisson". We heard the roaring of a rapid about 300 yards further up, went there and saw it was occasioned by vast heaps of boulders impeding the river's course between which the water rushed with great fury.

Cutts and Walker went on as far as the top of the rapid and saw a tolerably even ford and not too deep—they took a stout pole each and got over and held a long pole for us to take hold of and we all got safe over—the water was dreadfully chilling and in one place very deep and dangerous. We never found a little brandy of more service. We had now to cross a breakout and sand heaps, after which we reached the southern shore and having ascended to the plains, the dogs caught us a kangaroo and seeing a back log on a dry spot we camped for the night.

The Mackintosh is now at low ebb, which enabled us to get over it and I hope it may continue so, or how shall we re-cross such a current. We have had several dry days and the morn looks well tonight. The plains are heath and a fine sort of grass tree, not growing in tussocks, which the natives have burnt. They would I thought hardly come to burn a small patch, and I expected certainly to find a portion of good country not far off.

<u>Thursday, Nov. 13th:</u> Wet morning—wind south westerly and very thick in that quarter. Went on nearly south up the open country and found it all of the same kind to the north of a forest below us—soil poor and sandy with

pieces of milky quartz lying on its surface where our further progress was stopped by another tremendous river nearly as wide as the Mackintosh and very deep. Its course was from south-east and it seemed now at a low ebb, having a wide sloping bank now dry over which its waters flow and as we proceeded along in an uncertain mood whether it would be desirable to cross this large river or not and increase our obstacles, we espied an enormous trunk of a tree lying directly across having in its fall rested exactly in a rock under the water and although great part of the upper side of the tree was under the water and the current was pouring over it at a great rate Cutts thought it practicable for us all to get across by crawling upon our hands and knees along the tree and having got safe over we all followed, but the danger was much increased by the time the last person had to get over as the river had risen more than six inches during the time.

This is the widest river I ever crossed on a tree, being upwards of 50 yards. The weather was now squally with a heavy fall of hail. We ascended from the river and found on the open heathy plain beyond the Waratah or bush tulip in full bloom which is an evidence of its being a more favoured climate than some parts of the Surry Hills for those trees about Burghley are only now in bud. I call this large river "The Brougham". It joins the Mackintosh a few miles lower down and they must together form a very large rive and we thought ourselves fortunate in having encountered them singly. We had now arrived at the foot of a long heathy range which ran nearly in our course and expecting to obtain much information by ascending it, we did so with some difficulty and from the summit observed that the plains (which I have since named "Cranbourne Chase"–extend about eight miles in length nearly in a north and south direction and in some parts upwards of two miles in width. The river Brougham crosses the chase obliquely from southeast to northwest belted by forest the whole distance–a mixture of the green and brown.

The Chase has a cultivated and diversified appearance from its having been lately burnt in several extensive tracts looking fresh and green in those places and in others so completely covered with blooming heath that it resembled vast fields of clover divided by rows of shrub serpentine every brook which intersected it from the mountain ranges on either side. I felt much disappointed that it was not a country at all desirable for the

Company's purposes and the more so on looking over the Range I was upon (which I call Eldon Range) for I could discover nothing westward but heathy plains and lofty woody ranges beyond which limited my view to about four miles and not a spot of burnt ground. Then I proceeded for some miles nearly south along the top of Eldon Range, which is a lofty herbed wedge of heathy and hilly country, as my object next was to get upon its loftiest dome to extend our prospect.

We did so after much trouble and exertion and from it saw the "South West Hill" which is a high woody ridge insulated and far in advance of the ranges near the west coast first observed by me from Mt Pearse and bearing from thence south west but we could not see what kind of country there was about that Hill as we were still too little elevated to see over the near woody ranges to the north west.

We also saw the intersection of the two great gullies forming what is called the Paperman's River or more intelligibly the junction of the Huskisson and Mackintosh and that there is much open and apparently heathy country on both sides of the Mackintosh lower down.

We saw May-day Plains and the Vale of Belvoir–the Cradle Mountain was eclipsed by a loftier range in the foreground, but we saw the Barn Bluff bearing east by south, and little thought at that time that we should be obliged to pay it a visit. The air was very keen here and we were assailed with violent squalls of hail and sleet and being all nearly exhausted by fatigue and very wet and cold, we returned to the shelter of some rocks where we saw some dead trees to make a fire and remained upon Eldon Range all night.

Having now arrived within a few miles of Mt Heemskirk which I knew would command all the country round, if it should be possible for us to ascend it, I determined to see how far we could go, and if possible to get upon the top of that grand eminence that one might obtain all the information we possibly could to the south west of Mt Pearse.

Friday, Nov 14: Very little sleep last night for cold, which such a fire as we could obtain on the top of a mountain could not obviate. We went along Eldon Range nearly south and turned south southwest over the top between several hillocks forming a basin in which there is a lake about a quarter mile in diameter with an outlet to the south forming a cascade down the southern end of Eldon Range. This mountain range is composed of puddingstone rock, in which there are large round red and white pebbles cemented together in huge masses and in general covered with a kind of white clay, producing dwarf heath, mountain tea tree and rushy grass and of so tenacious a quality that in many places are fountains playing in the air in streams half an inch in diameter.

Having arrived at the south end of the summit of Eldon Range we discovered a tremendous gully with another large river, which we readily traced to its junction with the Mackintosh; Mt Heemskirk rose on the opposite side of the gully, traversing far above the other mountains surrounding it and was clouded halfway down, seeing which, and as it now rained and the wind being from the north west (the worst quarter) I feared even if we should be able to get upon it, that it would be some days before it would be free from cloud.

We observed large flights of white cockatoos below and considered it an indication of there being an open country not far off. The great river below was completely open to our view coming from south east passing through a great gateway formed by its having decidedly cut a passage by lopping off Mt Eldon from Mount Heemskirk which the perpendicular rocky chasm bears evidence of, and leaving the south end of Mt Eldon it enters a district of low heathy hills winding round them first in a south west and then in a north west direction until it joins the Mackintosh. This river I call "Canning".

The only route we could take to reach Mt Hemmskirk was southwest as being most free from precipices as we could judge. We descended in that direction very many heathy slopes, all-running with water rendering our travelling very dangerous. The rain now falling in torrents and in two hours we got down so near to the River that we could see there was no chance of our getting any farther, having arrived at a rocky precipice far above the water which seemed deep enough to flat of 74 and at least 60 yards over and could see nothing but perpendicular rocky cliffs on the other side.

We could go no further on, not one step, for there were precipices both east and west as well as south. Another considerable river entered the Canning to the westward of us. The Canning was roaring and foaming along in a terrific manner and our only chance of getting across seemed to be to go up and descend more to the westward but as this was our eighth day I did not think I ought to risk another day, particularly as we had no hope of getting back except by heading the two large rivers we had already crossed having had nothing but heavy rain ever since. I therefore returned again up to the Lake on Mt Eldon, a hurricane with a deluge of rain pursuing us all the way.

We were often obliged to rest with our loads before we could regain the top and dreading another such a night as the last I went directly down east into Cranbourne Chase although we were so dreadfully wet and fatigued we would willingly have remained among the scrubby peppermint trees by the lake. We were more than an hour descending the open heathy range although we went down at a great rate, not being able to avoid sliding many yards at a time, and having alighted on the Chase we pushed across through heath and grass tree partly burnt, and partly water-logged to a forest of tall peppermint trees where we hoped to find some firewood, wading several creeks more than knee deep.

We at last entered a shrubbery of tea trees when we pitched our tents. The dogs soon caught us three remarkably fine kangaroo on the burnt ground close by and the men declared on dissecting them that they had never seen any so fat before, which circumstance leads me to think that there is something peculiar in this spot which causes the kangaroo to become so fat and that the natives burn it knowing its good qualities. I therefore named it Cranbourne Chase or the Natives' preserve.

What I call heath includes in this place a great variety of plants and I observed along Eldon Range that there is an abundance of fragrant heaths some of them nearly resembling the wild thyme which sheep are so fond of upon the South Downs in England and a kind of coarse grass and there is no doubt that such herbage adds much to the fattening of kangaroo met with in the part of the country.

It is possible that the natives by only burning one set of the Plains are enabled to keep the kangaroo more concentrated for their use and I can in no other way account for their burning only this place unless it is to serve them as a halting place on migrating from the coast to the interior a question which a view from Mt Heemskirk might have solved.

Saturday, Nov 15th: It has blown a hurricane all night from northward, poured with rain to such a degree that we expected every instant to have been swamped. How we are to recross the rivers now it is impossible to imagine, but here are plenty of kangaroo if we shall be obliged to return. I cut on a large peppermint the "Cranbourne Chase 1828" and having packed up some of the kangaroo we proceeded eastward to see if we could cross the Brougham.

We waded through an extensive swamp of tea tree and cutting grass and crossed a break out more than bank high on a fallen tree. We were thus insulated and traversing a gum forest actually inundated in many places and everywhere streaming with the overflowing of the river, so that we were bewildered to know where the river was, and obliged to feel our way along crossing multitudes of streams of various depths and at last we came to an open place where the water is as knee deep. Round the trees were we stood and beyond (where void of trees) it was running at a dangerous rate.

The men stood deep in the running stream and resolutely felled a large tree with their tomahawks, but it fell short, seeing which and being heartily tired of our present critical situation and the uncertainty that it was the river after all, and that we might have only landed upon another island in a state of inundation, I told the men I would return if possible to where we had been the night before, which, after much sousing we all managed to do but in a dreadful pickle having found it much worse returning than going to the river.

A pole 20 feet in length did not touch the bottom where the men were felling the tree. It was perhaps a fortunate circumstance that the tree did not answer for us to get across, as we could see another run of water beyond which we might not have been able to get over.

This was a shocking day for any unfortunate creature to be out in, nothing but violent gusts of wind with hail and rain. The dogs soon replenished our camp with kangaroo. My bread, which I had baked at Burghley (11 lbs) lasted till today but had become mouldy. The men employed themselves baking half a dozen thin cakes or dampers upon bark for each person before the fire, as the ground did not admit of baking in it being so wet.

Sunday, Nov. 16th: Distressing weather. It has rained nearly all night and we have no hope of getting away from here unless we follow the mountain ranges until we can head the Brougham. We have actually passed the night ankle deep in water and our retreat would have soon been cut off, for had it continued to rain so heavily we could not have gone to the mountains at all.

It is wonderful we are able to exist in such a plight. We got on our legs, every joint feeling stiff, hands cut, scratched and sore, clothes torn to rags, wet and cold and on we go with our loads. We struck the tents, wrung them out, and started in the pouring rain for the foot of Mt Eldon at the south west end of the Chase walking for the most part across a nearly level plain of heath and grass tree with many creeks overflowing their banks, and when near the mountain, we crossed a torrent which descended with a noise like thunder down the rocky channel it had formed.

We then entered a scrambling scrub of running privet through which we struggled and waded knee deep in water for some distance and came to a tract of gum forest when we heard a roar of water proceeding down a gully, which we had observed from the Chase. We crossed it on a tree and found it a large branch of the Brougham. Here the dogs found a dead wombat–probably killed and partly devoured by a hyena.

We gathered the Waratah, upon a little plain beyond, in full bloom and upon a slender shrub 20 feet in height we saw some exquisitely beautiful yellow flowers–something like wallflowers, soon after which we began to ascend the side of a gully south east, toiling up a very steep gum forest in which are a few large stringy bark trees. A heavy storm of hail as we went on forcing our way upward through a dense thicket beset with wireweed upon a kind of white and yellow clay with a surface streaming with water as slippery as grass under our feet. We at length gained the summit of the range and rested on an enormous mass of pudding stone and it is worthy of remark that the rock felt quite warm and reeked with the moisture of the last shower, a decided proof that the earth is warmer than the atmosphere.

On looking over this hill, eastward we saw a much higher eminence, heathy and rocky which we supposed to be part of the same range, and endeavoured to reach it, but were soon aware of the impossibility for on descending to get nearer to it we saw one of the most outrageous torrents we had ever beheld at the bottom of a deep and nearly perpendicular gully, which it had formed in the solid rock. Its noise was deafening and its whole surface in such a perfect foam that it resembled a River of Cream.

We could only wonder and avoid going too near this terrible fellow which we knew could be no other than the great Brougham but seeing a clear road to the southward we went along the heathy mountains range, in nearly a south easterly direction, crossing many considerable torrents—branches of that river and hoped thus to reduce it to a more manageable size.

As we proceeded we discovered an open heathy country between the mountains lying north east which it would be desirable for us to get to, and after several hours travelling along the range, we came to a gully with a loud torrent in it and the day being far gone we halted and were enabled to make a good fire, finding plenty of celery topped pine but the ground sloped at an angle of 50 degrees and we were obliged to sit up all night there being no wood elsewhere.

We had walked the last hour in despair of finding any place to stop at where there was either wood or shelter.

Monday, Nov. 17: Much rain in the night and still continuing. Descended the gully, crossed a violent 20 feet creek knee deep and went up through a dense scrambling scrub and over a heathy slope which conducted us to the Brougham running here north west. We walked by it some distance up, till seeing a rocky bottom where it was not too deep we ventured in and luckily got over safely. The current was quite as much as we could bear up again with every precaution and between 30 and 40 yards wide.

We missed all the dogs here and they did not come after us with all the shouting the men could make until we had left the river an hour.

We came away due north and pursued the lay of the open heathy country northeast. We crossed several large streams between the heathy hills, which we could easily trace from the waterfalls with which the mountainsides are adorned. The dogs chased several kangaroo here but they were too fleet and dogs have not so much chance upon hard as upon soft ground where the kangaroo's feet sink in. The heathy country appears to be desirable for the natives as it affords them kangaroo, wombats and opossums, and it appears to have been burnt by them some time ago, of which the numerous dead stumps now standing in the gullies bear ample testimony. The soil is light and sandy with small bits of quartz bestrewing the whole of its surface so completely that to convince ourselves that it was not hailstones undissolved, we were obliged to catch up some and examine it, whence the name, which it has received of "Hailstone Heath".

There are large rocks scattered about, the size of houses which are of so friable a nature that the action of the weather has rendered the exterior of them as round and smooth as if they had been worked by a mason. Their appearance quite enlivens the descent, they assume such a variety of shapes, and resembling ornamental buildings and little shrubberies in general surround them. These rocks are of a slattern texture and composed of quartz and hornblend.

We now saw before us that a lofty ridge (running apparently from north to south) must be surmounted and could observe that its summit was rocky, and was partially covered with snow. We went on as far as a sheltering peppermint forest at the foot of the mountain at the east end of Hailstone Heath, where we arrived after crossing two deep creeks up to our elbows and being all very tired and wet and having had no sleep the previous night I halted and fell asleep (wet as I was) with sheer fatigue.

This afternoon was finer than the weather had been for several days and the sunset was magnificent directly at the back of Mt Heemskirk which it exhibited with a grand effect, every spire of its rifted rocky sides, its rugged gullies filled with snow and the numerous knobs and domes crowning its summit were all displayed to our view and there was not a cloud to be seen which seemed an earnest of better weather.

Tuesday, Nov 18th: Squally morning with snow and sleet, wind west. Went up the hill about north east passing by some huge domes of white rock as before described after which we left the heathy country and went through a forest of peppermint arriving which we found immense plant resembling Pine Apple Trees (such as seen in hot houses in England) require only a long trunk to make them like these curious trees which are upwards of 20 feet in height and having these long stems or trunks they are enabled to obtain air and light by protruding between the branches of other trees along the hillside.

These stems are not naked but retain the last year's leaves, which gives the plant altogether a grand appearance but it occasioned us much trouble to get along, as their edges cut like a knife or saw. They seem very hardy and if they are real pineapples, they would require very little trouble in their cultivation. We cut off some large leaves and brought them away. We ascended to the top of part of the lofty ridge and had some observations of the country we had left including Mt Heemskirk and two lofty peaks east of that mountain which I have named after the Princesses Victoria and Sophia. Descended, crossed a gully and ascended to the snowy top where we experienced a cutting storm of snow and sleet, during which the dogs caught a kangaroo and we stood up to our knees in snow while it was skinned and cup up and Mr Fossey and myself carried on portions of it, having but little pork left. The snow now fell so thick all round that we could see nothing whatever and were completely puzzled which way to go, or what to do as we had arrived at the edge of a tremendous gully many miles in width.

We wandered about in the snow storm with a great deal of labour and looked over northward and then southward as the storm would permit and saw nothing but precipices and gullies every way. At length the clouds began to disperse and we thought that the great gully might be avoided and that we could head it by going to the southeast. McKay led the way and we went on at as quick a pace as we could to keep ourselves warm as well as to endeavour to get out of such a perishing part of the country and comforted ourselves with the idea that we had rounded one portion of the formidable gully, but were soon as much at a loss as before.

The weather again became so thick that we did not know which way to go, and at last retreated into another gully to the south east where finding some scrubby gums we halted and collected together all the firewood we could procure to keep us alive through the night, which was as miserable a one as ever we experienced.

Wednesday, Nov 19: It has snowed all night and so much has fallen that we are completely hemmed in by it. Our fire was kept in with difficulty. All the trees are bending with their loads of snow and all the tea trees and other shrubs through which we must push our way are covered or buried with snow and resemble one solid body higher than our heads. It still appears very black and horrible to windward. Heavy masses are continually falling about us, blown from the mountains top.

We had snow melted for breakfast, which having warmed us a little, for no more firewood could be got at, we pushed our way through and descended to a strong creek running to the north and having crossed it had a most difficult job to climb up a steep rocky hill in the deep snow nearly east to regain the top of the tier and avoid the gullies, where we found snow three feet deep and as we laboured through it were overtaken by a cutting storm of sharp sleet which obliged us to retreat over a precipice and take shelter among some rocks, whence, when the storm had blown over a little, we saw Mt Block and Mt Charter, and I knew by the bearing that the terrible gully which obstructed us, was the same that we had seen from Mt Block running towards the Barn Bluff.

We hoped to avoid crossing this vast ravine by going more to the south east which we did, and rounded several minor gullies but the weather again became so thick that we could do nothing till about one o'clock when we had arrived as we supposed near its upper end. The snow storm somewhat abating we saw we were in a worse predicament than ever and that we were cut off entirely in consequence of our having to travel completely round to the east of the Barn Bluff to avoid the gully and that ravine seemed to be there more perpendicular than even where we were, but this was no place to stand still in even for more than one moment's consideration for the storm now came on with more violence that ever and completely doubled us up, as we were now standing half buried in the snow.

It cut our faces and hands to pieces and when we attempted to retreat, we found the snow had filled up all the marks of our approach. A partial gleam of sunshine having thawed the surface of the snow it had since frozen and we had been labouring in it like walking upon pie crust which broke at every step and let us in up to the middle, the edges of which cut the men's legs like glass, particularly McKay who broke the way for the party, seeing which I endeavoured too, but the snow formed in such hard lumps under my overalls which were forced up to my knees that I was completely fettered by it and in the greatest pain imaginable. One hour's exposure in this weather would kill any man if he stuck fast and remained inactive.

The poor dogs were regularly plated with coats of mail formed by ice at the extremity of the hair but they travelled better than we could, as the ice would support them. Our faces were swollen and smarted excessively. Our hands and feet benumbed. Now we had no alternative–retreat into the gully or perish and we made for the horrid ravine as our only refuge. We began to descend its almost perpendicular sides, finding great support from the ice bound snow as we went down from the ice bound snow, amidst jagged and slippery rocks, from which were hanging vast "icicles" like inverted obelisks as large in diameter as the trunks of trees, a proof that the frost is exceedingly severe in these elevated regions.

It took us four hours to descend this grand valley, hurrying as fast as we could and finding the great Mackintosh at the bottom was fordable we gladly forded it, fearing the melted snow and rain might prevent us in the morning. The dogs caught a wombat and we found some grass tree patches and dead timber where we had a good fire.

Thursday, Nov. 20th: Rain all night–very little hope of getting to Burghley for four or five days. This our fourteenth out–only a little flour and tea left. Mackintosh was now swollen and unfordable. Eyes swollen and scarcely able to see, faces felt as if scalded. Went up side of valley about north across some grass tree patches. Turned to northeast up a likely open clothed with mountain tea tree and tolerably good travelling. After ascending three hours we rested. We did not seem to be half way up. We saw nothing before us but perpendicular rocky cliffs and were obliged to fall a tree to get over it &c. We then ascended through stunted tea tree and grass tree and arrived at the snowy region once more, where we found it dangerous travelling from the masses of half thawed snow giving way under our feet as we crawled over the rocks.

Seeing we could head another gully by deploying to the right, we did so, and came northward across the top of the ridge deep in snow to the brink of another horrid precipice, where we halted a few minutes hoping the clouds would disperse and allow us to see what was before us, but that not being the case I determined to persevere to the north. We were obliged to turn to the right and ultimately got down to a gully in the gully where we found some black butted gums and halted for the night by the side of a noisy torrent which ran west, north-west where we had a wretched night.

It now became a serious question we should extricate ourselves at all, and determined to start very early tomorrow and have a long day before us.

Friday, Nov. 21st: Thick drizzling rain from west. Crossed creek and went north over a ridge covered with scrambling scrub. Descended sliding down places nearly perpendicular amidst mountain tea tree and came down to a torrent that made us stare. Its fury was beyond anything we could conceive of water. It had however luckily brought down two large trunks of trees which crossed each other nearly at right-angles and on them we crossed, amidst a roar which nearly deprived us of the sense of hearing. It was some time before the dogs would follow.

We went up a very difficult mountainside, often being obliged to climb rock in the face of a cascade as the whole was streaming with water. Abundance of luxuriantly growing pineapple trees. After much toil we began to fear the perpendicular cliffs of slate above us would oblige us to go back. We found a passage though rugged and dangerous and reached the top of this vast mountain where the fog was so thick that we could see nothing but the snow that we laboured through.

I was determined to keep the ridge as long as possible in the hope that the weather would clear and let us see our way. It did so sufficiently to discover that we could travel northeast along the ridge and we plunged along in that direction. At length the clouds began to disperse and we were delighted at seeing a grassy valley of great extent directly before us, something like the Vale of Belvoir, &c, &c.

We felt we were in the land of the living once more and could get kangaroo and made a direct line for the valley–sliding down the snow with great alacrity and after descending two miles we seemed to have arrived in another climate, warm and sheltered compared with where we had been the last four days. In fact, it was an escape from a snowy prison. I had never seen so much snow in my life. We found a halting place–dead timber, tried to get a kangaroo but dogs so hungry they helped themselves and refused to show. We therefore had some flour and water and as the evening was clear I hoped to obtain a view, which would tell us where we were &c &c.

I ascended a rocky ridge and was delighted to find that we had arrived at the north side of the Cradle Mountain and saw the lake, which Mr Fossey had described as an opening between the hills to the north leading to Middlesex Plains. In the eve we had plenty of kangaroo. Cradle Valley extends from west-southwest to east-northeast about six miles and is about a mile in width. It appears a wet place and the grass appears in general of the rushy kind, but intermixed with bladed grass in several parts. I understand from Mr F. that Hounslow Heath is a similar country and of vast extent and that it would form a great addition to Middlesex Plains as a summer run. There is much pencil pine of a large size in Cradle Valley and the neighbouring ravines.

Saturday, Nov 23rd: A fine clear morning–little wind from north and quite sultry (?). Left Cradle Valley, proceeding through an open forest by the side of the river, which is running to the north from the Lake below the Cradle. All stiff and sore–faces, legs and hands still swollen and all obliged to rest often.

We had good travelling across Middlesex Plains, stopped and had some kangaroo roasted on the ramrods in the Vale of Belvoir and with great exertion reached the May-day Plains and halted for the night.

<u>Sunday, Nov. 23rd:</u> Left May-day Plains soon after sunrise and arrived at Burghley all very hungry and fatigued, where we obtained the food and rest which we all stood so much in need of.

It has been a mortifying circumstance that we should have had no clear weather, while toiling over some of the highest mountains in the country, to enable us to see what the distant country was. We have yet a large field to explore between the Huskisson and the Mackintosh and to the north of the Huskisson.

(Sgd. Henry Hellyer)

Note: The latter part of this copy of Mr. Hellyer's report is much abbreviated in the original text, but has been expanded for this transcription.

CHAPTER 4

COMPANY OPERATIONS–FISCAL REPORTS & MANAGERS

Before analysing in some detail the Curr management style, let us get an overview of the Company managers, assistants and other associates found in the early VDL Company.

a. *Edward Curr* first arrived in VDL in 1819 as the partner of John Raine, a London merchant, but he had failed in his selection of a suitable partner and thus, in business. Raine single-handedly lost all his assets and his personal business. In 1822, Curr returned to London and wrote, *"An Account of the colony of Van Diemen's Land, 'principally designed for emigrants'"* on the trip home (it was published in 1824). In London, an investor group (promoters) had assembled into a syndicate named The VDL Coy. William Sorell (the Lt Gov. of VDL colony had returned from Hobart to London in May 1824 and told the Colonial Office of the desperate need for capital in VDL. Curr was introduced to the investor group and was later appointed chief agent at an annual salary of 800 pound. He won Bathurst's support in April 1825 for the VDL Act (6 Geo IV, c. 39), and the granting of its charter. The act simply described the land, as "250,000 acres in the form of a square in the north-west of the colony", and so Curr's first job was to select suitable land for agriculture. Curr arrived in Hobart 1826 and was to be followed on the next boat with livestock, implements, emigrant labourers and some livestock.

Curr hastened north with his assistants and surveyors to locate suitable land. The governor (Sorrel's successor–Lt-Gov Arthur) had been instructed to work with Curr while the boundaries were surveyed and then issue an occupancy license. Curr decided to seek separate land grants because of the nature of the land and the apparent inability to obtain one suitable block. The controversy over selection of land continued until 1830, when the company received six parcels amounting to 350,000 acres. Curr believed he had selected ideal land, but he soon realised that the most of the land was unsuitable for sheep grazing. Curr agreed to pay the required £10,000 for the land, and urged his directors to seek another grant in Port Phillip. Curr lost all of his flock in 1834 due to cold, disease and wild animals. By 1839 the government was concerned about the inactivity by the company and the lack of investment, Curr had moved his family to Circular head in 1827, where he built (at company expense) the distinguished homestead named '*Highfield*'.

Curr did manage to clear land, dig wells and build fences, huts and other buildings, on the granted land, but failed to take the opportunities presented in structuring a medium-term business policy and showing financial responsibility to the stockholders of the company. When Curr sailed to England in 1833, the company directors decided to abandon large-scale sheep rearing, reduce expenditures at each property and institute a tenant scheme to provide the company with rents and a market for stud stocks.

Curr returned to the colony in 1834 and concentrated somewhat successfully on the sale of livestock–Durham cattle, Suffolk Punch (sheep) and Clydesdale horses. The tenant scheme finally got underway in 1840 with small numbers arriving in 1842.

Acrimonious disputes between Curr and the colonial government, and slow progress overall caused dissatisfaction amongst and between the London board members, until Curr was given a year's notice to quit as Manager in 1839. James Gibson arrived in Circular Head in 1841 and Curr moved himself and family to Melbourne. His 17 years working on behalf of the VDL company, were generally unappreciated by the board of Directors and left the company in financial ruin. His successor, Gibson, another Englishman untrained in colonial farming and inexperienced in operating a large disburse group of socio-agriculture activities, fared little better than Curr and recommended to the Board the company's liquidation in 1850.

b. _John Ingle_ had arrived in VDL in 1804. An individual, wealthy from speculation in land, offered his opinion at investor meetings in London at the time of the VDL Company formation, that investment in 'the VDL Coy should be highly regarded'. He became the first 'Governor' (Chairman) of the Court of the VDL Company.

c. _Henry **Hellyer**_ arrived in Hobart in 1826 as architect and surveyor of VDL coy properties. When Curr decided to relocate the Company headquarters to Circular Head (from Burnie/Emu Bay) in 1826, Hellyer commenced some exploration in the northwest, especially St. Valentine's peak, which had first been observed and commented on by Flinders. This discovery by Hellyer was a decisive one for the company because Hellyer also wrote of the 'extensive, open and desirable company'. This news had elated Curr and he decided to select land in this vicinity but later Curr opined that Hellyer 'saw everything with a painter's eye but with an affliction which is blind to all faults', However, Hellyer agreed to survey the land selected by Curr in 1828. Due to his sensitive nature, he suicided in 1832. The Hellyer exploration reports have never previously been presented in full and are included in this text, within the Exploration Chapter, so the reader can gauge for himself or herself the accuracy of Curr's opinion.

d. _Alexander Goldie_ was appointed agriculturalist to the VDL Coy in 1826 at a salary of 200 pound and with the support of Lord Bathurst. Goldie lost control of convict workmen at Circular Head in December 1826, and requested a military detachment. Goldie was demoted for this over-reaction and placed in charge of VDL Company farm and stock departments at Hampshire and Surrey Hills. He resigned at the end of 1829.

e. The company engaged _Stephen Adey_ in 1826 as superintendent of stock and farms. Adey remained in Hobart whilst Curr went with his surveyors to Circular head. Adey resigned after only two years in the colony

f. _Joseph Fossey_, a surveyor, was appointed assistant-surveyor to Henry Hellyer, in England in 1825 at a salary of 100 pounds. Fossey and

Goldie were based in Launceston and took a rowboat to Cape Grim and then explored the region by walking south. Fossey later developed this track (to become known as the *Great Western Road*) between Cape Grim (Woolnorth) and Circular Head, and for his work received a grant of 2,000 acres. He resigned in 1830.

g.   *James Gibson* arrived with his parents and brother in Tasmania in 1832. His father died in 1839 and James returned to London where the directors of VDL Company appointed him their agent and manager in VDL because of his experience and education. He returned to Circular Head in 1841. He took over from Curr in 1842, with strict orders to economise. He secured a government survey and 300 convicts from Franklin. The convicts were organised into three probation gangs, two paid by the government, and directed to build roads connecting the Company's scattered properties with the settled districts. He sought (and obtained) the proclamation of a port–Burnie, at Emu Bay–together with its survey. From the proceeds of the sale of lots, he spent 3,000 pound on churches and schools, and establishing about 60 tenant farmers, with promises their produce would be bought by the company at fixed prices for seven years. He was terminated as Manager in 1852.

h.   *James William Norton Smith* was appointed manager of VDL coy in 1869(following Gibson's termination), after similar work in New Zealand. He found the Company depressed and encouraged active participation with Tasmanian agencies and joint development. He supported exploration and as a result the major tin discovery at Mount Bischoff was discovered, even though it was just outside the Company's boundaries. As a result of this discovery, outside the company's lands, Norton Smith built the 44-mile rail link between Waratah and Emu Bay, as a means of participating in this rich mining venture. This move also assisted in revitalising the company. During the rural depression of the early 1870s. Norton Smith became manager of the 100,000 acre Woolnorth property. The property had begun as the 350,000 acre land grant in 1826, but from sales to tenant farmers, it had been reduced to only 100,000 acres. Norton Smith recommended the floating of the Emu bay & Mount Bischoff Railway Co Ltd in 1900. He resigned (following a dispute with his directors) in

1903, at which time; Andrew McGaw (see below) was appointed manager.

George Arthur became the nemesis of Curr, and as the governor of the colony, was in continual conflict with Curr's changing needs and overwhelmed with the constant demands of government. George Arthur became the third 'assistant-governor' and assumed the mantle as colonial spokesman of Lord Bathurst's tough stance on the VDL company issue. Arthur's attitude was one of providing public service to all but not pandering or over-responding to 'pressure groups' such as VDL Coy. In his opinion, Curr and his co-investors had received a very generous apportionment of government land, and Arthur had bent the rules in Curr's favour as far as he could. Arthur resisted the British direction for public work being undertaken by contract, and preferred instead to use convict labour, as part of his remedial and fiscally conservative programme. Arthur was never overly sympathetic to the VDL Coy (when compared to the positive support Gov. Darling had offered to the AAC Company in NSW). He considered the VDL Company "far too big and too far away for him to easily control" (Governor's despatches 1826). As well VDL Coy wanted to install 'yeomen' farmers and introduce free immigration which Arthur did not think was either suitable for the colony or the colony was ready for such an approach. In spite of his opinions, Arthur showed no obvious bias and could not be faulted for his endeavours with the Company.

i. *Andrew McGaw*. McGaw, the VDL manager from 1902 to 1947, had a certain opinion of his employer: "This had to be the most unfortunate of all capital ventures in early Australia, due to poor selection of land, early mismanagement, and bad luck–the rich Mount Bischoff tin-mines was discovered just outside the coy property boundaries". McGaw was a chartered surveyor until in 1902; he was appointed chief agent and manager of the coy. McGaw diversified operations, and opened the Burnie sawmill in 1905 (the Burnie Brick & Timber Co, became a VDL Coy subsidiary in 1907), utilising timber from the coy properties. McGaw also became Warden of the Marine Board of Burnie in 1907. He retired from VDL Coy in 1947.

Having determined the appointment and background of some of the key Company personnel in those early years, it is appropriate to examine more closely the service of Edward Curr. Curr brought problems for himself and his employer because of a faulty temperament that cannot be disguised, together with a limited imagination and a self-serving ability that put him in disrepute with all he came across.

• Curr's Curse

Any fledgling company can be expected to have management problems early in its establishment until a definitive *modus operandi* is developed and strategic goals are developed. The VDL Company was not only expected to have problems but could not have got by without them, by the simple nature of its organisation structure and operations.

VDL Company was formed on the whim of an expedient plan to secure a steady supply of quality wool from a friendly or better still, an in-house source. The company was well capitalised, this being one of the prerequisites set down by Lord Bathurst, before he would sanction the Royal Charter for the company. As well as being flush with funds, the syndicate had been promised, albeit with conditions that were not going to be difficult to meet, 250,000 acres of arable land in the Island of Van Diemen's Land, which was known for its generally rich fertile soil, its fine sheep grazing and its surplus yield of grain. What is more, the company had secured the support of the previous governor of the colony, John Sorell, and the services of an 'experienced' agriculturalist that had excellent connections in the colonies of VDL and NSW–Edward Curr.

Did not Curr even commit to invest money in the company to show how convinced he was of the success of the enterprise?

So where were the problems?

An egalitarian like Curr could only set the tone of operations because he was autocratic, pompous, arrogant and disrespectful of the authorities. The company started off on the wrong foot and continued in that vein.

Curr argued with the authorities, all the way from the Secretary of State Bathurst, through the Governor (Arthur), the Colonial Secretary (Hamilton) down. The grant instructions (written by Bathurst) were poorly constructed and Curr would only have accepted them without question in order to secure the basis for moving ahead, securing the funds for the project, being appointed company secretary and VDL agent and the VDL Company operating manager. Self-serving and manipulative–do whatever it takes to get what you want, and then start questioning and being disagreeable

Some of Curr's failures are derived from the lack of planning, an eagerness to show results to his investors without careful consideration, and access to a large pot of money with which to develop favours and extravagances.

It would be a mistake to evaluate or judge Curr on today's company management standards, but even in 1825; the term planning was not out of fashion or unknown. By standards of the day, a company that was intending to raise one million pound in subscriber capital, would have planned well for its operation, had a goal or goals and have thought through the steps to achieve those goals. But little thought was given to the overall planning function. Curr had 'land' but did not know just where it was or how much? The land was grassed, but to what extent or its carrying capabilities was not known. Curr was expecting to grow wool, quality wool, but knew not where he would be buying livestock. He had been promised (by Bathurst) convict assignees, provided the company, housed, clothed, fed and secured these people, but he did not know how many or when he would get them. Curr brought with him several 'assistants' who were specialist 'agriculturalist, surveyor and architect, and with whom he was expected to form a triumvirate management committee, since the biggest obstacle to good management practice was the distance between the Circular Head office, and the Court of Directors; and between Curr and his managing director. This was truly a tyranny of distance.

Curr sent these young fresh-faced, (the oldest in the group was Curr who was 27) inexperienced 'assistants–Lorymer and Hellyer–out to 'explore the northwest region'. These 'trainees' were straight out of the dirty streets of London, brought into the country of giant trees, impenetrable vines and undergrowth, and told to find suitable arable land. Even Hobart town was too wild for them, so imagine what they felt about the northwest jungle of Highland Tasmania. They were the first white men to penetrate the forests in this region. Wild animals, deep ravines and 'savage natives' would welcome these city folk, and whilst they appear to have tried their hardest to find good country for Curr–what was not there could obviously not be discovered, and Curr took umbrage at their not finding the fertile open plains that he expected to be there. These assistants gave (generally ill-informed) personal opinions of the land and its suitability, but Curr didn't like their opinions on such important matters, thought they were wrong, did the opposite to what they recommended and then criticised these assistants for trying.

The records of these explorations offer rare insight into how an Englishman, untrained and impractical, approached the task of 'exploring' and evaluating this new land. They obviously wanted to please Curr, and their masters in London, and their reports are detailed, with flowery language and a constant search for the superlative–the deepest gorges, the highest trees, the most impenetrable undergrowth, the sheerest cliff face, and the tallest peak.

The reports are presented in full as the means by which the reader can determine whether Curr misjudged the assistants and turned away from good advice.

The academic Dr. H. J.W. Stokes, who wrote briefly about the VDL Company for the Tasmanian Year Book sees Curr in much the same way:

"Curr expected to find the Hampshire and Surrey Hills sections of his grant, to be amongst the finest grazing country on the Island, and planned to commence his settlement there. However, the first visit to these areas, indicated to him, a thin soil of indifferent quality, with rocky outcrops but an abundance of water. A second visit by Curr two years later, had him rethinking his negative opinions, and he later reported to his directors that his opinion got better following each visit."

Curr had decided to think of this area as being very beneficial, and misinterpreted Hellyer's report, which honestly portrayed the region. However, Curr found it easier to blame Hellyer for a few words of gloss than admit his own belief in something that he wanted to find in the region, but didn't.

Stokes also opines on the Curr character "He was quick to sense an insult, and tended to see in the actions of others a desire to persecute him, and he believed (with almost manic intensity) the Tasmanian government was doing all in its power to thwart the company. As a result Curr, adopted a belligerent, disrespectful attitude that resulted in the Governor (Franklin) refusing to have any further dealings with Curr."

In 1839, Curr refused to accept the direction of his directors in relation to a concession being reached with the Governor, and in September 1840 was given a year's notice of termination. The disagreement was over the payment of wages to a local magistrate. Curr had originally agreed with the governor to pay these wages, but that was when he wanted something in return. But having got what he wanted he changed his mind about the 'cost' and for over a year confronted the governor. The Colonial Secretary reported to the Colonial Office who advised the VDL Court about the standoff. Even then Curr challenged his employers until they took the stand that Curr should be dismissed.

Stokes observes that Curr stood out as energetic and determined, especially when compared to the many malcontents and incompetents who were going through the revolving door of the company employment office in London before being transferred to the colony.

The first report to be written by a company worker, following a lengthy visit to the colony, came from Jorgenson in 1828(*History of the Original, Rise and Progress of the Van Diemen's Land Company–1828*). Although a fascinating account of the origins of the company, it is shallow on intent and even silent on the problems association with the early 'management' team in the selection of the land grant. However, the Jorgenson comments must be put into proper context. In 1827-28, the time of writing his booklet, he was a convict assigned to the VDL Company. He took a dislike to Curr who had limited his exploration trips within VDL Company Land. So the negative comments by Jorgenson against Curr may not have great basis in fact, although there are no recorded disagreements of the statements in Jorgenson's writings

Jorgenson claims, the company (through Curr) made the best selection of land from the generally poor resources available, but comments indirectly on the Curr style by suggesting the company had chosen him for his expertise as set out in his book about VDL country. "This gentleman (Edward Curr), writes Jorgenson, was introduced to the notice of the Directors from the circumstance of his having published a work on the VDL colony, and it was naturally supposed that he must be somewhat acquainted with the localities of a place who had written on the subject, and published his writings. We, however, do not subscribe to this mode of arguing. We are also very modestly told that Curr had traversed the island from one end to the other and that he must therefore be conversant with the state and nature of the country and acquainted with most people in it."

Jorgenson could not locate anyone who knew Curr or who spoke of him kindly, nor could he recognise many of the facts related in the book on his own travels. Jorgenson claims the Curr book was written whilst Curr was 'trying to beguile the tedious hours of a gloomy winter's passage round Cape Horn'.

"Mr. Curr's publication has nothing to applaud, but much to condemn". (Jorgenson p12)

Jorgenson puts a different twist on the Curr disagreements with Lord Bathurst and Lt-Go Arthur "Curr, anxious to fix a settlement in the Port Sorrell district, put a very different construction on Lord Bathurst's words than did the local government. It is clear that the Secretary of State Intended the company's lands to be should be as distant as possible from existing settlers, so as to give no cause for just complaint. The Governor maintained a point of sound argument over the company's agent, but the company persisted and the Governor resisted until this current moment" (the resolution took place in 1830). Mr. Curr urges that, in any event, and against any contradictory argument, the company will have the Hampshire and Surrey Hills, although when he personally saw the lack of impressive soil, he blamed the episode on his assistant's selection.

On the question of Curr's perversity on convicts and quit-rents, Jorgenson comments: "He hound means to impress on the mind of Lord Bathurst that it would be a very considerable saving to the Government were a number of Convicts to be assigned to the Company. This led to an arrangement, whereby each prisoner would save the government £16 per annum. The result would have been that had this arrangement progressed, the entire quit-rents due to Government might have been erased, whilst other settlers, who were in need of convict assistance, would not receive the same concession. Jorgenson recommended that the arrangement be terminated, in the same manner he remonstrated with the disadvantage to other settlers, that this one company received 350,000 acres of land, without cost.

Jorgenson finds little to admire or pay respect to in the origin and formation of the VDL Company and obviously went out of his way to criticise the failings of Edward Curr. Jorgenson returned to London, wrote his report and the VDL Directors probably placed Curr on the 'to watch' list. Relations thereupon deteriorated between the Directors and Curr, and less than 10 years later, the directors had the excuse they needed (they did need an excuse because Curr was a stockholder as well as being Company secretary) to terminate Curr from their employ.

Jorgenson appears to have correctly and objectively interpreted the times and 'failures' of taking opportunities as well as the failings of Edward Curr, but A. L. Meston who (in 1925) wrote '*The Van Diemen's Land Company 1825-1842*' takes a different line and draws very different conclusions.

Meston concludes "Curr, the company's colonial agent, found the colonists suspicious of absentee monopolists and found the Governor prepared to put, on his instructions, the interpretation least favourable to the Company"

Meston also concludes, "The grant of land was outside the settled areas and its powers confined to growing fine wool. The regions of land grants offered were quite unsuited to raising fine woolled sheep, the surveyors had to contend with forested mountains and severe weather to find the few likely areas.

Meston appears to be rewarding Curr for his misdemeanours and lack of moral integrity, and mouthing Curr's defences to his directors for a series of disastrous episodes. Meston misinterprets Curr's self-serving approach and overlooks the damage done by Curr to the Company for almost the first 20 years of its history. Leaving a legacy of ineptitude, Curr affected the next 50 years of company operations

Meston excuses Curr on the basis of "The trial of strength was not merely between persons but between systems of colonisation, and Curr was the agent of the obsolete one". There must be responsibility shown by a recipient of a land grant of 350,000 acres of land in a new colony. Even Jorgenson claimed "the grand desideratum for the consideration of the Tasmanian Public must be whether it is of greater advantage to the colony to see a large portion of territory brought into a state of cultivation, which otherwise might have remained idle for ages to come, or whether to observe that improvements made by the company may cause distress to the inhabitants of the other parts." Jorgenson comes down in favour of the obligations of the administrators to develop the colony, even if it results in a profit or advantage to the investors.

That the overall goals of the Company were based around wool was logical but that they be restricted to 'fine wool' is not, unless careful and full evaluation had been made as to the climate, breeds, fodder, and management of such an operation. The 'Pastoral Age' in Australia between 1820 and 1850 saw the release of 73 million acres of (under licence or lease) in New South Wales and 4,500,000 acres in VDL. The average run in NSW was only 30,000 acres, the squatters being only 2,000 strong. By 1830 Australian wool had become established on the English market, over 2 million pound of it having been exported. In 1834, the quantity had doubled, and by 1841 the quantity had doubled again to 8 million pound. However, in 1850, 30 million pound was being received into England, or half the total English import of wool. Although we are jumping ahead just a little, it may explain a central point in our story—why did the VDL Company directors not push harder for this land grant opportunity to be a successful wool source for the company promoters and stockholders. Obviously they were having their wool import needs met from other colonial growers, probably at a cheaper landed cost per pound weight, with less problems, probably better quality and landed in England at a price (on a consignment basis) that allowed careful selection, instead of being forced to buy 'company' produce.

Meston states that the Court of Directors mostly ignored Curr's advice, even though the advice was based on local knowledge. We know from Jorgenson's observations made at the time–1828–that Curr's advice was tainted and self-serving, and was one man's opinion, rather than the management committee ordered by the Company Court. Curr himself abandoned the idea of the management committee since he did not want to have to democratise the decision-making process within the operating area, and he sent his assistants off on long trips whenever a meeting was called for.

Meston makes the interesting point that two powerful influences, and some knowing events, powered the formation of the VDL Coy in 1824

a. James Dixon, published his narrative in 1822, and reported, "The country is peculiarly adapted for sheep, and that animal thrives well and increases astonishingly. Taking its climate into consideration, VDL is much superior to NSW where the burning heats in summer dry up everything".

b. Early in 1823, Commissioner J.T. Bigge released his third Report on conditions in NSW and VDL, and one of the recommendations made, based on John Macarthur's work, and the results obtained by him, was that "settlers possessing capital and a real intention of pursuing the same beneficial course of industry" should receive grants of land in NSW 'in proportion to the number of convicts they engage to employ and the numbers of sheep and cattle they took with them". Of course, Macarthur was being more than a little disingenuous with Bigge, as he was already planning on a heavy involvement with the *Australian Agricultural Company,* which was given the royal charter just shortly (a few months) before the VDL Company.

John Ingles, who had spent much of his time in NSW where he assembled a 'fortune' offered intelligence (to the first 11 VDL Company syndicate promoters), that the downturn of the woollen industry in England was due to the deterioration of quality of the fleece which also resulted from an irregular supply, which in turn caused 'a rapid rise in the price of wool' (Meston). Of the 11 original promoters of the VDL Company syndicate, all were closely connected with the woollen industry in the west of England, 3 were members of the House of Commons, 1 was a director of the Bank of England, and 1 was extensively concerned in army clothing and the cloth trade. Of the remaining promoters, James Bischoff (soon to become the Managing Director of the Court, and reporter on events at the company) was a London woollen merchant engaged in exporting woollen goods abroad; John Maitland had been Chairman for 40 years of the wool trade board in London and the rest were wool merchants and manufacturers, and a banker or two

This was certainly a powerful lobby group and one to which the Government would listen carefully. The application for a grant of 500,000 acres (states Meston) was made on the 22nd May 1824. Bathurst personally received the promoters on 5th June to discuss their plans. Meston writes that 'the frenzied speculation of the time' made Bathurst cautious, and the promoters withdrew to consider their response to Bathurst's three main objections, which were:

1. The company's entrance into the market (along with the AAC) would raise the price of sheep and cause financial injury.
2. 'That if fine wool sheep were exported, the wool would deteriorate';
3. 'There was insufficient unallocated land in the colony for the grant, without interfering with the present settlers.

The answers were provided by John Marsh (one of the promoter/investors) who showed that there was already a gradual improvement in the wool quality, and by John Ingles who could state from personal knowledge that there was an abundance of unallocated land, the possession of which would not interfere with free settlers. Ingles, on the third point, advised the syndicate to ask for their grant to be given in the northern half of the Island and two-thirds of it east of the West Tiers.

They also told Bathurst in response that the grant would be 'for the purpose of breeding from the best flocks which can be selected in Europe' (Meston p 13).

Meston then records how Curr originally became involved with the VDL Company promoters. "A small book on VDL had just come off the Press and what the promoters read gladdened their hearts. Not knowing Curr, the promoters discussed Curr with former governor Sorell. Sorell spoke in the highest terms of Curr's integrity, of the estimation in which he was held by all the reputable colonists, of his knowledge of actual conditions and of the accuracy and reliability of his facts. We know from other sources that Sorell had only met the young Curr once, during a 'country trip' by Governor Sorell, and had never spoken to him at any length.

Curr told the group that 'VDL is blessed with a salubrity of climate which no country can surpass and which is found to be favourable to the rearing of sheep. He told them that there were several extensive tracts of good country, not difficult to access, well watered and of which no great part had been allocated. Of the western side of the island he knew little because it had not been explored, but he thought it improbable that such an extensive area should possess no good land'.

Meston writes "Curr's extensive and intimate knowledge of the Island and his boundless energy made him so useful that within two months, he was made Secretary *pro tempore* of the group".

Meston then reports that in February 1825, the directors renewed their application, sending evidence of unallocated land suitable for their purpose, the results of their enquiries and asked again for 500,000 acres or what Lord Bathurst thought fit. Sorell, who stood high in Bathurst's estimation, supported the plan and the overall project and Bathurst was able to inform the syndicate that he stood ready to take the plan to fruition, by presenting the Bill to the Parliament.

The directors of the AAC (*Australian Agricultural Company*) took their concerns about too much demand on sheep supplies affecting the colonies to Bathurst. Bathurst urged the two charter companies to work out a solution before he imposed one.

Meston records the HRA the settlement of this dispute between the AAC and the VDL Company. "The AAC thought the limited sources of sheep would inflate prices if both companies' bought at the same time. The AAC wanted the VDL Company not to buy for a three-year period. The VDL Company refused this treatment and responded by wanting the AAC to buy sheep from Germany and they (the VDL Company) buy from Spain. To resolve this impasse, Bathurst brokered an agreement between them whereby the VDL Company purchased from Spain, and the AAC purchased from Germany, such restrictions remaining in force for three years".

Correspondence in the HRA offers an interesting insight into the Curr-Arthur dealings and the growing animosity between them. Curr told Arthur that it might take 1-2 or even 43 million acres of land from which the company could select 250,000 of arable and grazing land. He was taunting Arthur, who was already highly indignant at what he considered sharp practice and asserted that Curr had played upon the ignorance of the Colonial Office and had used his personal knowledge of VDL to obtain a concession detrimental to the interests of the Colony. Whether we regard this act as a clever piece of chicanery, there is no doubt that Curr gained a very valuable concession for the Company.

Even Curr acknowledged the potentially good deal when he wrote to his Court (in late 1826) "If these conditions of giving the Company 250,000 acres of useful land be correctly acted upon, the badness of the great majority of the north-west corner of the land will have this obvious advantage that the further the limits of the land extend the nearer they will approach the settled districts".

Curr had another gain over Arthur when he argued successfully, "The land covered with a dense forest of heavy timber and producing no grass, even if the soil is good, could not be classed as useful land within Bathurst's definition. Although such land can be cleared and be thus turned into good grazing land, the cost of doing so would be excessive. He was entitled to take only such land as could be put under the plough with little or no expense for clearing, or, could be used for pasture".

• Jorgenson on the topic of Value Adding for the Company

Jorgenson suggests the directors were concerned about the lack of profits in the company and considered trying to get exchange land at Port Phillip. However, he opines that the company, in a few years, must make tremendous gains from the extensive grant bestowed on them. Considering the price of land (the government was demanding not less than 5/–per acre for inferior land), the grant and the increase of stock, the company's estate 'will be of a value to exceed the whole capital subscribed, and one can reasonably calculate on an annual dividend of ten or twelve percent, on the actual value of the estate, rather than on the capital subscribed'.

Being headquartered in London, with its 'Court' being a prestigious posting to hold, it is not surprising that director's relationships would influence VDL Company's business activities. Marion Diamond writing of Benjamin Boyd in '*Australian Financiers*' suggests, "In return for participating in a weekly director's meeting, each director of the Royal Bank of Australia received an annual fee of £100. Such fees were an annual charge against the revenue of the Bank. These directors of the Bank were drawn from a wide area of business in Scotland and England. Several had Australian connections; John Mitchell, was also a director of the VDL Company and was brother to the surveyor-general in NSW, Sir Thomas Mitchell. Interlocking directorates such as this were not uncommon in the 'City' of London in the 1840s, and widely influenced the placement of business, as well as loans, share swaps and investment trails.

Let us turn now to a review and cursory examination of the annual reports between 1825 (the first report) and the 1960s

Annual Reports

We will track the progress and performance of the company, in this section, through the annual reports issued by the Governor and his Court, every year from 1825. The first annual report was not printed but it was reproduced in the writing of James Bischoff in 1832, following a visit to the colony. The Bischoff Report is of such significance it is reproduced in the appendices to this work, in full.

Although it may be mundane to work through each year, the devoted reader may well be inclined to look to the highlights of each year as a means of gauging whether the Court was doing its job, and that, in particular means guiding the Manager.

Before we commence with those annual highlights, there is a question of accounting standards and record keeping, to be examined.

Between 1825 and 1851, the Company capitalised expenditures on the land grants to the extent of £162,024 (the figure of £600,000 quoted by Kerry Pink–refer Chapter 8–Setting *the Record Straight*–is incorrect).

Present day accounting standards would have partially applied in that period (how many ways can one capitalise costs of developing an asset?), but it appears, that in an effort to make the Colonial operations more 'investment oriented', the bookkeepers in Circular head over capitalised various expenses. Without a doubt the operation made a loss from the very first year, as there was no real 'product' income until 1834, and in the interim, all of the salaries and overhead expenses were being paid by Bills drawn against the London office. If budgets or forward estimates were prepared, they have been lost to the company's vast archive collection in Hobart. Expenditures between 1825 and 1851 would have consisted of salaries for managers, explorers, surveyors, agriculturalists, general workmen, land clearing, building company houses, and clearing land for tracks, roads, stock routes, wharves, boat hire, the office building in Circular Head and a collection of staff and workmen houses. Probably some farmland development for planting crops, grains, and livestock supervision was included. What was not included according to the 1851 'liquidation' Committee Chairman was livestock purchased, machinery purchases, stores, or the value of convict labour. We know, now, what was not included but even the auditors of 1851 who were entitled to know what had been spent from 'day 1, did not know.

The Auditors supplied the 'Liquidation Committee' with a consolidated statement of revenue and expenditures for the company between 1826 and 1851, and it does not present a pretty picture.

Cash Inflows:

Shareholder calls	265,292
Livestock Sales	10,987
Wool Sales	22,723
Wheat Sales	343
Fees on transfer of land	1,351
Sundry inflow	<u>1,213</u>
Total Cash Inflow:	**£301,913.14.3**

Cash Outflows:

Land Improvements.	162,024
Purchases of Livestock	22,209
Purchases of Stores	41,768
Dividends Paid	8,881
Salaries paid in VDL	18,168
Salaries paid in London	14,006
Parliamentary fees	3,017
Visits to the Colony by directors	13,526
Office expenses–London	6,330
Directors Fees	4,021
Legal expenses	1,292
Office furniture–London	807
Quit rent paid	608
VDL Library	581
Sundries	<u>2,813</u>
Total Outgoings	300,792
Cash on Hand	1,121
Total accounted for:	**£301,913.14.3**

These figures are noteworthy for what they tell us but more especially for what they don't tell us. Imagine being faced with 'bankruptcy' and being told by your financial officers–'we don't know where the money has gone'.

The best figures the auditors could provide the Liquidation committee was that capitalised development expenses amounted to £108,054. The balance of 'land improvements' was spent on: shipping £307; livestock £28186; machinery £1,108 and stores/account tenants £32369.

The ability of identifying what the £108,054 pound was spent on was not within the London committee's abilities and the then current auditors questioned why the earlier auditors had not sought detailed accounting records. That was a fallacious and self-serving cover-up. No auditor should have been able to certify the accounts, year after year, without qualification to the effect that (a) the colonial expenditure could not be identified on a line item basis; (b) the colonial accounts should have been either audited locally in VDL or a format provided by the auditors for completion by the bookkeepers in VDL; (c) that the company was unable to meet its financial obligations, as and when they fell due; and (d) the liquidation value of the assets obviously would not realise the book values and the accounts were therefore overstated.

The company by 1851 was obviously trading irresponsibly, as the amount due to tenant farmers was 86% of the total amount shipped by the tenants to the company under its guaranty buy-back of produce from the farmers by the company. That the company could not pay what was owed to the tenant farmers was only part of the problem. The bigger problem was that the buy-back scheme was only an incentive to rent the land at 2s per acre for unimproved land, which 'rent' was not offset by any land clearing work carried out on the company land. The company had not made any preparation for retailing or on-selling the farmer's produce, and in 1850 the total annual produce received into store sat in the store, rotted and had to be dumped in Emu Bay. This episode cost the company £31,484.

What the reconciliation of revenues and expenditures for the first 25 years (set out above), failed to disclose is that the cost of wharves, survey, the church, the jetty came to over £20,000. These figures are apparently 'covered up' in the land improvements total, so we may never know how the development expenses were capitalised, but there is no doubt that Curr, as Manager, wanted his directors to think he had spent the annual money drawn on London mostly on capital works.

This was not the only deception plotted by Curr. Curr covered his tracks well on capitalising as much 'operating' expenses as was possible.

He had a novel way of informing the directors how well he was running the colonial operations. The Curr method was very different to the structure adopted in the 'Blue Books', which were the official records of government income and expenditures in the colony. The 'Blue Books' could not and did not value the 'work' of convicts–although overall, their contribution to GDP was substantial. Curr would inform his directors of how much of production was used for 'internal'-worker purposes, in addition to the quantity being available for sale. In most years, the Curr 'value' of grains, meat, timber etc was close to £13,000 although the records show that between 1840 and 1850 the average gross sales from these products in cash terms was only about £5,000. Curr wanted to inflate the actual production by claiming that physical production was much greater than actually occurred but the worker rations would account for the difference. Only very gullible directors would accept this explanation and by rights the Curr listing of expenditures and their account allocation should have been questioned as well. What Curr was doing, was overstating capitalised expenditures, reducing the loss and falsely building up an asset.

Another aspect of the 'liquidation' committee's report is particularly troubling–not only do they opine that the underlying financial figures are questionable, but then the report says 'the book values are too high in relation to current sales values'. This, of course, is the classic trap for managers to fall into. Set the results of your operations at optimistic levels, and make it look as if you have spent wisely and performed admirably, as was Curr's want, but don't let the results impact negatively on your balance sheet. Overcapitalising expenditures makes the 'profit & loss' statement look good, but overstates the balance sheet, and comes back to haunt the manager in the event he is forced to sell those assets for their book value. As was the situation facing the 'liquidation committee' in 1851, the company could not realise the properties for the book value and so there would be a further loss on liquidation. So what does one do–just as the Committee recommended. Close everything down, terminate all the staff–take what one can for the assets, or lock everything down until times improve.

Although we can't blame Curr directly, even in his absence he thwarted the company's efforts to liquidate the assets. His hand was clearly there on the very self-serving bookkeeping practices.

The reader will have noted, from the statement of cash flows, just how little revenue had flowed, during that first quarter-century, from operations. Only 10,000 pound in livestock sales were reported for the 25-year period 1826-1851. Sheep, cattle, horses, swine and deer were the company's livestock reserves, and they had bought the sheep from Spain at an average of £4 per head f.o.b., but there is little evidence that sheep sales of potentially fine breeding sheep, just unsuitable for the Island climate and conditions, would ever make the company successful.

It could only have been with the director's knowledge and consent that the company management was playing with the figures. The 1850 Return of Livestock showed the following:

Description	Sold	Deaths	leased to tenants	Final#
Horses	20	8	0	117
Cattle	175	10	0	2605
Sheep	1965	322	648	6873
Deer	25	0	0	81

For a pastoral company that had 25 years of experience and 350,000 acres of land to be only running the above number of livestock is rather sad. That deaths accounted for a minimum of 5% of the end of year sheep count is also a reflection on management. That only 343-pound value of grain was produced for sale, (other than for in-house use) is a sad expression on planning within the company. Livestock valuation for the Livestock Return of 1850 was 27,507 and after stock losses for the year of 1851, the end of year valuation was 26,622, but the same livestock, without any sales reported was valued at only 25, 017 at the end of 1852. What are more troubling are the changing valuations of the improved properties:

1850	108,054
1851	117,915
1852	95,129
1853	118,400

There is no explanation in the Annual Reports, or are there any explanatory notes to the financial statements. Stockholders must have gazed with horror at the changing book 'valuation' of their major asset, and wondered 'how' and 'why'. The director's hope they only express shock at declining values but are impressed sufficiently by increased or rising valuations that they decide to subscribe to the next call and keep the company afloat for more money to be wasted.

The auditors were changed often–possibly because they didn't want to be associated with a failing company that was creating waves with its financial statements. Each auditor obviously had a different technique for handling transactions and balances.

In 1851, the '*Abstract of the Balance of the Colonial Books from the commencement of Company to the 31st December 1851*' reports tenant produce account with a balance of 34,885 pound and a profit and loss account balance of 23,242. However in 1852, with a new auditor, there was a similar statement . . . '*Abstract of Balances from commencement to December 1852*' but with no reference to tenant' produce account, but the profit and loss account now has a balance of 61,450 about 10,000 pound greater than the previous year, but the overall bottom line balances are the same. So trying to follow what happened–in 1850 there was separate recognition of indebtedness to the tenants; in 1851 that indebtedness was 'written off' to the profit & loss account, and a further loss of 10,000 pound was recognised in that same year. This 10,000-pound loss was made up to a small extent of revaluing land and livestock, but most of it was the result of operating expenditures not being capitalised.

Keeping in mind that we are now reviewing and discussing the broad range of business enterprises pursued by VDL Company, it is interesting to note that, only the tenant farmers wanted to lease land and grow vegetables, or grains. The company showed no interest in doing so on their own account. Clearing the land was too' expensive' for Curr, who could not get his mind around a grain production of just a few thousand acres–he had 350,000 acres and wanted large scale activities, at no cost, if he was to do anything at all. Curr thought the future was rosy when his land leasing income reached £3,000 in 1838. But it could have reached this and more had he commenced in grain production, cropping, vegetables, course wool, timber, tobacco or hops. Of his 350,000 acres, he could have and should have examined every opportunity for raising revenue. The directors should have told him 'work towards being self-sufficient by 1840, but instead the company made its annual call on shareholders (£1 per share) until 1851. All of these funds went straight into a 'black hole'–the funds were not properly accounted for and therefore could not be properly audited. This situation came to a head when the 'liquidation' committee could not identify where the Company had made the £300,000 of expenditure on property improvement. It had been capitalised into each property but neither the Directors nor the auditor could say, on what items the funds had been expended. The Company was becoming a prime example of when things start going wrong, it all seems to be going wrong.

Of course, even the auditors should not be blamed for a less than perfect accounting, recording and reporting system.

By reference to the book containing 'bills drawn', one can see that there is no notation on the bills as to what goods or services had been purchased, nor was there any supporting vouchers or documentation, to assist the enquiring mind. The references were vague and took the form:

'#4 Nov 11, 1826 30 day sight Walter A Bethine £40.0.0'

One would have thought an entry in the daybook or journal would have referenced this payment and identified its purpose, but we find no such extravagance.

Let us return to the regular annual returns. Before 1850, they were essentially P.R. documents intended to persuade the stockholders that all was well, and they should accept the company had to operate at a loss for another ten years, and they continue to pay their calls because the company was growing stronger and stronger because so much of the expenses was being assetised.

As we have seen above, by 1852 the company was in crisis. And the directors finally recognised the extent of the problem. In the annual report for that year, the directors recommended (a) the abandonment of all farming; (b) the sale of all livestock;(c) the collection and receiving of all outstanding debts; (d) the reduction in salary of the Chief Agent/Manager ('if he has no staff and no livestock, he need not be paid the same as if the company was fully functioning'); (e) termination of all company workers except the Manager, the two school teachers ('all of whom can remain at lower salaries'). The directors pushed the point of the liquidation proposals by noting in significant positioning in the report that 'total bills drawn were

£4,823 whilst wool sales were a sorry (net) £779. What had worried the 'liquidation committee' was that overall land sales during the year 1851 were 4,144 acres for only £8,047, with annual rents of £818.219.0 and the livestock sales for 1966 sheep, 193 cattle and 65 horses brought only £2,139. This proved the point to the Chairman of the committee that

o   The valuation of assets in the accounts was too high,
o   That it would take many years to liquidate the assets, and
o   The company could never be profitable unless it changed direction, radically.

The committee, in reporting on the 26th September 1851 (reported in the 1852 annual report) recommended that the land be broken up, and sold, but in the interim it be leased, without the guaranteed buy-back of produce which lost 1200 ton of potatoes and 4,000 bushels of grain.

The timing could not have been worse for trying to structure the company and head operations in to another direction. The gold discoveries in Victoria had just been announced, and most settlers were attracted to the gold fields and not the isolated northwest coast of the Island colony. However the decision was made and they moved in that direction. Gibson still headed the team but he it would not be long before he too was terminated with a year's notice.

The annual reports of 1853 and 1854 were simplistic documents with no news, no advice to stockholders and little information. The company was on its last legs and disclosure was the last thing on its mind. However Directors fees were still being paid at normal rates for attendance in the prestigious boardroom. Wool sales had dropped from £1764 in 1850 to £989 in 1853. Annual cattle sales were holding fairly steady at between £1654(1853) and £1764(1850). Stock numbers, due to a failing breeding program (not because of good sales volumes) were in decline. From the table above in 1850, stock number s by 1853 had declined to 6,873 sheep, 2605 cattle, 117 horses and 81 deer.

The Annual Report of 1855 reported the 'saw mill erected near black River (Circular Head) was in production with 80–acres of good timber set aside for harvesting. Town lots in Stanley and Burnie were being marketing at a 5% commission, and as if the directors thought the tide had turned they reported newspapers in the colony had announced gold had been found at Macquarie Harbour, not far below Cape Grim on the West Coast. Directors wrote that there might be the chance of finding gold at Woolnorth.

The directors also announced that a steamer ferry was now running regularly between Launceston, Emu Bay to Circular Head. 'This would open up potential for coastal trading' they said.

There is no Report available for 1856, and the Annual Report for 1857 noted the arrival of a new company manager. It also noted that the road had been opened from Circular Head to Launceston, with new land sales taking place at Circular Head.

In 1858, town lots at Stanley were selling for £40 each quarter acre. Highfield House (originally built by Curr in 1826 had been leased

(together with 330 acres) for £500 per annum. The population on Company lands had increased from 912 in 1851 to 1242 in 1858.

The 1859 Annual Report recorded the recent sales of 40-acre lots around Burnie and Circular Head at the good rate of £2 per acre. Town lots were still selling at various prices, at rates apparently acceptable to the company. During the year, there was the first sale of split wood and timber to Melbourne. This was the year in which Sir Edward Poore, a London Director, visited the Colonial operations and wrote his report, which is included in this work in the Appendices.

It was in 1860 that James Gibson was terminated–he was given a year's notice in 1859. Nichols, a former employee and colonial representative of London based Dalgety & Co. was appointed Manager, and he reported that the prices of all agricultural products in the Colonies was quite low, but should improve in the next year. He reported that gold exploration was being carried out (under contract) on the company's properties and that quantities of tin, iron, coal and plumbago had been found.

The Directors also recorded that a submarine cable from Circular head to Melbourne had been laid and was operational.

For 1861 the directors showed a little more optimism and reported that they had rented the 200,000 acres comprising Surrey Hills and Hampshire Hills at £400 per annum, bring total rents to 3,000 pound per annum. Not quite time for rejoicing but things were moving ahead, especially as the news broke that a small gold discovery had been made sat the Hellyer River.

Other leases included the 150,000-acre 'Woolnorth' property at £300, and the lease renewal of Highfield House at the rate of £500.

Missed Opportunities

Keeping in mind that we are now reviewing and discussing the broad range of business enterprises pursued by VDL Company, it is interesting to note that, unless the tenant farmers wanted to lease the land and grow vegetables, or grains, the company showed no interest in doing so on their own account. Clearing the land was too' expensive' for Curr, who could not get his mind around a grain production of just a few thousand acres–he had 350,000 acres and wanted large scale activities, at no cost, if he was to do anything at all. Curr thought the future was rosy when his land leasing income reached £3,000 in 1838. But it could have reached this and more had he commenced in grain production, cropping, vegetables, course wool, tobacco or hops. Of his 350,000 acres, he could have and should have examined every opportunity for raising revenue. The directors should have told him 'work towards being self-sufficient by 1840, but instead the company made its annual call on shareholders (£1 per share) until 1851. All of these funds went straight into a 'black hole'–the funds were not properly accounted for and therefore could not be properly audited. This situation came to a head when the 'liquidation' committee could not identify where the Company had made the £300,000 of expenditure on property improvement. It had been capitalised into each property but neither the Directors nor the auditor could say, on what items the funds had been expended. The Company was becoming a prime example of when things start going wrong, it all seems to be going wrong.

Of course, even the auditors should not be blamed for a less than perfect accounting, recording and reporting system.

By reference to the book containing 'bills drawn', one can see that there is no notation on the bills as to what goods or services had been purchased, nor was there any supporting vouchers or documentation, to assist the enquiring mind. The references were vague and took the form:

'#4 Nov 11, 1826 30 day sight Walter A Bethine £40.0.0'

One would have thought an entry in the daybook or journal would have referenced this payment and identified its purpose, but we find no such extravagance.

Let us return to the regular annual returns. Before 1850, they were essentially P.R. documents intended to persuade the stockholders that all was well, and they should accept the company had to operate at a loss for another ten years, and they continue to pay their calls because the company was growing stronger and stronger because so much of the expenses was being assetised.

CHAPTER 5

THE VDL COMPANY–GAMBLES, OPPORTUNITIES & FAILURE

Governor Macquarie (of NSW) was not only a great social thinker and builder (public buildings, roads and communications), he fostered developments that were to lead to big things and secured free export of wool to the English market and led to the establishment of the industry in Van Diemen's Land by organising the shipping of sheep there. His early coldness to free immigrants did not affect his interest in free enterprise.

S.J. Butlin writes in *Foundations of the Australian Monetary System*

"The expansion of farming, whaling and wool-growing found its capitalists in Macarthur, Marsden, Wentworth, Blaxland, Blaxcell and Lords, and its labour force grew rapidly as the numbers transported rose. There was a steady rise in imports, reflecting the flow of capital from England, and if exports were still small, consisting, apart from wool and whale oil, of casual shipments of timber or coal, local entrepreneurs were freely talking of new and varied local industries, and significantly, seeking in local distilling a market for grain which already threatened to exceed what the gaol would demand".

As governor-in-chief-, Macquarie had arrived with some special thoughts for 'guiding' the colonial economy whose growth was something over and above the growth of the gaol economy. The free economy should be promoted over the gaol, ultimately to replace it, and therefore he

(Macquarie) should encourage and promote the interests of the emancipists. To this end, he planned a scheme for a local, albeit government bank, and when that was disapproved, he moved to crush the private note issuers. He imported a currency and retained it within the colony by 'localising' it. A losing battle of restricting private notes led to the 1816-17 'illegal' formation of the Bank of NSW. His answers usually led to 'privatisation of industry, whilst recognising the limits of the local economy and the early need for an official intervention by way of encouragement. This approach applied to the BNSW, to the trade in Commissariat notes, and as it did to the system of land grants for those holding capital.

The economy was essentially in the hands of a few wealthy entrepreneurs and was to be guided by a few wealthy capitalists working on behalf of the local emancipists. The creation of a Legislative Council in 1823; the freedom of the press; large free immigration, the separation of the VDL colony and, under Governor Arthur, its growth as a primary penal settlement, were merely extensions of the mushrooming 'free' economy on the mainland.

It was this scenario and encouraging signals that promoted and provoked the pastoral expansion of the late 1820s and into the 1830s. The boom stage, following 1835, was staged to succeed the strong initial economic expansion between 1810 and 1830. Even in a small island of Tasmania a similar pattern was emerging to that in New South Wales, where until 1830, the limits of settlement were confined to that area within the nineteen counties. In Tasmania, writes Butlin (*op cit*) 'the expansion of the occupied area was of necessity small, since there was little new pastoral country to occupy'. The Tasmanian economy, especially in terms of imports, exports and import surplus, was not to lag behind the mainland for long, nor be limited by its small land mass.

RECORDED IMPORTS AND EXPORTS 1831-1840

	NSW			Tasmania		
Year	Imports	Exports	Surplus	Imports	Exports	Surplus
1831	490152	324168	165984	298774	141745	157029
1836	1237406	748624	488782	558240	420123	138117
1840	3014189	1399692	1614497	988356	867007	121349

On the other side of the ledger, there was the still growing British expenditure in connection with the convicts; the formation of 'investment' companies and trusts, including mortgage companies, in Britain through which funds could be funnelled into the new colonies, as well as the proceeds from the growing number of absentee investors, and the import of cash and goods on account of the migrants. 'These were but some of the channels through which came the flood tide of capital' (Butlin *op cit*)

It was left to the local banks to underpin this great pastoral expansion, amongst which the Banks of Launceston and Hobart (Derwent Bank) were most active. This expansion is shown in the growth of loans by the BNSW where in 1830, loans sat at £36828 whilst in 1836 they averaged £222787.

Butlin records "It was in Tasmania that local initiative in banking was first shown. Throughout the 1830s the Island experienced brief ups and downs in economic activity and after this first outburst of enterprise fell more and more behinds the mainland in the race, in part, at least, because Tasmanian residents saw more profit in mainland adventures. During 1831-34 there were constant complaints of poor business, of restricted bank advances, of the intolerable burden of interest rates, and the urging of local banks into a single 'Island-wide', united Bank.

The VDL Company performs typically of British investors & speculators

There are seven letter-books in the Tasmanian Archives relating to the Derwent Bank. These contain some remarkable enquiries for investment opportunities in the VDL colony. This Bank received many enquiries from Britishers wanting to emigrate, with their capital, to the colony.

In response to one enquiry to relocate to Tasmania from Scotland and commence a 'sheep farm' associated with various other small-scale activities, the enquirer, a Major G.D. Mercer, recently retired from the British Army (typical of many such transfers and relocations), was advised by the Derwent Bank Manager "Your ideas are the same as those of all men, who have never visited a colony just arising from the wilderness. You are anxious to build mills and make salt, and to lay out money, which will never bring you in any return. It is with these English ideas that too many emigrants and all companies yet formed have ruined themselves".

In other words 'the VDL Company is typical of the ebbs and lows of agricultural investment in Tasmania.

The manager went on to point out "In a young colony we must go step by step and not get into manhood before we can run on our legs. When money can be otherwise more advantageously laid out as it can be in land, in sheep and cattle, in bank shares, or lent on mortgages, mills and salt must be left to the miller and small capitalists who, by their personal labour and with few or no servants make their trades answer".

One can imagine a responsible person associated with the VDL Company saying of their company:

"We set out to breed fine wool sheep and to grow fine wool. That was our Charter and to encourage the level of investment required, we were given 250,000 acres of tillable land to commence operations. However, we argued with the governor to the point that we received 350,000 gross acres, few areas of which were at that time suitable, without extensive improvement, for running sheep. The committed capital of £500,000 was supposedly to be spent on improving the land–much of it in the company-township and port, and some on staff housing, livestock, offices, boats, supplies and equipment. In retrospect, we should have sought the advice, opinion and assistance of experienced local farmers, who knew much more about the land and colonial conditions than did British managers. In this respect, at least, the Company would not have lost its entire flock in the cold and wet conditions of 1831-32. In other respects, the low wool yield experienced within the colony for much of the 1830s could have been improved, and at a much lower cost than was actually the case. On the other hand, the poor diet offered the sheep could have been improved by grazing them on the better pastures within the company's land and in that way the mortality rate would have been much lower. As the Bank Manager said, it was those English ideas, and ego driven management that brought financial ruin to the Company. The banker also said 'you must walk before you can run' but the Company was not keen on this approach. It follows that once you make over-ambitious projections (as Curr did to the Directors) then one is bound to be held accountable and so there was constant pressure (within the limitations of a long sea voyage and almost twelve months between writing for instructions and receiving a response) upon the colonial manager to perform, better and better–more stock, less cost, more revenue, less wastage and loss. The managers then took to thinking of all the hair-brain schemes possible to make money and one by one tried them all. Long-term planning, covering short-term losses in order to make longer-term gains, was not a policy available to the managers. They were all on a bonus program, which instead of having the effect of driving profitability had the effect of driving risk-taking ventures, which ended in failure and expensive failure usually.

These risk taking ventures and their associated financial failure included:

a. Assigned servants transferring to the Colony, indentured to the Company.

b. A tenant farmer scheme with fixed lease terms and a guaranteed buyback of produce at top market prices

c. A town ship residential land sale with no concurrent agreements for building homes or for offering jobs to the buyers.

d. The creation of a port at the Company town-ship, initially designed with a wharf only suitable for a rowboat and large enough to take local produce. With the advent of wharfage needs for ores, additional expenditures were needed for the expansion, before any wharfage charges were realised.

e. A railway line running from the Mt Bischoff Tin Mine, 40 miles south of the port and in a rugged mountain area, to the Port at Emu Bay, made from wooden rails that did not survive the first season.

f. Geological surveys were made firstly by a government paid surveyor and then more extensively and at significant cost on behalf of the company. No commercial finds were made within the company boundaries.

g. Great quantities of commercial timber was logged and left in situ because no outlet had been found in the colony for sales of timber, and the company could not afford to ship the timber back to England for sale there, although extensive timber sales were being negotiated. Curr did not want to share his proceeds by paying a consignment fee and so very miniscule revenue was received on account of the substantial timber reserves on company lands.

h. Livestock sales by the company were made 'on account' but because of the cyclical economic conditions, many buyers used the livestock but had no means of paying for it. The company's 'bad debt' expense was relatively high.

i. Wool sales were made in England by private contract and it is noted in the accounts that the company, received (from its woollen mill owning stockholders), less than commercial value for the wool.

The growth within the colonial economy had to this point been driven by overseas investment. The most important source of such investment was the British Government expenditure on the convict settlement via the sale of bills drawn on the British Treasury. Such bills could by drawn by the Commissary or the payroll officer of the military, or by the Dockyard or Lumber Yard, or the Female Factory, or the Government Farms responsible for supplying fresh meat and vegetables to the Commissary. These treasury bills were supplemented in the 1820s and 1830s by the bills drawn against the Australian Agricultural and Van Diemen's Land Companies, together with those of the missionary societies and a few private traders whose credit was usually good. Even so, most immigrants found it more satisfactory to bring out their capital in the form of English banknotes, coin or actual goods.

The VDL Company used a number of 'depositories' in London to effect the payment of its bills drawn in the colony. Notations of these institutions are found in the Annual Reports.

- Balance carried at Messrs Currie & Co
- Interest received on account from Messrs Overend, Gurney & Co.

In VDL, balances were held at

- The Bank of Launceston

Sundry Balances in London were held at the Union Bank, which also had correspondent accounts in Australia

- Union Bank (in London)

The Bank of Launceston became a prominent financial institution in the second metropolis of Launceston, when the Derwent Bank declined to open a branch in the town.

Other institutions closed in order to avoid competition and these included the Bank of Van Diemen's Land and the Hobart Savings Bank. In 1832, the Bank for VDL moved to absorb the Bank of Cornwall in Launceston and open its own branch, but the branch proved unprofitable and closed its doors in 1834. The former bank business was taken over by the new Tamar Bank. The Derwent Bank then moved to open a branch but was declared a 'failure because of its inability to meet the competition of the Bank of VDL'. (*Hobart Town Courier 25 May, 1832*)

The Tasmanian economy prospered and declined, in regular cycles as influenced by conditions in New South Wales, in particular, and by conditions overseas (Britain).

As in NSW, the economy of the Tasmanian colony, in 1840, began to slide into a five-year depression. 'Banks and businesses failed; Hobart, Launceston and the townships between silted up with unemployed workers'. (Hughes: The Fatal Shore p521) The end of transportation to New South Wales meant that the whole yearly exodus of convicts was directed to VDL. In 1839, less than 1500 convicts had arrived in the small colony. By 1842 the figure was over 5,300. Hughes writes 'the system could not handle them, and the island could not absorb them. Worst of all, in the midst of all the confusion, it was left to Franklin (the Governor) to change the whole system of convict management.'

The colonial office, under Lord Stanley, had decreed 'from 1842 onward, the assignment of convicts to private settlers in VDL must cease. It was to be replaced by the 'Probation' system, whereby all convicts would be worked in government gangs around the island. The settlers now had two complaints–the economy was in a bad state and the settlers were losing their access to this free labour. The Stanley system was designed to combine penitentiaries in England, with transportation abroad. At first the convicted would spend time in *Pentonville*, be offered conditional pardons, and be sent to Australia to completed their sentences. Once there, the men would be 'disbursed to settlers across the country districts of VDL and NSW. They could take their wives and families, thus the 'stigma' of transportation was abolished.–This new program could be part of an immigration program. No longer to be called convicts, they would become known as 'exiles'. This was not a new idea, it being first raised in the Molesworth Committee in 1837.

The system became operational; in 1846, 517 exiles arrived; in 1847, a further 536 landed and in 1848, 455.

Edward Curr had led the Port Phillip pastoral community against the cancellation of transportation and the loss of 'free labour' and was initially happy with the 'exile' program. However, by 1846, his opinion had changed to 'exiles were depressing the wages in the colony, and it would affect the flow of free immigration'. Stanley's successor, Early Grey, offered to intervene and ensure a suitable mix of free and 'probationary' labour was available. He offered to 'send one free immigrant for every convict, and the wives and families of exiles as well'. Curr changed then his mind. In fact, England's general economic depression of 1847 intervened and caused a surge of free immigration. From 1847 to 1849, over 30,000 emigrants sailed from England to NSW. The demand for exiles or even convict labour ebbed.

• Varieties of business Activities

Meston attempted to put the VDL Company operation into focus: "The Company's main object was the growth of fine wool. This the directors maintained on all occasions without contradiction and this Bathurst recognised when he ruled that the criterion of the land to one allotted was its capability to pasture sheep. Curr and the company had a total objection to timbered land. All the good land in the northwest district was, almost without exception, clothed right down to the seacoast with dense forest. Near the coast the prevailing trees were eucalypts, white gum and stringy bark, towering aloft, often 250 feet; further inland sombre beeches, the myrtles of the colonists, of great size, replaced these." Hellyer offers some indication of the density of the forest from the report he prepared for discussion with the government on what could be defined as useful land. "On one acre, there were 2384 trees, 12 of which exceed 12 feet in girth and 4 exceeded 30 feet in girth. On another acre, there were 1,976 trees, 28 of which exceeded 12 feet in girth, eight of 21 feet and eight of 30 feet. This was typical of most of the forest". (Hellyer: Report–ref Appendix to this study). Each company official had a variable opinion of what constituted good land. For example Goldie, who for many years had been the company's agriculturalist, having arrived in the colony with Curr, but who had resigned after serious censure by Curr, attributed the company's failure solely to the policy adopted by Curr. "I think I could rear sheep at the Surrey Hills to advantage with little artificial food and shelter".

Curr would be caught out again when he presented a request to Lord Glenelg to exchange the Surrey Hills land for other land to the east. Lord Glenelg would ask, how do I reconcile the Company report of such poor land at Surrey Hills, with the written report to future buyers of VDL Coy land, when the 1833 booklet, writes so glowingly of the 'Woolnorth area" . . . 'The proximity of Woolnorth to a good harbour will enable produce of every kind to be conveyed to a market speedily, and at no very great expense. There is probably no place in VDL better'

Then the 1832 annual report was equally misleading. Both publications were the work of the Managing Director, James Bischoff, who deliberately misrepresented the circumstances of the company.

It would be incorrect to view every fatuous attempt to make 'quick' profits as a business enterprise but if we take these shallow and ill-conceived ventures away we are left only with the following *business ventures* of note:

- Land sales
- Emu Bay Railways, and
- VDL Minerals

We can dispose of the VDL Minerals fairly rapidly because it did not last long; cost the company a lot of money, cost the company manager his job, and really gained nothing.

The Company Land sales lasted all the way from 1830 to the 1960s and produced fairly encouraging results.

The Emu bay Railways, like its successor, the Zeehan Railway produced little by way of cash flow and also cost the company a great deal of money and was directly aligned with the mineral company.

The VDL Company Land Promotional Brochure

The analysis of VDL Company Annual Reports in Chapter Four covered much of the land sales activities and the result but the company produced an undated document in about 1870-1880 outlining its *Freehold Farms & Town Lots for Sale* and it is worth examining the booklet. The date can be set fairly closely because the printed text gives the company address as Blomfield House 85, London Wall, London, but that address has been erased and replaced by 35 Copthall Avenue, London EC2. This move was made by the company prior to the turn of the century.

The brochure reads "The VDL Company is one of the oldest companies engaged in Land Development in Australasia. It was incorporated in 1825 for the purpose of development and cultivation of 350,000 acres of land in the northwest district of Tasmania. The company's policy has been to clear and cultivate its lands, and thereafter to sell ready-made farms to settlers. Only about 270,000 acres remain in the company's hands for this purpose.

(The reader will note the extravagant wording of this brochure and see that it is not dissimilar to that which was written by James Bischoff in 1842 and which brought him undone.)

The land is extremely fertile, well watered, drought free, and well served with roads railways and shipping facilities.

Farming of all types is carried on and affords profitable and congenial employment

The values of land vary according to locality and proximate market; partially cleared farms are about £8-10 per acre up to £35. Every farm has a permanent water supply

Sections will be sold by cash or advantageous mortgage terms, providing payment over 14 years at a low rate of interest

"Emu Bay Estate

20,000 acres remains and is suitable for dairying and general farming. Farms are from 50 to 250 acres–all rich agricultural land. The Port of Burnie (the chief shipping port of the NW coast) is located on this estate Cargo boats carry agricultural products, timber and minerals to Melbourne and Sydney. Burnie is connected to all principal Tasmanian Towns by rail, including Launceston, Hobart and Stanley. Burnie is the premier port on the northern coast and offers excellent opportunities for immigrant traders.

Prospects are for butter factories and freezing and cold storage works with Melbourne being only 18 hours by steamer.

Hampshire Hills Estate offers 7,000 acres for selection starting at only £3 for each unimproved acre. The Emu Bay Railway runs through the estate and affords excellent means for transport of produce.

"Surrey Hills & Middlesex Plains Estates

This estate offers about 134,000 acres; it is recently surveyed and provides sections of between 1,000 and 2,000 acres. The estate is an elevated tableland of rich, basaltic soil, well timbered and abundantly watered. The native grasses offer good grazing and the land is suitable for growing good crops. It is suitable for grazing and dairying with good local markets. The Emu bay Railway traverses the estate to Zeehan and Mount Bischoff. The township of Guildford is centrally located within the estate and Burnie is only 37 miles. Blocks commence at £1 per acre

"Circular head Estate

Only 9,000 acres is available in this area of highly improved farms, near the Port of Stanley. The land is suitable for cattle rearing and fattening. The area includes an experimental apple orchard of 250 acres. The areas first settlement was made here in 1825.

General Information

Tasmania possesses one of the most beautiful climates in the world, and has an abundance of sport including Kangaroo and Wallaby hunting, shooting and fishing.

Intending settlers should first gain experience of Colonial methods, by working for a time, say a year or two, on a colonial farm. The VDL Company is engaged in farming on its own account, on a large scale, and embraces agriculture, stock rearing, fattening and orcharding. The company will endeavour to assist suitable applicants in regard to their acquiring a practical knowledge of colonial farming and a successful career."

The preparer of this little booklet with its charming photographs made the northwest coast a haven of beauty, productivity and a profitable operation just waiting to happen.

There are many gratuitous and untrue statements made but even so it achieved little purposes, as the masses did not venture forth from their cosy lifestyles in England to the wilderness of Tasmania's frontier.

Although the land was slow to sell the company eventually reduced its acreage from 350,000 to 50,000 in just fewer than 180 years.

What is noteworthy but doubtful as to authenticity is the change of direction and mission claimed by the company in this booklet. From being a producer of fine wool, to be a land developer is a quantum leap but one, which needed to be made, especially if the company couldn't produce sheep and therefore did not need all of the land. Edward Curr may well be taking the credit for the successful; if slow land sales program as he never believed his selection was worthy, although Dr. Stokes and Kerry Pink absolved Curr from any responsibility in that regard and blamed Bathurst for all of the company's woes (refer Chapter Eight–setting the record Straight)

The Ship-owning ventures of the VDL Company

Graeme Bloxam has examined the records leading to the company's business venture as ship-owner, and records" Curr first attempted to buy the Schooner *Caledonia*. Curr failed in this purchase and instead chartered two small vessels–*Nelson* (13 tons) and *Ellen* (24 tons), reach costing 20 pound per month including captain and crew. Curr did manage to commence the company's fleet with the purchase of a whaleboat for £25. Curr used the whaleboat to explore the northern coastline, including the Emu and Inglis Rivers, Circular Head and Rocky Cape. Curr managed to convert the charter of the *Nelson* into a purchase for £200. In 1826 the brig *Tranmere* arrived at Circular Head from England. Ownership was claimed in the company's records of that year although Lloyd's register only shows it as being chartered. 'She' remained at VDL until 1828. Curr wanted to buy the *George Arthur* but it was priced at £1,000, which Curr thought unreasonable. Curr, as an alternative, purchased the 27-ton clinker for £450 in 1827. The directors in London purchased an 88-ton schooner *Friendship* and it arrived in 1829. The *Nelson* had been lost in mid-1827. A new vessel was ordered from Sydney yards in 1833 and named *Edward* after Curr who had gone to England to report to the Board. Upon this arrival, an older vessel *Fanny* was sold to Stephen Henty of Port Phillip fame. Then, in 1839, Curr arranged to build two vessels at Circular Head–*Joseph Kripps* and the *Eagle*. The day before Curr left the company's employment in 1842, he launched another new vessel, named *James Gibson*.

By 1843, the company had lost most of her fleet and decided to cease owning ships and from then on only employed chartered tonnage. At least the shipping venture lasted almost 20 years, longer than many of its other numerous enterprises.

The Emu Bay Railway

Lou Rae writes in her 1991 work 'Emu Bay Railway' "The VDL Company's involvement with tramway and railway operations had been a learning but generally unrewarding experience and after many frustrations and much bad luck, it was pleased to sell its interests to an eager Australian syndicate. The controversies and tribulations surrounding the early Emu Bay Railways were not dissimilar to the problems faced by the VDL Company on its establishment some seventy years previous."

A Business Plan that Worked

Before turning to the numerous and diversified business enterprises, most of which were developed in a rush to secure short term profits, and possibly fend the company away from bankruptcy, it would be of interest and value to review a business plan that actually worked.

For such an introduction we turn to Brian H. Fletcher and his 'Governor Darling–A Governor Maligned', and in particular to his brief analysis of the Australian Agricultural Company. Both companies received their charter in 1824 and their progress and development should have run parallel. One company surged ahead with a clear goal, albeit ambitious, in kind, whilst the other company cried about its terrible plight (which was of its own making), licked its wounds, caused general chaos in its relations with the government and most authorities, and never achieved any goal. Compare and contrast the path of the two companies.

Fletcher writes "Governor Darling informed the Directors of 'his earnest wish' to assist the Company 'by every means consistent with his duty'. In 1828 he reiterated this assurance and claimed to have responded more generously to the Company's demands for convicts than to the requests of private settlers. He had also despatched a military guard to protect the company's property and then sent a magistrate to Port Stephens to perform judicial duties. When the local manager made accusations against the Governor of being uncooperative, the Court in London did not support him and commented–from the facts, we would have come to a very different conclusion."

One area of disagreement related to the coal mines on the AAC property. The Governor did not think they should be privately controlled, and arranged through Bathurst to carve off certain lands for leasing to a mining operator. In response to company appeals in London, Murray, Bathurst's successor, struck a new working agreement with the directors and gave the company 2,000 acres of land in fee simple which included the government mines at Newcastle and the Company was to have a virtual monopoly over coal-mining in NSW for thirty-one years.

Fletcher confirms "The combined area of agricultural land sown on the Company's estate and in the colony increased from 45,000 acres in 1825 to 71,000 acres in 1828. Further growth continued to take place, as Darling was very aware of agriculture as a source of employment and as a means of providing foodstuff. On several occasions he made labour available to assist with the wheat harvest. He ensured that land suited to agriculture was reserved for that purpose and endeavoured to enlarge the grain market by supporting proposals for the establishment of distilleries. He was also anxious for the settlers to diversify their crops and favoured the experiments that were being conducted with sugarcane and tobacco. He wisely did not encourage settlers to become involved with risky crops such as vines, poppies, hemp etc as 'to interfere with the immediate pursuits of the settlers' would prove counter-productive whilst 'they do not have a competent knowledge'. At a more general level Darling patronised the Agricultural Society, which a group of leading settlers had established.

Darling also, upon the advice of the Society increase the duty on imported spirits and tobacco, in order to raise the profit margin for farmers. He limited government farming and grazing, thereby increasing the market for private farmers. He also directed government departments purchase local produce by tender. As the *Gazette* reported on 22nd October 1827,'what other rulers might have only dreamt of, the present Governor is actually accomplishing, for the benefit of the public, and the sustained advancement of the colony'.

If Bathurst's direction to improve the VDL flock was to be achieved it would take better sheep husbandry, but the difficulty here was that most farmers were on small holdings and most of these small farmers, had been once under sentence. The majority knew little about farming lived on a subsistence basis and were easily ruined through adversity. There was thus little chance, whilst this situation continued, for enlightened methods to be used or of agriculture improving its standing, and whilst the governors appreciated the problems in upgrading the flock quality, there was little they could actually do to achieve this goal.

Darling took another view of the challenge and wrote to Bathurst "it is desirable to direct a greater share of the capital and intelligence in the colony from grazing to agriculture". Darling, like his lieutenant in VDL believed in free enterprise and also thought it best to allow the economy to regulate itself.

The point of these references is 'what a difference' a good relationship between the company (in particular Curr) and the governor would have made. The governor had within his jurisdiction the ability to encourage the development of VDL agriculture and therefore assist and encourage the tenant farmers on VDL Company property, to experiment with new crops or foods, and thus broaden the opportunities for the small farmers, to review its policy towards fine wool, and encourage a cross-breeding program (as Marsden had done in Sydney) and develop sheep suitable to the harsher VDL: climate for both wool production and meat production. If the London market for course wool could be held at about 12 pence per pound, (landed), then building up the yield of wool per sheep from 6 to 12 pound would double the return to these graziers.

Developing the Properties

Before reviewing each of the enterprises owned and pursued by the VDL Company in what we would term today vertical and horizontal integration, it would be of value and interest to understand the extend of the development work done on each property between 1826 and 1851, and in so doing try to understand where £4108,000 had been spent; in addition, we need to understand why the company suddenly decided to abandon farming and sell the properties, and this review may, too, cause our understanding of whether the land selection had been such a disaster or if other circumstances were present in contributing to the deterioration of the company's fortunes.

To learn more about the properties of 1851, we rely on the written report and evaluation by the newly appointed manager, James Gibson, keeping in mind he was another in the sequence of British Managers, transferred fro England with little understanding or appreciation of the Colonial climate, conditions, or circumstances.

Gibson, reviewed each property individually:

(a) <u>Circular Head</u>
"Excepting the township of Stanley, of about 250 acres, and Highfield House, with the garden and the deer park, the whole of the peninsular is let to tenants, at rentals from 5s to 20s per acre, and upon renewal, will bring a considerable addition to the Company's income

(b) <u>The Township of Stanley</u>
Á plan of the town has been prepared showing the new allotments laid out these having different values according to their situation. The Lagoon and Tea Tree Scrub, forms portion of the town, and can be easily developed if drained, and will serve as a valuable reserve

The town boundaries can be extended when required either along the Bay or by dividing Chapman's field into allotments

(c) <u>The Mainland</u>
This area consists of about 2,000 acres and remains available for rental, in sections of 80 acres, which will bring about 7s or 8s per acre per annum in rent. This area is heavily timbered so tenants will require longer-term leases of ten to fourteen years

(d) <u>Mineral Spring</u>
This healthy portion of land is rented for ten years and is known as 'the Inlet'. This area of about 1,000 acres is mainly marshes but if drained could be used for cultivation. Another adjacent area is a mineral spring which will be rented to invalids from other colonies because the water is impregnated with iron, contains magnesia and sulphur and, when fresh, a quantity of carbolic acid gas.

(e) <u>The Rivers at Circular Head</u>
The Black River, which forms the eastern boundary of the Circular Head block, is navigable for a distance of two miles by vessels up to 100 tons burden. 'Slate, brick clay and quartz rock are found on the banks and it will ultimately prove the outlet to an extensive tract of country on its eastern bank, and also to land at the south of the Circular Head grant, which is now being rapidly occupied, under the new government land regulations. A reserve of 200 acres should be made at its junction with Bass Strait, for the formation of a township; and 100 acres, should be set-aside for the same purpose at the neck of land, which connects the peninsula with the main.

(f) <u>'Woolnorth'</u>
This tract of country is the least valuable of the company's estates. Renting it out, as has been done, is the best arrangement because at the end of the lease it will revert to the company in a partially improved state.

(g) <u>The Islands</u>
Walker's Island is barren and Trefoil, from its limited area (224 acres) is of little value. Collectively they are the least valuable properties owned by the company.

(h) <u>Emu Bay</u>
The Emu Bay estate contains a large extent of rich land and would sell very readily. I think the company might be benefited, and the rest of the property enhanced in value by putting a quantity of it

up for sale. A new township would be formed here, adjacent to the River Cam and the Hampshire Hill Road.

(i) <u>Surrey & Hampshire Hills.</u>
Two thousand acres of Hampshire is rented and more can be disposed of on similar terms; very soon the property will become of much annual value or be likely to fetch a high price.

The elevated character of surrey Hills (much of it being over 2,100 feet above sea level) causes changes in the weather, sand joined to the difficult access from the rest of the colony, distracts much from its value, but I think it could be let in subdivisions, upon satisfactory terms.

(j) <u>Middlesex Plains</u>
Although situated at an elevation of 2,700 feet, this estate is better grassed and more valuable as a stock run than any similar extent of land at the Surrey Hills, whilst its proximity to the settled districts is another advantage.

James Gibson's Recommendations

Following the assessment made of each property made Gibson (refer above) for the 1854 Annual Report, he drew a number of conclusions to restore liquidity to the company.

a. Sell the forest (of approx 2,000 acres) at Circular head, or it could be let on 10 to 14 year leases.
b. Rent out the East Inlet on a 14 year lease
c. Sell town lots at Emu bay (Burnie) and Stanley, each six months, with the reserves recommended
d. Sell the Forest Land at Emu Bay, and allow the company to handle the timber transporting and sales
e. Rent out Middlesex, Surrey & Hampshire
f. Emigration: Encourage emigration to company lands, and offer good terms and support for land sales to these emigrants

g. Steam Communication: Encourage a regular steam communication with Launceston and Melbourne and this will do much to improve the value of the properties at Circular Head and Emu Bay Private enterprise will undertake this role before long, but the company could bring it about earlier by offering a bonus to the owners of the first boat, and remaining in business six months.

h. Roads & Bridges: An act of the Tasmanian Legislature has provided for the construction of cross and bye roads, by imposing a rate upon the land in those districts where the inhabitants bring themselves under the operation of the Act. The company will then be relieved of all trouble on this score, excepting the payment of the assessment. I recommend that bridges be approved across the Mersey and Forth, in order to move livestock and persons on horseback to pass at all seasons of the year and make Middlesex and Surrey Hills more accessible. The bridges could be erected of local timber and the cost of each will not exceed £200.

i. Wharves and Harbours: The wharf at Circular Head has been repaired but needs extension. The harbour at Emu Bay will require expenditure to make it more secure

j. Minerals: Quartz Rock is plentiful around Surrey Hills, and extends to Emu Bay; Malachite, a rich copper ore, has been found at Circular Head; Coal has been discovered at the Rivers Mersey & Forth, and other veins will run into the company's lands

k. Valuing the Different Estates

Mr Gibson estimated the total company assets (property–land & buildings) to be not less than £200,000. Cash balances are over £8,000

What Gibson was telling the Directors was that the company had partially turned the corner. The market in the VDL colony, especially following gold discoveries in Victoria and NSW, had picked up and was being to attract emigrant and new settlers. A broader opportunity was being developed for the company produce, such as timber and minerals, but the production of livestock, wool or grain, did not enter the equation.

Sir Edward Poore Reports:

The directors resolved, at the end of the Gibson visit, and "in order to leave no means untried to improve the company's affairs, to induce a Gentleman, Sir Edward Poore, to be a special commissioner, to go over the whole of the several properties, to confer with the chief agent on all matters relating to the selling and letting of land, the prospecting of minerals and the bring home his report thereon".

Sir Edward sailed in October 1858 and returned in July 1859.

Poore arrived in Launceston in January and starting from Deloraine, rode by way of Surrey & Hampshire Hills to Burnie, thence by steamer to Circular Head (and thus Highfield), and by horseback to Woolnorth. Poore wrote that 'in order to preserve his independence, he avoided Mr. Gibson as much as possible'.

In brief Poore reported as follows:

"In my opinion, a large portion of your land is of excellent character, and much of the waste (land) capable of great improvement.

I could not ascertain the existence of any minerals except for large quantities of excellent slate.

I could not confirm gold had been discovered on the Island

The slate mining has been presently abandoned, although with freights to the mainland, now at competitive rates (Circular Head to Melbourne is 25s per ton; Sydney and Adelaide 35s per ton) the venture should be reconsidered.

An essential condition of the occupation of wastelands is a certain amount of fencing. One of the tenants, Messrs Grant & Fields has erected a good amount of quality fencing.

There has been little surveying done recently.

Highfield House at Circular Head has been repaired of late but not thoroughly.

The farm buildings generally are in good repair and are serviceable.

The Wharf At Circular Head will need further repairs next year.

The forestlands, south of Stanley, are most valuable and will be excellent for future cultivation. Nearly the whole is fine land and has great capabilities. The timber is good and of large size.

'Woolnorth' is fully rented to Messrs Grant, and is almost entirely wasteland, capable of vast improvement but already a good sheep run. A suitable (non-English) grass able to be controlled by fire would carry 30,000 sheep instead of only the 6,000 carried at present. This would raise the rental value to £1,000 per annum. Such a grass is available in Sydney, as I learned from William McArthur; it is called *Indian Couch* and fattens cattle readily and grows rapidly, and would thrive on 'Woolnorth' soil.

The Surrey & Hampshire Hills should be subdivided into at least 2 runs using natural separation) and rented out. Up to 10,000 cattle could be thus maintained.

Middlesex Plains is rich black soil, which, if grassed, would produce a large amount of good feed.

Stanley should become an important place for trade and shipping. Large amounts of surplus grain should be produced and shipped to markets.

Trade is very dull at present, due mainly to American timbers being imported. Firewood in the near future will be valuable and saleable for in excess of 20s per ton. This will increase rather than diminish the value of the company's properties.

The principal roads are macadamised and in good repair. Burnie, in Emu bay, is likely to become a large shipping port, as it is an open roadstead. It would benefit from the erection of a wharf. The cost of £500 could be raised by subscription for this purpose from towns' people.

Overall, when the colony is more prosperous and the general state of trade more propitious, it would be well to dispose of certain company lands.

When town lots are sold, buyers should agree to build upon them within a certain time, in which case a lower price can be justified without being detrimental to the company, as adjoining lots would increase in value. One thing that will make the company's properties much more valuable is 'population'.

I suggest that the land be let by tender (and not necessarily to the highest bidder), and that company-sponsored mortgage finance be made available to buyers. I am attaching to this report a more detailed map of the properties showing the soil types, buildings and general condition."

This was a very useful and thorough report by Poore and begs the question—why did it take until 1858 for someone with an open mind and some little business experience to carry out a survey of this nature. Curr could have arranged for a similar survey except his ego would not allow someone else to offer an opinion which may show his inadequacies and ineptitudes to the full. That Gibson recommended this step and went to the trouble of personally evaluating the company's assets in anticipation of a further review and study puts him into a separate race of British Managers. The company may still have a future and thus avoid liquidation.

The company, it appeared, had bottomed out and turned the corner. Although there were relatively minor hiccups between 1858 and 2000,the company tread water and survived.

It is interesting to look at the annual reports commencing 1900, and use this information as a lead into the topic of changing ownership.

The year 1900 recognised 75 years of existence for the company, and the annual report for that year was much more positive and upbeat that most previous years. Amidst the discussion of the coming federation, the directors hoped the company would share in the national advantage coming from Federation. They mentioned that the construction of the railway connecting Burnie with Zeehan and the West Coast Mineral Fields had made further progress during the last year and it was hoped the coming year would see its completion. The Engineer in charge submitted a lengthy report.

Even after 75 years, the company was able to report only "the profit on the year's <u>livestock trading</u> has been only £2,664.6.1, being a gain of only 834.5.6 over the previous year

Rents on land increased marginally but future years should be much better

Timber: A consignment of over 100 logs of myrtle timber from the company's estates was made, and should be repeated in the coming year.

The Company ports were benefiting from the very active & positive trading condition throughout Tasmania. The overall increase of company exports was £192,512 due to higher wool prices and in minerals the increase was £581,585 due to higher output as well as better prices.

Even the minerals/Mining activities were in good shape. The export of Copper increased by 69% in quantity and 97% in value due to better copper prices. Tin prices and output also improved according to the directors,

By <u>1910,</u> the directors were reporting:

That rents had increased to £11,194.1.6; up from 10652.17.6

That Livestock prices (for fat cattle were down) and the net profit was only 4031-pound compared with 4135 for the previous year

Land Sales realised 862 acres for £7,001.6.4. The company sold land to the State government for them to build a breakwater at Emu Bay Harbour.

Emu Bay Railway traffic increased from £58,685 to 59,422

The Federal Government had imposed a land tax on the company's UCV, costing the company £2,669. The "directors deprecates action on the part of a British Colony which must have so damaging an effect on the best interests of British investors".

After what the colony had contributed to the company in 85 years, the directors should have been grateful for being sable to contribute anything back to the Commonwealth.

The directors declared a twenty-shilling dividend and paid £10,000 in dividends to its stockholders.

It is interesting to note that in the 1910 Balance Sheet, which was beginning to resemble a modern day balance sheet, the valuation of the company's remaining 339,995 acres (out of the original 350,000 acres) was set at £186,314, still less than Sir Edward Poore's opinion of 1858 (his was 200,000-pound. Livestock and machinery had declined to a total of £12,163.16.3, whilst cash was still being kept at *Glynn & Co* in London and the Bank of Australasia in Tasmania. Audit fees had risen from £17 in 1845 to £21 in 1910.

In 1922, annual rents had declined to £6415, land sales were only bring £14,640 for 10,567 acres, and farming produced only a profit of £910.

The directors reported that the 'Woolnorth' swamp was being drained.

In this year the company land had been revalued and the remaining 258,496 acres was valued at £230,267;livestock had increased to 19616-pound, although cash was at a very low level. For the first time the company was making provision for Australian Income Tax, and the Commonwealth Land tax payable by the company had been defeated in the High Court and the State Government was now imposing the same tax, as well as a state income tax. In addition the company was now paying a corporations tax in England.

In 1930 rentals had still not recovered, farming operations incurred a loss land sales amount to £113320 compared to just £20 the previous year. The company had sold 123,000lb acres at a little less than one-pound per acre, which incurred a loss since the properties had been revalued in the previous 10 years. This sale of the Surrey Hills property had been a long time coming. Negotiations had been taking place over a five-year period because the parties were unable to reach agreement on price and terms. In the end the company met the buyer's (APPM) demands sand the sale took place, enabling the company to repurchase a great deal of its issued stock. This transaction left the value of remaining property (only132, 830 acres remained) at £95,750. The company managed, in spite of its huge windfall sale of land, managed to only pay ten shillings in Federal Income tax for the year

The 1940s & war years showed the company returned to losses, in spite of thew strong farm conditions. Rents remained steady but farming results showed a gross profit but a net loss because extra charges had been made to "the farming account by way of rental for lands in hand used for farming and pastoral purposes". (Governor–C. Hampton Hale 1942 annual Report)

This is a most unusual accounting transaction, although it seems to have had only marginal impact on the total state, federal, local government and corporate taxes paid by the company. The transaction and balances for the year are cloaked in confusion although this writer's reconciliation shows higher costs associated with similar revenues in the various areas of operations. The balance Sheet value of property once again declined due to further sales in the late 1930s–in 1942, the remaining 92,666 acres was only valued at £45,963. Livestock and plant was reduced to £10,240. The company was, by 1942, merely a shell of its former self, still not making good profits, and satisfied solely with pastoral and grazing operations–the timber and port activities having been closed out in the 1930s.

The Governor's Report to stockholders states that there was a bumper harvest in potatoes in the district, but VDL Company was not in the potato business, and the new freezing works at Somerset processed a record 31,000 fat lambs, but again 'Woolnorth' had none to sell. "Very good potato seasons are not helpful to dairying and cattle sales" (Governor Hale–Annual Report) The Governor did not comment on the fact that London office costs and Director's fees were greater in the year 1942 than the salaries, wages and expenses in Tasmania. The company appears to be going backwards, again.

<u>1950</u> and a new Governor brought better news. Rents had increased; farm operations showed a healthy profit and land sales had commenced again. Once again farming operations were charged with a 'rent', thus inflating rents received sand understating farming profits. Director's fees increased and tax provisions doubled. Property values further declined, although property maintenance once again was capitalised in Fixed Assets. All of the B, C & D class shares had been bought by and converted to 'A' class shares of which there were now 250,000 shares fully paid ay 5s, so a return of capital (In 1949 there had been a 1s.3d return) had been completed in the 1940s, probably greatly to the company's benefit.

<u>1960</u> and more changes to the accounting processes; The company had sold a further 30 acres of land but revalued the remaining land, so that 64,606 acres now had a value of £121,619. The directors had reduced acreage from 350,000 in 1830 to less than 65,000 in 1960. Farming showed a profit of only £7,046 compared with £2,946 in 1959. Potatoes had been grown as a cash crop and earned £1,333. The 'bull' stud operations were profitable and the sale of two bulls caused the livestock to be revalued by about £20,000 to £45,782. The directors do not disclose how many cattle or sheep are being carried to make up the livestock valuation. At one time it was a sense of pride for the stocking rate to be identified.

A general observation is that the company had returned to lesser than desirable British management and secrecy about the operations prevailed. It was once again a company in confusion and in need of reassessment before a third party affected a takeover.

CHAPTER 6

CHANGING OWNERSHIPS

Any company, formed by a group of Mill owners, must make provision for changing ownership of shares. Mills are bought and sold, owners die and new owners come to replace them, but the share in the VDL Company were not then, as now, easily saleable. There was no formal mechanism in the Charter to allow the stock to be bought or sold, transferred or assigned, and that is why as part of the accounting reports there is recognition of the current equivalent of 'treasury stock' where shares, with unpaid calls, have been forfeited and the control reverts to the company.

An interesting study is to understand the history of charter companies, and their replacement by regular corporations. Company law also grew and changed as trading activities became more widespread. Part of this business law involved the commercial bankruptcy of companies, and we will answer the question whether the intent to 'liquidate' the VDL Company in 1850 would have been possible under then law as a voluntary process as opposed to an involuntary 'bankruptcy, wherein the company could not meet reasonable expectations of credit terms, or negotiate bills drawn on a timely basis or any default on the company bank loans.

However, we know about the share ownership in the early years and can track the controlling ownership between 1826 and 1971 when it left British hands and found its way into the hands of an Australian family. Then in early 1980, ownership changed once again to Italian control, even if that family latterly made a permanent residence in Australia, for a short time. Two more changes took place, first to another English investor and then to a New Zealand company.

Changing ownership was aligned to numerous business interests.

- The first and longest running investors were holding shares in order to secure regular supplies of fine wool. Such ambition was not met with any degree of reality, but most of these woollen mill owners, continued to hold their shares, in the hope they would either receive a return on their investment or a return of capital, or an eventual receipt of the Golden Fleece as fuel for the mills.
- The Australian shareholder was not overly interested in making a profit. Having married an Englishwoman, the interest was in the social benefits that being the 'Governor' of the Court of the Van Diemen's Land Company could provide. He built, at company expense, a fine home on the property for himself and his wife, and she recommenced a company interest in horse breeding. But this was a short-term uncommercial interest.
- The Italian investors had also been persuaded to the stock by the grandeur of the title, although the investor group and their adviser decided not to 'buck' the rules of the London Stock Exchange who were already making a quiet probe into the company stock trading and ownership, not the FIRB, whose role it was to stop illegal takeovers of Australian companies. The status of the VDL Company had become complicated and murky. A charter company, it was bound by the British Company's Legislation, and the listing was controlled by the LSE. However, the asset was in Australia, and being pastoral land, was subject to control by the FIRB, and although listing had never been gained in Australia, the Companies Law of Australia applied because the VDL Company had been reregistered in Tasmania under local laws.

Press coverage of the company by the local press was regular and the prospect of change in operations or ownership was also a subject for special press attention.

Our first reference point for ownership is a Report on initial proprietors, dated 1826. They categorised themselves as:

M.Ps–4
Wool traders & merchants–9
Merchants–other–4
Bankers–2
Excise Commissioner–1

Thus this would confirm Bathurst's conjecture that the company was formed by a majority of Woollen Mill operators, Wool merchants, bankers and general investors. The company remained in such hands from 1826 for the next 100 years. The company's poor financial performance and the wide spread of shareholdings made it difficult for shares to be traded, and by the depression years we read in the Annual Report that there were a lot of 'widows and orphan shareholders who relied on a regular dividend'. For years the company had operated at a loss and any dividends, small and intended only to keep calm at annual general meetings, and such dividends were paid out of capital.

So the share register remained relatively inactive for a century and a half, with many shares falling into the control of 'estates'.

The late 1960s saw a transfer of 'control' from English stockholders to an Australian–Mr Blythe Ritchie. Ritchie had married Gaile, after he had spent time in England following a few years in an American Agricultural College. Ritchie's father was a Western District grazier in Victoria and Blythe had grown up amongst horses, cattle and merino sheep and went to the USA to learn a 'different style of agriculture'. Gaile's family owned stock in VDL Company and encouraged Blythe to assemble a controlling interest and try to put the VDL Company in better shape. Upon assembling the necessary shares, Ritchie was appointed Manager to replace the ailing Mr Morrison, who had been associated with Woolnorth for a quarter of a century.

Under Ritchie's management the 'Woolnorth' property had been the scene of several successful rodeos. The rodeo promotion was a result of Ritchie's personal interest in the sport, developed during his stay in the USA. Ritchie frequently employed as station hands such top rodeo circuit riders as Bonny Young. Ritchie built a rodeo yard at the property, which 'was the most up to date in Australia'.

Ritchie made a number of changes to Woolnorth including completion of the project to drain the marsh area between 'slaughter hill' and the sea. Ritchie also built, with company funds, a magnificent 'company director's house' overlooking the flatland to the sea. It was built exclusively from Tasmanian timbers and measures 100 'squares'.

The 'Launceston Examiner' reports on May 2,1974 that the "Woolnorth' property was on the market unofficially and another Australian–a Tasmanian businessman–Lloyd Bonney was the 'prospective purchaser.

The newspaper reported that Bonney had recently sold his Circular head property along with his trucking and cement business and wanted to acquire an investment property. At that time, 'Woolnorth' was carrying 5,000 sheep, 2500 cattle and between 60 and 100 horses.

The Bonney sale did not proceed but Ritchie kept looking for a buyer. In 1979, Jonathon Todhunter a London 'hustler' of European funds for 'investment' sought out Ritchie to 'make a deal'. Todhunter's father was an executive director of the London-based ICI and his mother was a member of the Lempriere family–a pastoral house in Victoria with Tasmanian connections. Ritchie had sold the 'Woolnorth' wool through Lempriere Company and they were aware of his interest in selling his 'Woolnorth' interest'. Todhunter had a number of wealthy 'clients' in the Milan to Verona corridor in Italy and maintained an office in both Milan and Munich for the purpose of raising 'deposits' of cash from wealthy Italian families. Both these offices were merely fronts for apartments, but gave a good impression of an international organisation. 'Front' was all Todhunter wanted from his 'international offices' and his 'head office' in the prestigious Stock Exchange building office in London. Cash collected by Todhunter was taken over the border at Chiasso in Switzerland and deposited in U.S. dollars into the Todhunter account with the United Bank of Switzerland. The lire he received from his 'clients' was changed at 'black market' rates into American dollars from U.S. service men at the base north of Milan.

Todhunter took his proposal to buy 'Woolnorth' to a number of 'clients in Milan, until one of them, Valmorbida, directed him to the wealthy, ego-driven Count Cicogna in Verona. The Count took the bait; expressed instant interest and Todhunter took the opportunity of trying to close the transaction. The Count had to raise the money, whilst Ritchie had to get approval to sell his shareholding. The count was aristocracy, with liveried waiters to serve dinner in an old 'palace' he rented. Cicogna and his son-in-law, Guilio Dolcetta. Ritchie had got his price (close to $3A million) but was not likely to allow it to be spoiled or foiled by an ambitious assistant in the FIRB or the LSE.

On 19th March 1984, Todhunter released a press statement claiming that 'after 159 years the VDL Company had finally become Australian'. He claimed 'an anonymous principal shareholder, formerly resident in Italy and owning 1.5 million of the 2.5 million 25p shares has moved to Australia'. He was referring to Guilio Dolcetta who with the Count's daughter had moved to Sydney. Todhunter claimed that for FIRB purposes (permission was sought and granted after the event and without a full, frank or honest disclosure to the FIRB or the LSE), although the company 's domicile remains in the U.K, 'the transfer of shares could be approved'. The Australian Financial Revenue stated "the company remains the height of discretion on the untoward disclosure of information, but was able to learn that the present directors included Todhunter as Governor/ Chairman; Valmorbida and Dolcetta as directors and the Company Manager in Tasmania (Graham Gillon) as another director and a Burnie (Tasmania) CPA, Neville Hyland, as Secretary. The irony and falsity of the Todhunter press statement was that the register shows Dolcetta only held 1100 shares as directors qualifying shares, Valmorbida had 110,000 shares in his name whilst Cicogna, through a nominee company, remained in Italy and controlled the other 1,350,000 shares. Dolcetta was a proxy holder for the nominee company.–Barclays Nominees (Gracechurch) Ltd. The AFR concluded "Freedom from FIRB restraints means it can expand without being limited, should it wish to do so, as well as releasing the company *from a number of trivial but tedious imposts*". The Italian years finished when the Dolcetta brother passed away in Italy and Guilio packed up in Sydney and returned home. The Count decided to sell the nominee interests as well as that held by Valmorbida. So much for an Australian company!

Ritchie and Cicogna both used the company and its assets for personal aggrandisement. Theirs was not the grand profit motive of yesteryear, but rather a self-satisfying fulfilment of buying part of Australia's rich colonial and pastoral history.

The new owners have a pure profit motive. Tasman Agriculture (according to their company brochure) "secured majority ownership of the company by purchasing 87.5% of the company's shares in November 1993. Using experience gained on its 52 farms in New Zealand, Tasman Agriculture has begun a dairy conversion program calculated to move 'Woolnorth' closer to developing its full farming potential"

After 178 years, Woolnorth is trying to develop its potential. From English hands to Australian, to Italian and now New Zealand. Just about everyone has had a try—why not the New Zealanders?

CHAPTER 7

SETTING THE RECORD
STRAIGHT

Only two writers have recently tackled the history of the VDL Company. Kerry Pink is a long-time resident of Burnie, Tasmania and has directed his journalistic efforts over the past ten years to local Emu Bay and region community history. In addition he has written a history of other local corporate institutions such as Kauri Timber Company and the Renison Tin Mining Company. He is presently retained by the VDL Company to prepare a history of the last remaining company farming asset–the 'Woolnorth' property.

The second writer is an academic, Dr. H.J.W. Stokes, whose article *The Van Diemen'sLand Company* appeared in the 1971 Tasmanian Year Book.

Both writers have relied heavily for their detail on Company operations on Meston's History of the VDL Company 1824-1842, and as we have seen in the earlier chapters Meston declares a strong bias in favour of Curr and so do these two new writers. This position is unsupportable in a full view of the VDL Company and its history. A more objective position is available but neither Pink nor Stokes accept any alternative position.

• The local version of the Company history

Kerry Pink, a retired journalist from the Burnie Advocate has developed an intimate knowledge of the company activities in the former company town of Emu Bay, now Burnie.

In more than 8 books about the region, and its history, Pink has identified most of the important events associated with the company.

In 'Beyond the Ramparts, he writes "The principal objective of the company founders was to help relieve England's woollen mills from their heavy dependence on expensive imports from Germany and Spain and also to profit from their colonial investment. The company was to fail, miserably, on both objectives because Arthur insisted on restricting the company's land selection to the country west of the Mersey River, and not as Curr wanted, in the timbered native grasslands in the eastern half of the Island . . .

The VDL Company, which received its Royal Charter in 1825, sought a grant of 500,000 acres of native grassland that would graze sheep and cattle with minimum expense and time. Despite its early misfortunes, mistakes and financial losses—a litany of wasted endeavour and unfulfilled hopes—the VDL Company has survived for more than 1600 years, still operates as a Royal Charter Company and still farms part of its original land grant, the 54,600 acre 'Woolnorth' property at Cape Grim.

The advantages to the colony of granting land to the company were to be the importation of thoroughbred livestock, free settlers to a convict dominated island, cultivation of waste lands, construction of roads, bridges and ports, and the establishment of settlements in uninhabited country."

Pink offers a short assessment of the major faults of the company, "Curr's workload was massive made all the more onerous when he soon discovered he could not rely on the judgement or actions of his senior staff, particularly their early assessment of potential sheep pasturage, and climate, in a colony completely foreign to their English background. That knowledge could only be acquired by experience, and mistakes made in the gaining of that knowledge were to cost the VDL Company dearly (Pink, *op cit* p25).

Curr, himself, was responsible for supporting his assistant's selection of the Surrey Hills and Hampshire Hills as the centre of the company's pastoral operations. Sheep were first taken to the area, from Emu Bay, in 1829, using a rough track cleared through the forests. The opinion of Hellyer and Fossey, two Curr surveyors was impressive." *The country is so admirably laid out by nature that it assumes very much the appearance of a nobleman's domain, both to extent and good quality'* Curr never saw the country personally before selecting it as part of his 250,000 acre selection. Even when Curr advised his directors "*The Surrey Hills can never be first or even second rate sheep pasture'*, the directors decided to accept this region of land. This would not be the first nor most expensive blunder Curr supervised.

CDL Company directors were required, for cash flow purposes, to make annual calls of £1 per share for almost the next 20 years, until finally in 1850, the directors appointed a committee to investigate the liquidation of the company. Pink estimates "By 1851, the directors had authorised expenditures during the past 25 years of over £600,000 on the colonial enterprise, whilst receipts had only reached £34,054

Curr's dismissal in 1841 was preceded by the suicide of Hellyer in 1832 and the resignation of all other original officers by 1830. The new manager, James Gibson, instituted a policy of tenancy, on company lands–7-year leases at 2s per acre per annum. By 1843 some 68 pioneers had taken up 82147 acres of land. Even with the company offering to buy their tenant farmer's produce and sell to them provisions, supplies, tools etc, the company still lost money. The cessation of transportation, the directors believed, would make the company land attractive to new free settlers wanting to buy land for farming.

The Company meeting in February 1851 decided to stop farming operations and concentrate on land sales. Small areas around Circular Head were sold in lots averaging £2 per acre. 'Highfield' the Curr house was advertised for lease, mainly because Gibson, who was now recommending the formal liquidation of the Company's assets moved to Launceston, before his dismissal in 1859.

The main asset of the company was sold in 1936, when the remaining 38,000 acres of the 'Hills' area was transferred to APPM for about £1 per acre. This became the key source of timber for the Burnie paper manufacturing industry. Only 50,000 acres of the original 150,000 Woolnorth acres remains at this time.

Pink in *Against the Tide*, writes "the paramount factor in the decision by the VDL Company to select Circular Head as the site for the first European settlement on the northwest coast of Tasmania in 1826 was its suitability as a natural deepwater harbour".

Pink, in this latest book, repeats the myth "under its royal charter, the VDL Company was granted 250,000 acres of crown later (later increased to 3250,000acres) and it envisaged a flock of a quarter of a million sheep, grazing on native grasslands."

He also repeats what he wrote in a previous work "the company was forced to select its grant in the northwest corner of the islands west of the Mersey River"

The report by Curr's associates were not contradictory however, John West in *History of Tasmania* records 'the first loaded cart sent from Hobart through the Midlands to Launceston in 1807 had made the journey without a single tree being felled. On the other hand, Captain Charles Harwicke who made a cursory examination of the coastal fringe on the northern coast for Governor Sorell in 1823, described the region as 'quite impenetrable and totally uninhabitable (Report dated 23.01.1824)

Although Sorell had commissioned the Hardwicke report on the hinterland and northern regions, he had left the colony before the report was presented to Sorell's successor, Governor Arthur. In spite of strong hearsay from sailors, and not having received the Sorell report, Sorell, stood before the court of the VDL Company in London and opined ">>>>>>>>>>>>>>>>>>".

Pink in a further history of the local Burnie area–*Campsite to City*–takes further historical liberties and pro-company bias when he writes (P1)

"The company's first misfortune was being forced, under protest, to select its land in the northwest quarter of the Island. Its greatest mistake was to attempt to undertake a specialist rural enterprise, the production of fine wool, in an area that was virtually unknown. While the fertile volcanic soils, lush pastures and temperate climate of the northwest cleared of its dense forest after decades of toil, were to surpass any area of Tasmania for grazing and cropping, the region was not suited to the production of fine wool. Unlike the milder Midlands and eastern districts of the Island which produce the best and highest priced wool in the world, the climate of the northwest is wet and cold for too many months of the year for production of fine fleeces."

One may be asking just what is the real explanation for the first and biggest problem faced by the VDL Company.

It is not too simplistic to argue that a person (e.g. Curr and Sorell) who are trying to gain an advantage (in Curr's case, he was seeking a position of importance and a financial advantage) will make representations a little extreme of the absolute truth in order to show his importance, knowledge, wisdom and substance, and then later having been given the challenge that he so badly sought, had to verify his claims. Curr was in that very position. From the operation of a small land grant just north of Hobart town, and not having met Sorell whilst in the colony, Curr conspired with Sorell to impress the Court of the Company and to sell them on VDL as an ideal location for a pastoral property. Sorell, as the former Governor of the Colony, and not personally aware of the northern regions of the colony, stated that Curr was a 'good chap, experienced and competent' whilst Curr claimed that Sorell was the epitome of gubernatorial excellence.

Curr was young (only 26 at that time), eager to impress and wanting to portray himself before the Board of opportunity as technically competent, willing to be a co-investor with these other wealthy entrepreneurs, and begging for the chance to show what he could do for the company. 'Profits, a good return on capital, growth in assets through rising land values, as well as a steady supply of top class wool at low cost, were all things Curr claimed he could make happen. That there could and would be practical difficulties, did not fit into the equation and that is why, before any land selection had even commenced, the company had bought a supply of sheep in Spain and they were being shipped to Hobart–the cart before the horse, or the sheep before the pasture.

As unfortunate as the Pink misstatements are, the Stokes version raises a real question of academic accuracy.

The Year Book article is extracted from an unpublished thesis by Stokes, but we are not told whether the extract was prepared by Stokes or a third party within the Bureau of Statistics. Any criticism or judgement is tempered by this lack of information. However, the Stokes' article includes a number of statements, which must be questioned.

"Sufficient self-styled 'authorities' were found to convince both the company and the government that there was ample land suitable in its natural state for grazing in the unexplored northwest quarter of the Island."

If this statement were even halfway correct, Curr could be forgiven for being misled by 'outsiders'. But these 'authorities' comprised only three in number: Sorell, Curr and Hobbs, the latter having firstly sailed around the northern coastline before walking overland between Hobart and Launceston.

These could hardly be classified as 'independent 'authorities' and since Sorell and Curr were in league to convince the directors of the value of VDL, and Hobbs had been sponsored by Sorell, he too is hardly an independent or reliable witness.

Stokes went on to understate Curr's experience and claim to first hand local knowledge when he writes "Curr had only limited experience of farming in Australia". In fact Curr had received his small grant of 1,000 acres from Sorell and had farmed in the favourable climate and soil conditions found only on the east coast of the Island and in an area not Far East of Hobart town. Stokes, like Pink. Seems inclined to favour Curr and make Curr the underdog. In reality Curr was self-serving, and by overstating both his experience and the value of the VDL landscape and conditions to meet the company intentions, he did himself, his employer and his co-investors a grave disservice and one, which could have sunk the company by the time Curr was terminated.

As further evidence of the 'soft' approach against Curr, Stokes writes, "Curr believed that the government was doing all in its power to thwart the company and adopted a belligerent attitude in his dealings with the authorities that strained relations almost to breaking point." Again Stokes is apologising for Curr, since relations did reach a breaking point. In 1839 Governor Franklin refused to have any further correspondence with Curr and Curr was severely reprimanded by the Directors. Curr would have clearly understood, especially after a year of close personal negotiations with Bathurst what the Secretary's intentions were. That Bathurst did not exhaustively detail every statement or parameter within the final written 'instructions' is not a sign of ambivalence or weakness on Bathurst's behalf, but rather that full details were not known, by either party and that a full year of personal discussions between Curr and Bathurst and his staff should have been sufficient, at least between conventional 'gentlemen' to settle the issue of where 250,000 acres should be selected from. In effect, Curr had made a monumental blunder and was too egotistical to admit he had made a mistake or misled the directors. He could not back down

Stokes also refuses to admit or state just how serious the financial situation had become. He writes 'a general meeting of shareholders in London in February 1826 decided to abandon the farming operations in the colony.' In fact, the meeting decided to appoint an in-house committee of three stockholders and one director to set down the steps for 'liquidating' the company's assets, and report back to the next annual general meeting. The committee found it unable to recommend 'liquidation' since the assets would not realise sufficient funds to meet the liabilities, even excluding the stockholder's capital.

Stokes completes his article by stating "Nothing ever occurred (in the company's history) to justify the vast sum invested in the Van Diemen's Land Company by its founders.

Answering the Pink and Stokes version of the VDL Coy history

Mr Pink misunderstands the circumstances of the company's formation. It was not a wealthy company; it was formed on the basis of a capital commitment suitable to sway Lord Bathurst. The shares were issued upon application. There was only a nominal payment upon the issue being made, subject to the land grant. The original application had been for 500,000 acres and an issued capital of one million pound. This was cut both as to the amount of land and the authorised capital. The grant approved by Bathurst was for 250,000 of 'pasture or tillable land' which when selected grossed up to 350,000 acres. The claim that Bathurst 'forced' the company to select land in the northwest corner is totally incorrect.

Bathurst, as Secretary of State for the Colonies, had devised a well-considered plan for developing outlying areas of the colony. Port Phillip and Morton Bay had been opened up, together with Port Macquarie, and it was part of the policy to open up new areas at that time unsettled (and often unexplored), whilst utilising the surplus quantities of convict labour. Thus Bathurst was reminded that the northwest region of VDL was uninhabited, unexplored and remote. So the chance of giving a small section of that region away via land grant with lots of strings attached was too good an opportunity to miss. Neither Curr nor his Directors were 'forced' to accept the proposal, and the official records confirm not too much resistance was offered to Bathurst's proposal and quid, pro, quo.

The Directors were overwhelmed. The AAC had not long before been awarded one million acres of land grant at Port Stephens in NSW, for which they raised a million pound in capital. The City of London was rife with speculation. Opportunities abounded everywhere. The directors must have thought–let's jump on the bandwagon. What was confronting them was very simple. A group of woollen mill owners and operators were part of an industry group, usually meeting irregularly unless there was an industry wide problem. There was now an industry wide problem–the industry could not get regular supplies of raw wool, other than at unreasonably high prices from Spain and Germany. England was not keen to trade with these countries especially in such an important commodity as wool, and one by which it could be held ransom over trading terms and conditions. The wool from New South Wales being imported into

Britain, was suggesting a replacement source of various types of wool was about to emerge in Britain's favour. So this industry group assembled with a common goal, common ambitions and a gem of an idea to work with. 'Let's follow the trend commenced by the AAC. We will request a grant of land to be matched by us with development capital, with the sole aim of providing a regular and steady supply of raw wool to our own mills and at a rate cheap' (enough to support the British tariff on imported wool, which was being strenuously objected to by dominant NSW growers such as Macarthur and Marsden).

It took a year of negotiations with Bathurst to assure him of the credentials of the investor group ands what they wanted to accomplish. It was Curr and Sorell who convinced Bathurst that VDL could accommodate their needs. Bathurst picked up on this and he designated the northwest region as the one in need of exploration, development, inhabiting and 'stocking'. It really was a take it or leave it situation that neither Curr nor his associates wanted to leave. Being given a half-million acres of land ready to take livestock, produce wool, ship it back to England as fodder for the mills, was all the directors could think about. What could go wrong? 'We are rich'—a half million acres of land have been given to us'.

The company could transfer its own indentured workers. It would encourage (as set down in Curr's booklet) emigrants, it would dig for minerals, and it would be a trading house in an area without competition. It would own ships. The possibilities were endless. But what went wrong.

Curr was a law unto himself. He was young, ambitious and eager to get started and then get rich. He had invested in company shares. He had been there and farmed on his own account. He was ready, was above needing any specialist help or training. He was the first in a line of British managers, who had no experience of the country, or the climate or the conditions, but who could not bring themselves to ask for local help. Curr had made enemies in the colony within a few weeks of his arrival. One can picture it now. 'I am the head of a large landowner, a great company waiting to plunder the small colony, which takes our name'.

Curr, no doubt was his own worst enemy and the worst person the company could have chosen to represent it in the colony. He confronted and confounded officialdom in Hobart to the point that the governor would not even talk with him. He was manipulative over his interpretation of the Bathurst instructions and agreement of the terms of the land grant. Arthur should not be criticised for implementing a policy imposed on him. Arthur was not in favour of the policy of British capital buying land grants at the expense of hard working free settlers. Bathurst's instructions were very clear, if not painfully detailed, but without conflict in interpretation.

Curr was on a giant ego trip. He had something to prove, and prove it he would. When Pink quotes Curr as saying 'the land was of no value, and would prove too expensive to develop', he was quoting just another Curr exaggeration. Curr wanted quality pastureland, although in his argument with Arthur he demanded 250,000 acres of tillable ground. Curr's opinion of forestland was that 'it had no value' and was typically poor unproductive soil. Curr also claimed that he might have to take a gross one-quarter of the Island if that was the only way he could get the promised land grant, as he interpreted the instructions. His constant rowing and argument with Arthur was pointless. The governor could only be expected to carry out the Bathurst instruction, and Curr, must have known that his threats to Arthur would be made known to Bathurst, as would his unreasonable demands. Bathurst was not going to retreat from the position the British Cabinet had approved, nor from a policy that was proving successful elsewhere.

Neither was Curr going to retreat from his position before his directors and admit he had made mistakes over his personnel selection, over his confrontations with the officials, not in his land selection, nor in his intemperate statements to the board that VDL was the ideal place from which to choose a large-scale pastoral grant. Curr's ego and need to remain the manager in VDL was taking its toll. It eventually brought him asunder. He challenged the government once too often and stood up against the Board and ignored their precise, conciliatory instructions. He was given a year's notice and the Board perpetrated the mismanagement by appointing another Britisher to the post.

Before we turn to a simple but crucial question prefacing the land selection, let me assess the circumstances driving the VDL Company in its first twenty years of operation. This review should set the scene for understanding what was driving Curr and the Directors in intemperate ways.

Fletcher (*The Australian People 1788-1945*) relates p.1 "The material resources of Australia, would be largely to the benefit of British capitalists. British *public* investment was limited and did not matter much. The commissariat and other government expenditure of the convict era were seldom applied, and then in only small quantities, to developing colonial resources. Capital outlaid on soldiers (83 years) and convicts (80 years) ran into many millions in the eighty years of convict transportation. But it was not dug into the soil, except for a small amount during the Macquarie era. But it was British *private* investment that was to make the Anglo-Australian economic structure.

There were six stages for government-encouraged investment in the colony.

- In the first stage, British policy encouraged large investment by pastoral and mercantile companies chartered by special imperial statute; both the Australian Agricultural Company and the Van Diemen's Land Company were floated with grants of large areas of land in 1824.Similar encouragement was forthcoming for individuals with money to invest.
- A second stage was developed following the Forbes Act of 1834 under which English Banks were encouraged to bring funds to the colony and make loans, with security, for the purchase of the large amounts of crown land being released and sold by the government. Whitehall had decided that 'capitalists should buy land at auction instead of being gifted it free; since the cash terms for the traditional 640 acres was beyond most local investor' means, the banking system covered the shortfall.
- The third tier of policy was developed following the gold rush when a further move by large British banks into the colonies was encouraged.
- . The fourth stage followed the first borrowing of colonial government funds in London. This opened up a new phase of direct investment, based on the idea that if the colonies were

credit-worthy to the City of London, then it must be a sound place to invest directly.

- The fifth stage saw the growth of the large London-based pastoral houses, who were a one stop house for funding pastoral business, taking wool on assignment to the auction houses in London and becoming much broader financiers than the Banks were willing to be.

- The sixth stage was towards modern Australia when the British Mining giants funded massive developments of gold, coal, silver-lead, zinc, copper, iron and other metals.

Thus contrary to the Kerry Pink analysis, Bathurst was following a formal government approved plan to not only open up new country but also encourage direct British private investment in the colonies. It was Curr and the Board who mistakenly saw the pot of gold at the end of the Bathurst rainbow and did not match their greed with sound business acumen. This lacking in sound practice and policy lasted for at least the first one hundred years of operation and cost the company any chance at fulfilling its goal to be a successful company. Curr was but the first messenger of disaster; he was followed by numerous other, all controlled from the powerhouse of Board opinion in London.

The company went through two distinct stages and the rationale for directing company operations differed from stage to stage. Stage One took place when the British mills were reliant on European countries as sources of raw wool. Stage Two followed the apparently limitless export of wool from the Australian colonies to England, at very competitive and attractive prices, and thus replaced the uncertainty of the European supplies, and also avoided any need for reliance on the VDL company supplies. At this point, the mills and their owners who were the promoters of the VDL company, did not need the VDL exports, and so their interest changed from the company being a regular supplier of wool, to just another investment opportunity. They soon realised that as an investment opportunity, the VDL Company was not going to be a star, and their interest thus waned.

Why did the VDL Coy Board not change their initial goals?

It is of interest, in view of the early and continued failure to ask what was the goal of producing fine wool, and why was this goal not abandoned before disaster struck, and then seek wool production, in moderation, of various standards as was being undertaken by experimentation by Marsden in NSW?

The facts are that based on the advice of both Curr and Sorell that the Island was suitable for raising fine wool, Bathurst inserted into his 'Instructions' that there were two goals of the VDL Coy; firstly that the company would produce 'fine' wool, and secondly, that the Company would upgrade the sheep breeding program on the Island.

And so a fundamental question must now be—Why was it necessary or appropriate to produce fine wool? Or, at least, wool of a grade finer than what the mills were buying, and receiving, from Germany and Spain!

H.B. Carter in *His Majesty's Spanish Flock* offers us some insight and answers to the important question.

> Carter writes P383, "The French, in buying 6.8 million improved sheep, were looking for firstly a substitution of improved flocks for the same number of common sheep; secondly, the French, from this move alone, could expect to gain about 32.3 million francs because of the enhanced quality of her home-grown wools; thirdly, in the hands of the skilful French manufacturers, French fine wools would acquire a new value and in proportion to their increase would enlarge the export of cloths and stuffs which, about 1810 returned already 22.7 million francs; fourthly, if the imported Spanish wool was valued at an average of 12 francs per kilogramme and the imported German and other wools from mixed breeds at 7 francs per kilogramme, then France by herself would be relieved from paying 57 million francs per annum to foreign nations."

So Bathurst's thinking would have been: a. By granting the woollen manufacturers co-operative a significant quantity of crown land and by causing them to think in terms of production only of fine wools, then, the government will have restored regular supplies of raw materials to this important national industry, as well as reducing imports of raw materials from Europe and eliminate the potential of being held to ransom, and not only save a lot of money for the manufacturers but eliminate a great deal of imports and thus assist the balance of payments problem.

The question of 'why produce only fine wool, and why, when it was found that the northwest region climate was too cold and wet for producing fine wool, was not the breeding program amended so that a wool grade, more appropriate to the region, was not developed and pursued rather than continue to try to grow at ever increasing loss to the Company, the 'fine' wool that was not marketable? This failure was a loss not only to the Company but a great loss, in opportunity cost terms, for the woollen mills and their owners.

If the persistence by the company was motivated by the intention of honouring the terms of the Charter, then it was misplaced. The company breached the Charter in a number of other minor ways, and who, in fact, was likely to go through the 18 items of approved operations including producing wool from grazing sheep and determine that they were not in fact producing fine wool. On the other hand, what is the definition of fine wool? The 1830 definition and the ideas of fine wool are very different to our terminology today.

> The reader can make up their own mind about whether the company succeeded or failed in terms of its charter provided by Bathurst and to its obligations to its stockholders, employees and creditors.

Pink and Stokes take one position on the question, largely using Meston's valuable analysis, but this independent economic analysis is based on revisiting the many records of the company found in NSW and Tasmania, and mainly through the new interpretation of the annual financial statements made public between 1826 and 1900.

> Numerous conclusions and assessments can now be made, commencing with a semi-official version of the early events.

CHAPTER 8

SUMMARY & CONCLUSIONS

Let me commence this summary and conclusion by incorporating a brief summary of the company, as seen through the eyes of a company official.

One of the distinguished company officers, Henry Cattley, hand-wrote his own evaluation of the early VDL performance in 1863 and although the original document is now only in printed form and is included in the Appendices to this text, it is worth incorporating into the text at this point so the reader can compare both outside and inside opinions of the Company. A photocopy of the original hand-written paper is in the Tasmanian Library at Launceston, and access to that paper is gratefully acknowledged.

This is what Secretary Henry Cattley had to report in 1863:

> *"The original design of those who projected this company, was to form a settlement for the purpose of sheep farming, and the growth and exportation of wool, the breeding of stock,—as horses, cattle etc.*
>
> *For these purposes, many preliminary expenses were found necessary, such as the forming of a wharf and port for landing and shipping produce; providing a residence for the manager and erecting buildings for a certain number of artisans, surveyors and others who were sent out at the expense of the company, and for landing the stores to be shipped along with them.*

After a lapse of some years, and although a certain amount of wool was shipped yearly to England, and much superior stock raised and sold, by which the Island was greatly benefited, the farming did not succeed, the expenditure being found to greatly exceed the income. The whole of the stock was therefore sold off–the labourers discharged and the company limited themselves to the sale of land.

The formation of the company commenced by an application for an act of Parliament, which was obtained and is dated 10 June 1825-6Geo.IVCh.39

By this Act the Crown was authorised to grant a charter, which was also obtained and passed the great seal on the 10th November 1825.

It was granted to certain persons named, who afterwards became the first Directors and auditors of the company. John Pearse Esq M.P. became the first Governor, and Joseph Cripps the first Deputy-Governor.

There was no prospectus put forth, in the ordinary way, in consequence of a pledge exacted by the Government that "no shares would be issued to the public to become marketable property, until the charter should be obtained". The first yearly meeting of proprietors was held in London on 7th March 1826.

The charter recited that 23 persons (Cattley lists them all by full name, including his grandfather John Cattley) with others 'had subscribed amongst themselves £1,000,000 which they proposed to layout and invest in the cultivation of waste land' and it authorised a grant of land to them accordingly.

The rules laid down for the selection of land are found in a letter from Earl

Bathurst, dated 25th April 1825, as follows:

"The VDL Company will receive their grant to the NW district bounded on the north by Bass' Straits, on the west by the ocean, and on the east and south by lines drawn from either shore so as to afford the necessary depth of country etc etc". But the land so described being found of poor quality, the rule was afterwards modified and the present boundaries agreed upon.

In the first instance a small Royalty was reserved to the Crown attached to the grant. The company's title was perfected by a second act of Parliament dated 25th June 1847 authorising the Crown, by warrant under the Royal Warrant to empower the Governor of the Island to execute a deed under the great seal of the Island to grant to the company the land marked out, which the Act declared, should be "free and forever discharged from the quit rents etc in the letters patent as Charter expressed and before recited".

The Royal Warrant was dated 15th May 1847 and the letters patent under the great seal of the Island 27th July 1848.

The first persons sent out as Managers or Commissioners were Mr Edward Curr and Stephen Adey; but after a time Mr Curr acted alone. Mr Goldie accompanied them as Chief Agriculturalist and they sailed in the ship *Cape Packet"* with the surveying implements and a supply of everything requisite, for the purpose of selecting and locating the lands to be granted"

A number of artisans and labourers with the stores and implements required for starting the first settlement, followed in a brig of 180 tons purchased by the company and called the *Tranmere".*

The first settlement was formed at Circular Head. The first surveying expedition was conducted by Mr Hellyer assisted by Messrs Fossey and Lorymer, who penetrating the unknown country, discovered the Surrey and Hampshire Hills, Valentine's Peak, the River Emu etc. They formed accurate maps of all their discoveries and gave district names to the several localities by which they have since been known.

The shares of the company were originally 10,000 of £100 each on which, at present time (1863) £28.10.0 per share is paid up. By an Act just passed dated 11th May 1863, the nominal capital of the company is reduced to £300,000 and the shares to £30 each leaving to the directors the power of calling up only £1.10.0 per share beyond what has been paid to-date.

London June 1863   **(signed) Henry Huntley (Secretary)**

The disasters for the company were probably just financial wastages as every step the company made had a useful and worthy intent behind it. Usually it was a case of the wrong policy for that time. In addition the pressure on the managers to make a profit and show a return on investment was so great that shortcuts, brainstorms and impractical ideas were given the light of day without careful planning and without being tested before persons with appropriate experience. For instance, the Emu Bay Railway being constructed at enormous expense–it ended up costing over £400,000 when the original estimate was only £11,000, and then to make the rails out of deteriorating wood to save money; or to commence selling farm lots at Circular Head in virgin territory, without any person experienced in the local soils, and with guarantees in addition, was a recipe for trouble. The company sold farmlets of between ten to one hundred acre lots, on the basis that the men would be given company work in their off season, in addition to the company buying all their farm produce at commercial prices, was double trouble. For a start the small farmers' off season coincided with the off season for the VDL Company as well, so little productive work was available and this cost the Company a great deal of money–wasted money. Buying farm production without arranging for a market through which to on-sell the produce was another waste of funds, and this experience ended up costing the Company nearly £40,000.

Buying a mineralogist or prospector at the height of the gold rush in the 1850s, whilst knowing already that there were no minerals to be found on Company property seems another waste. Declaring that there were commercial quantities of slate on the Hellyer Hills area of Hampshire Hills property, 'sufficient to serve the whole world's needs' seems curious unless and until the quantities had been tested and a means found of marketing and delivering the product. There turned out to be insufficient markets, poor quantity product and undeliverable product (except at uncommercial costs). This was another waste of time and money. This was another dead-end, just another one of so many. We should conclude that many of these exercises were in the nature of P.R. events for the benefit of stockholders who were being asked annually to make a further capital contribution, without real prospects for gain.

What then was the cause of these excursions into blue-sky thinking? Pressure on managers of an agricultural operation to produce profits and cash is the primary blame. Poor selection of managers with insufficient commercial and local agricultural knowledge is the secondary cause.

Who lost out through these skirmishes into the wastages? Obviously the stockholders lost money, but also the company itself, through loss of prestige and reputation. Stockholders lost by not receiving a dividend or return on their already sizeable investment, but they also lost by having 'calls' made on the unpaid portion of the stock, which then required further capital investment by these already challenged investors.

To ask what if, may be quite counter-productive. We have already discussed some of the many difficult financial situations facing local managers, mostly outside the competencies of the managers. Distance between Tasmania and England made communication slow and subject to misunderstandings.

The core competencies that should have been expected of local managers (in the colony) were:

- Knowledge of local soils, climate and weather patterns.
- Knowledge of local livestock, their feeding and nutritional requirements and seasonal management.
- Knowledge of the VDL Company legislation and the limitations imposed on the company as far as its trading operations, money lending and land sales were concerned.
- Some knowledge of surveying and a penchant for exploring would not go to waste at the company.
- Special talents for land and livestock marketing–both for broad acres, farmlets and town lots, would be of assistance but most of all a broad-minded organiser, problem solver and adjudicator.

The company never did, at least not until McGill arrived in 1902, have such all-round management talent to help it through its problems, nor was there any form of training or 'succession' planning in order to maintain continuity at such a large company!

So, we can conclude that, if the sheep raising had been successful, and wool yields and quality had been commercially viable, and livestock sales had been successful to local farmers, then land sales would not have been necessary. Township and development may well have been a supplement to farm income and this expenditure could have justified the wharf development and a basic trading operation. If minerals had been discovered in commercial quantities on company land, this development too, would have supported the wharfage expenditures, but the railway lines were uncommercial and outside the business plan. This, like roads and bridges, their construction and maintenance (at least after the initial stage) should have been left to the local Government, and not privatised and restricted.

The company should have followed through on the farm-let operations of growing grains, vegetables, harvesting and processing timber and the numerous other activities the tenant farmers found for making money, for instance, tobacco growing, dairying and fresh vegetables were successful sidelines.

However, what might have happened between 1826 and 1900 is past history. The Company survived narrowly and remains in business today, at least doing successfully what might have been done one hundred years ago.

One may ask, is this really a 'study of failed intentions'? It is not too harsh to have expected better from a company that was 'gifted' 350,000 acres, raised a million pound in capital(in 1824 pounds) and needed only good management and the will to succeed. It had the AAC's success to follow in NSW and surely had access to the same opportunities of the large mainland land-owners who did not have the advantage of no debt, imported livestock and a dominant, monopolistic position in Tasmania to market livestock and produce.

The company failed because of poor goals, inadequate planning, poor management decisions and a change of intentions from wanting to produce 'in-house' wool, to finding that the directors could buy better wool at cheaper prices on the open market.

GENERAL BIBLIOGRAPHY

1. Butlin, N.G.–Forming a Colonial Economy
2. Shann–Economic History of Australia
3. Appleyard–Australian Financiers
4. Broeze–Mr. Brookes and the Australian Trade
5. Butlin, S.J.–Foundation of the Australian Monetary System
6. Australian Dictionary of Biography
7. Ellis, M.H.–Francis Greenway
8. Australian Encyclopedia